Music in Our Lives

ALSO BY JONATHAN L. FRIEDMANN
AND FROM MCFARLAND

*Music in the Hebrew Bible: Understanding
References in the Torah, Nevi'im and Ketuvim* (2014)

Music in Biblical Life: The Roles of Song in Ancient Israel (2013)

*Synagogue Song: An Introduction
to Concepts, Theories and Customs* (2012)

Music, Theology and Worship: Selected Writings, 1841–1896 (2011)

Music in Jewish Thought: Selected Writings, 1890–1920 (2009)

*The Value of Sacred Music: An Anthology
of Essential Writings, 1801–1918* (2009)

Music in Our Lives

Why We Listen, How It Works

Jonathan L. Friedmann

McFarland & Company, Inc., Publishers
Jefferson, North Carolina

LIBRARY OF CONGRESS CATALOGUING-IN-PUBLICATION DATA

Friedmann, Jonathan L., 1980–
    Music in our lives : why we listen, how it works / Jonathan L. Friedmann.
        p.   cm.
    Includes bibliographical references and index.

    ISBN 978-0-7864-9759-1 (softcover : acid free paper) ∞
    ISBN 978-1-4766-1896-8 (ebook)

    1. Music—Psychological aspects. 2. Music—Social aspects. I. Title.

ML3830.F76 2015
781.1'1—dc23
                                      2014044411

BRITISH LIBRARY CATALOGUING DATA ARE AVAILABLE

© 2015 Jonathan L. Friedmann. All rights reserved

No part of this book may be reproduced or transmitted in any form or by any means, electronic or mechanical, including photocopying or recording, or by any information storage and retrieval system, without permission in writing from the publisher.

Cover image © iStock/Thinkstock

Printed in the United States of America

McFarland & Company, Inc., Publishers
  Box 611, Jefferson, North Carolina 28640
    www.mcfarlandpub.com

TABLE OF CONTENTS

Preface 1

Introduction 5

1. Writing on Music	9	11. Art Music	93
2. What Is Music?	16	12. Consumer Music	102
3. Where Does Music Come From?	24	13. Creativity	108
4. Innateness	34	14. Music-Making	117
5. Character	40	15. Mind	125
6. Shape	48	16. Listening	133
7. Transience	57	17. Ownership	140
8. Language	69	18. Prejudice and Tolerance	147
9. Nature	76	19. Religion	155
10. Folk Music	86	20. Spirituality	163

Bibliography 181

Index 193

Preface

This book is composed of "morning musings." Written in the pre-dawn hours, it anthologizes musical thoughts conjured in silence and solitude. Each of its chapters is built from stand-alone essays linked by family resemblance. This admittedly unusual approach was not random, and its result is not piecemeal. From the outset, my goal was to create a text that introduces and expands upon key aspects of the musical experience, mostly from the listener's perspective. The roadmap was carefully drawn, and effort was made to carve a logical path from one chapter section to the next. It is my hope that the organic character of each section is preserved within the larger structure of the volume.

Unlike the authors of other general texts on music, I have not abstained from taking personal positions or asserting my own voice into the topics I discuss. Music is a vibrant, passionate, and opinion-arousing area of human life. Examining it in an antiseptic way would be contrary to the subject matter. Not every reader will agree with every idea proposed or example chosen. In fact, the discussions are brief and more or less open-ended precisely to encourage pondering and grappling.

If this book has a primary agenda, it is to stimulate self-examination. Too often, we rush to musical judgments without investigating the reasons for our reactions. This is partly the fault of music itself, which is typically felt so immediately and viscerally as to leave little space for contemplation. Musical moments are utterly experiential: the spotlight is shined on emotion rather than intellect. It is easy to overlook the multifarious factors leading up to and following a musical experience that give rise to seemingly spontaneous responses. The many and varied explorations presented are designed to flesh out the fascinating background.

Earlier versions of several of these essays were originally posted on my blog, *Thinking on Music*. Astute readers have noted the flexibility of my viewpoints and interests from day to day. I am an eclecticist by nature. I sometimes find myself retooling theories or switching sides in debates, and upon later reflection see value in the divergent opinions. As excursions in an ongoing search for understanding—what my friend and former professor Jon R. Stone calls the "scholar's quest"—the components of this book should be regarded as time-specific convictions rather than permanent views. In this way, the chapters subtly argue the possibility that conflicting (or even contradictory) positions can possess a little bit of truth.

The sundry platter of concepts and theories is plucked from a buffet of disciplines. Such an approach is necessary when dealing with a subject as holistic and multi-layered as the human experience of music, and is not uncommon among pedagogues. An illustration in point is one of my favorite historical examples, the story of Oscar Weil. Born to German-Jewish immigrant parents in Columbia County, New York, in 1839, Weil left home at eighteen to pursue violin studies in Europe. With the outbreak of the Civil War, he returned to the United States and enlisted as a private for the Northern cause. Injuries sustained in the war left him with fragile health and a permanently wounded hand, which ended his career as a concert performer. Upon retiring from the army, Weil went back to Europe to reinvent himself as a composer and instructor of composition. He returned to America a year later, settling in San Francisco, a climate better suited for his delicate health. His primary income came from teaching violin and composition. According to the editors of *Oscar Weil: Letters and Papers*, "A lesson from Mr. Weil was to the young student an educational adventure. He constantly journeyed from the immediate business of the hour into fields of general culture, into the discussion of books, painting and poetry. For he was deeply versed in the history and literature of the English, French and German peoples; and had brought away from his contact with these an imaginative power and a wealth of allusion which served to illuminate his own art. To him art was all comprehensive and music only one of its manifestations."[1]

Weil's instinct to connect music to other fields has become a popular modality in recent years, and lies at the heart of the present volume. We are in something of a golden age of music research. Technological advances have merged with philosophical interests to produce an array of distinct yet converging studies illuminating the musical nature of our species. Virtually every day, a new brick is added to the wall of interdisciplinary information, drawn from psychology, neuroscience, evolutionary biology, ethology, anthropology, ethnomusicology, and more. This book develops, supports, challenges, and diverges from this material, which is flourishing at such rapid speed that it is nearly impossible to keep up.

For all of these reasons, this survey does not pretend to be comprehensive. It is by no means the final word—or even *my* final word—on the subject.

By the time of its publication, I will have written dozens of other essays, and the world's output will have continued at its furious pace. This book is but my humble contribution to the endless exploration of humanity's relationship with music.

More than anything else, my expertise has been augmented through my writing. I agree with Isaac Asimov that writing is essentially thinking through one's fingers. There is no substitute for that depth of discovery. The greatest aspiration of this book is to excite others to pursue their own thinking and writing on music.

While the material included is mostly the result of inward reflection and independent digging through the literature, several people helped to give it shape, both directly and indirectly. I am grateful to my students at the Academy for Jewish Religion, California, whose participation in class discussions inspired several of the points pursued. Thanks as well to the loyal readers of my blog, especially Stan Stewart, Daniel Campos Putterman, and John Morton. Comments and encouragement from these fine musicians and thinkers have sharpened my arguments and sent me to realms I would have otherwise overlooked. All conclusions and imperfections are my own. I am most grateful for the boundless support of my wife, Elvia, the model music enthusiast for whom this book was written. Finally, I dedicate this work to my late mentor, cantor-composer William Sharlin, whose wisdom and constant pursuit of refinement are with me always.

Note

1. Flora J. Arnstein, Albert I. Elkus, and Stewart W. Young, eds., *Oscar Weil: Letters and Papers* (San Francisco: Book Club of California, 1923), 1.

Introduction

Literature on music comes in many types. There are technical studies analyzing the minutia of a composition or style, biographies and autobiographies delving into the lives of important contributors, scientific investigations into all facets of musical phenomena, harsh criticisms, and soft praises. Some look at music in specific populations, while others explore intersections of music and the broader society. Some offer overviews of "great" composers, while others list "legends" of Western and non–Western genres. There are ethnographic studies, philosophical treatises, theological discourses, feminist critiques, polemical diatribes, practical manuals, listening guides, resources for archivists, catalogues for collectors, textbooks on theory, workbooks on musicianship, encyclopedias, compendiums, dictionaries, and more.

If proof were needed of music's vital role in human life, this vast and varied amalgamation would be it. Countless gallons of ink have been spilled in pursuit of musical understanding, and more is added each day. Curiosity about things musical can be measured by the amount of books and articles published on the subject, which number in the millions. Writers of antiquity observed the mysterious hold music takes over our hearts and minds, and contemporary scholars and researchers continue to search for the reasons why.

In one way or another, pondering the "big questions" has given rise to the various sorts of studies listed above. What constitutes "greatness" in music, what factors contribute to musical preferences, what functions are served by musical displays—these and similar big-picture concerns lie at the heart of virtually all musical inquiries. While an analysis of music in a Polynesian ritual and a text on counterpoint in the style of J. S. Bach may have few surface similarities, they exhibit common underlying concerns for customs, aesthetics, conventions, expectations, cultural meanings, and so on. The same can be said for almost any disparate pairing of musical subjects. Music and those who produce it are endlessly diverse. Yet, without neglecting cultural specifics or blurring inherent functions and values, we can appreciate the shared human needs and tendencies that tie them all together.

Content

This book examines music through a humanistic lens. Rather than wading through musicological details or presenting "thick descriptions" of case studies, it aims to enrich awareness from the perceiver's end. Less attention is given to analysis and criticism, and greater emphasis is placed on the hows and whys of music in human life. With an assortment of interdisciplinary excursions and a tapestry of global musical examples, its pages travel through twenty key aspects of the musical experience.

Specifically, these are: the challenges and rewards of writing on music; the difficulties of defining music; evolutionary theories of music's origins; the innateness of music in humanity; the impression of character in musical selections; the shape of musical patterns; music's transient essence; the relationship of music and language; musical possibilities in the natural world; the nature of folk music; music's artistic basis; habits of musical consumption; music and creativity; the intricacies of making music; the mind and musical perception; listening preferences; music and identity; prejudice and tolerance in musical choices; religious interpretations of music; and music as a spiritual conduit.

Purpose

What, exactly, can be learned from all of this? Advocates for music education often highlight the side benefits of formal training, even for students who do not aspire to perform professionally. Among the reported nonmusical cognitive advantages are improved reading skills, higher standardized test scores, and increased spatial-temporal reasoning.[1] The scholastic value of simply listening to music is not as clear and certainly not as dramatic. Despite the popularity of the Mozart Effect and other research purporting a link between listening to certain types of music and augmented mental capacity, they mask a mixture of fiction and fact.[2] Yet, while quantitative benefits reside overwhelmingly with those who study an instrument, conscientious listening does have qualitative rewards.

Thoughtful listening opens up a unique avenue of self-awareness. This is not to be confused with "good listening," or the identification of technical aspects such as rhythm, dynamics, meter, melody, harmony, and form. Such knowledge is an essential part of musicianship and undoubtedly amplifies cultural appreciation. But there is more to musical reflection than memorizing Italian terms or recognizing stylistic indicators. Basic curiosity about why we even care about music can open the mind to deep discoveries.

Introduction

From the moment we wake up, our lives are inundated with musical sounds. Daily activities unfold to a partly selected and partly random musical soundtrack. Some music is intentionally heard from the car radio, mp3 playlist, or headphones at the gym. Other music invades the auditory system through advertisements, a neighbor's stereo, or loudspeakers at the grocery store. In most cases, the music stirs a certain, if not always conscious, response. The type and magnitude of that response can teach us much about ourselves.

The listening experience encompasses a potpourri of individual and environmental factors. How a person reacts to a single selection is determined by disposition, personality type, peer group, generational grouping, geographic location, access to resources, education, cultural heritage, past history, socio-economic class, personal associations, momentary temperament, physical setting, recording quality, volume level—just to list a handful. Peeling off any one of these layers and contemplating its impact on musical perception is an enlightening exercise.

Music is as ubiquitous as it is taken for granted. Because it is so omnipresent and tightly woven into everyday life, rarely does one pause to ponder its profundity; and since intellectual involvement is not a prerequisite for musical reaction, music seems more apt for experience than examination. True, music affects us whether or not we understand what is taking place, and musical opinions are formed with or without introspection. But as soon as we scratch the surface, we begin peering into ourselves.

Approach

The topics covered are comparable to the major themes present in other general texts, but the approach taken differs in four significant ways. First, I have inserted my own voice into the topics discussed, rather than taking a more impartial or disinterested viewpoint. Second, each chapter consists of "mini-lessons" designed to introduce and stimulate thinking on a concept or situation in as few words as possible. In my experience as a teacher and researcher, this fast-paced world of multi-tasking and light-speed information dissemination is best served by writing that is concise and focused. Third, allusions and analogies used to illustrate the book's various points are drawn from an eclectic range of extramusical sources, from philosophy to fiction to food. Apart from (hopefully) enlivening the discussions, this method is intended to make the sometimes-intricate content relatable to a wide range of readers. Fourth, the book looks at music as a universal human phenomenon. With rare exceptions, everyone reacts to musical stimuli and integrates them into sundry areas of life. The musically inclined and disinclined benefit from music in essentially identical and equal ways; absence of individual skill does not correspond to lack of capacity. Situating this awareness at the forefront, the pages that follow survey the roots and offshoots of our deep and complex relationship with musical sounds.

Notes

1. See Dee Hansen and Elaine Bernstorf, "Linking Music Learning to Reading Instruction," *Music Educators Journal* 88:5 (2002): 17–21, 52; Steven M. Demorest and Steven J. Morrison, "Does Music Make You Smarter?" *Music Educators Journal* 87:2 (2000): 33–39, 58; and Frances H. Rauscher, et al., "Music Training Causes Long-Term Enhancement of Preschool Children's Spatial-Temporal Reasoning," *Neurological Research* 19 (1997): 2–8.

2. See Rudi Črnčec, Sarah J. Wilson, and Margot Prior, "The Cognitive and Academic Benefits of Music to Children: Facts and Fiction," *Educational Psychology: An International Journal of Experimental Educational Psychology* 26:4 (2006): 579–594.

1

WRITING ON MUSIC

Writing on music is no easy task. First and foremost, music is meant to be heard and felt directly, not analyzed indirectly with the sterile tools of written language. Added to this, musical phenomena are self-contained and occur in specific contexts, making generalizations difficult to justify. There is also the constant tension between theory and practice, and the tendency to miss the full experience by favoring one over the other. Finally, there is the "musician's burden": the inability of the expert to receive music with the purer and less critical ears of the novice. The purpose of this chapter is both to acknowledge these obstacles and to chart a course beyond them. After all, this book is nothing other than words about music.

Real Music

Atticus Finch, the noble defense attorney in Harper Lee's *To Kill a Mockingbird*, coined a useful courtroom adage: Delete the adjectives and you have the facts.[1] The reality of a situation tends to be hidden behind layers of embellishment and prejudice. It suffocates under the weight of bias and interpretation, losing its neutrality and assuming a character dictated by the commentator. This is a natural function of human perception. We are not robots; our big brains are wired to assess rather than sterilely measure. The process is sometimes harmless and sometimes not. What Atticus strove for is the ability to isolate intrinsic essence from cluttering vocabulary.

Atticus's maxim finds a musical parallel in the writings of philosopher and musicologist Vladimir Jankélévitch. In *Music and the Ineffable,* Jankélévitch reminds us that music is made to be heard, not to be talked about.[2] In the intangible way music can be said to exist, it inhabits an abstract and ephemeral realm. Each listener associates sounds with personal images and feelings, which can be discussed in ornate—yet ultimately equivocal—detail. Music is a self-contained phenomenon, occurring apart from our attempts to decipher or characterize it. For this reason, Jankélévitch considers the music-language relationship a one-way affair: music can elicit endless talk, but talk gives nothing back to the music.

Musical description is a type of linguistic performance, in which the reader (or auditor) is manipulated to hear music a certain way. Once exposed to suggestive language, the possibility of "pure" listening becomes a near impossibility. This is true whether the adjectives are unsophisticated ("good," "bad," "pretty," "ugly") or flowery, as in Lazare Saminsky's appraisal of Ernest Bloch's *Sacred Service:* "[It possesses] an awed gleam of cognizance of the Supreme force that clasps the universe into oneness."[3] More than simply allowing us to experience music through another's sensibilities, figurative remarks irrevocably color our perception. To a certain extent, we end up processing the music as someone else wants us to.

Opinion and bias are inevitable outcomes of human cognition. A thinking brain is a judgmental brain. What the fictional Atticus and philosopher Jankélévitch stress is that objectivity demands resisting and overcoming: resisting the temptation to embroider the facts, and overcoming our susceptibility to such embroidery. The extramental thing—the thing-in-itself—is not language-dependent. It is what it is, as the tired saying goes.

Clearly, it is a fantasy to think that prejudicial adjectives will ever be expunged from the courtroom, or that music will ever be experienced in a non-verbal vacuum. One could even question whether it is desirable in all cases to dispense with a reasonable dose of colorful wordage. Nevertheless, we should pause to recognize that reality resides beneath the words.

Surviving Context

Some people are sticklers for context. They are hypersensitive about how words are handled and hyper-protective of original sources. For any statement, speech, painting, essay, song, novel or other cultural artifact to have legitimate meaning, it must be appreciated in, and only in, its native confines. Removing an idea from a specific discussion or an object from its historical period damages the intent and invalidates later applications. In the extreme of this view, ancient scriptures have no lasting relevance, reports on an event cannot describe anything else, and artistic creations from different periods or locations cannot be properly reproduced. Timeless wisdom becomes time-bound information. Ageless beauty becomes situational aesthetics.

It is fair to say that the extreme position is rarely (if ever) taken. Even sticklers treasure an occasional proverb or a piece of Classical music, though both were contrived for foreign audiences long ago deceased. Where the issue becomes problematic is when a comment is given wider relevance than the author intended. This is especially frowned upon in the guarded field of musical analysis, where fidelity to context is almost a maxim. True, ink spilled in the examination of one composer or piece of music is necessarily distorted when applied to a different work, let alone something more general; and egregious distortions can and do occur. But to insist that every musical insight be understood only in its document of origin restricts its potential readership and potential to enlighten.

If staunch contextualism were to prevail, then popular books like *A Dictionary of Musical Quotations* (Croften and Fraser)[4] and *Music: A Book of Quotations* (Galewitz)[5]—as well as specialized books like my own *Quotations on Jewish Sacred Music*[6]—would lose much or all of their value. However, most of us recognize that words written on a particular situation or creation frequently retain and accrue beneficial meanings when expanded to larger contexts.

An example is composer-musicologist Hubert Parry's warning, "Look out for this man's music; he has something to say and knows how to say it."[7] Parry wrote this after attending the premiere of Edward Elgar's *Enigma Variations*, but it could be describing any sincere and competent musician. Similarly, Beethoven unknowingly wrote on behalf of many composers when he included this statement in a letter to Louis Schlösser: "You will ask where my ideas come from. I cannot say for certain. They come uncalled, sometimes independently, sometimes in association with other things."[8]

The governing ideal of a remark may reside within specific parameters, but unconditional truths can still be happened upon. Indeed, various and sundry quotations find their way into anthologies precisely because their usefulness survives their context.

Part of this durability owes to the fact that observations made about any one thing take place within a grander sweep of experiences. No phenomenon exists in isolation and no reflection on a phenomenon is without underpinnings in a larger reality. In this sense, the constricted setting of a given quote already exists in a wider context, and the sagacity it possesses can speak to a wider context still. For instance, words about a Romantic composition may capture the essence of Romantic music, or elucidate music composition in general.

Of course, we should always be sensitive to the original target and meaning of a statement, and be habitual citers of sources. It is also obvious that not everything brilliant is applicable outside of the page it is printed on. But when it is, we should be free to adopt it as wisdom to think by.

Theory and Practice

Theory and practice in music are often portrayed as opposing modes of discernment. Theory is viewed as abstract, analytical and remote from the musical moment. Its tools and methods distill a work to its elemental components and provide the mechanical framework for a piece's construction; but they hardly account (or attempt to account) for music's affections or aesthetics. At its most austere, theory becomes what seventeenth-century philosopher Marin Mersenne conceived it to be: the reduction of music to the movement of air. Opponents of this approach, like social critic Morris Berman, point to its apparent spiritlessness.[9] For them, music is a happening, existing to be heard and felt, not dissected or diagnosed.

If we take the extremes of either position, then listening and analysis are two unrelated activities. The theorist rarely dwells on the effects of a piece while examining it under a magnifying glass. And the listener rarely ponders specific properties that are stimulating a musical response. However, theory and practice are not as distant as we might presume. Not only are they aspects of the same thing—music—they also address companion human needs for order and wonder.

The combination of formal design and amorphous impact is at the root of music's appeal. Though features such as pitch, timbre, duration and harmony are susceptible to meticulous examination, their cumulative effect cannot be accurately predicated, precisely measured or empirically determined. It is at the same time science and art.

Mathematician and polymath Jacob Bronowski made a related observation in his influential book, *The Identity of Man*.[10] Using science and poetry as contrasting pathways of human inquiry, Bronowski explained that while scientific imagination seeks to resolve ambiguities by conducting decisive tests between alternatives, artistic imagination encourages divergent paths without deciding for one or the other. Science is miserly, weeding out the proliferation of new ideas; art is generous, exploiting the vastness of ambiguities. For Bronowski, these two trajectories of the imaginative process—narrowing and expanding—form the basis of human consciousness.

It is intriguing that both avenues exist simultaneously in music. A musical selection is receptive to the scientific approach of the theorist, who separates, labels and quantifies its basic elements. But it is also open-ended, inviting subjective reactions and creative interpretations. These modes of engagement can appear mutually exclusive and certainly call upon different devices and frames of mind. Yet, when we apply Bronowski's insights, it becomes clear that theory and practice satisfy the concurrent and fundamental human needs for certainty and possibility. Science and art merge in music, enriching the entirety of consciousness.

Less Is More

There is an old opera joke that Wagner's music is better than it sounds, while Puccini's music sounds better than it is. The humor of this quip lies in the absurdity of judging music—the audible art—apart from how it sounds. It lampoons the elitist's assertion that accessible music is almost definitionally inferior to more esoteric works, regardless of what our ears tell us. Whatever truth there may be in this musicological system of merits and demerits—and whatever influence such assessments may have—it nevertheless highlights distinctions between listening and evaluating, and between scholars and ordinary folk. It is the difference between experiential knowledge—"I know what I like when I hear it"—and analytical discernment—"I discern its value when I measure it." These divergent modes of apprehension help explain the often-wide chasm separating popular musical opinions and the rarified views of music critics, theorists, historians and other professionals. "The expert knows best," so says the expert.

None of this is meant to negate the worth or even accuracy of musical criticism. When a musicologist or respected composer extols or disparages this or that opus, we should probably pay attention. But even the specialist will admit that too much information tends to tarnish the musical experience. What is primarily a medium of emotional expression becomes the subject of cognitive probing.

There is a standard line of thinking in the philosophy of aesthetics that visceral reactions to art are most intense in an art form other than one's own. For example, a painter will have a primitive rush of emotions when standing in a Gothic cathedral, while the architect next to her closely examines the stonework of the clerestory, the dimensions of the fan vault and so on. The painter excitedly declares, "This place is awesome!" The architect replies, "Did you notice the design flaw in that section of the ceiling?" Similarly, an architect seated in a concert hall will surrender himself to the mass of sound, while the musician sitting beside him busily scrutinizes melodic contours, harmonic density, tonal color and so forth. The architect blurts out, "This is marvelous!" The musician responds, "Trivial rubbish." The first is wrapped in sensual pleasure; the second is absorbed in adjudication.

It is sometimes said of the music theorist that he has a refined appreciation of the analytical and abstract, but a cultivated disregard for the affective and aesthetic. Of course, expertise in the science of music does not in itself preclude musical enjoyment. It is, after all, the music expert who is most interested in and enthusiastic about musical history, variety and subtlety. But, as the aesthetician readily acknowledges, interest and experience are not the same thing. To paraphrase Aaron Copland, the "gifted listener"—i.e., the musically educated—may hear more in a performance, but as the listener's knowledge expands so does her distance from the "primal and almost brutish level" of musical emotions. Again, this is not necessarily good or bad; but it does account for the disconnect between the novice's professed love for this or that conventional fare and the critic's supercilious remark that Wagner's music is better than it sounds.

Goethe's famous saying has relevance here: "Doubt grows with knowledge."[11] If we replace "doubt" with "critical analysis"—which is the essence of Goethe's phrase—we begin to recognize how difficult it is for the knowledgeable musician to replicate the relative simplicity and abandonment of the average person's musical encounter. Proficiency in the art tends to impede purity of experience.

Notes

1. Harper Lee, *To Kill a Mockingbird* (New York: HarperCollins, 1988), 97.
2. Vladimir Jankélévitch, *Music and the Ineffable*, trans. Carolyn Abbate (Princeton, NJ: Princeton University Press, 2003).
3. Lazare Saminsky, *Music of the Ghetto and the Bible* (New York: Bloch, 1934), 176–177.
4. Ian Crofton and Donald Fraser, comp., *A Dictionary of Musical Quotations* (New York: Macmillan, 1985).
5. Herb Galewitz, ed., *Music: A Book of Quotations* (New York: Dover, 2001).
6. Jonathan L. Friedmann, ed., *Quotations on Jewish Sacred Music* (Lanham, MD: Hamilton, 2011).
7. Hubert Parry, quoted in Christopher Wood, *An Elgar Companion* (Derbyshire, UK: Moorland, 1982), 180.
8. Ludwig van Beethoven, letter to Louis Schlösser (1899), quoted in Scott Power, *Musician's Little Book of Wisdom* (Merrillville, IN: ICS, 1996), 356.
9. Morris Berman, *Coming to Our Senses: Body and Spirit in the Hidden History of the West* (New York: Bantam, 1989), 40.
10. Jacob Bronowski, *The Identity of Man* (Garden City, NY: American Museum Science, 1965).
11. Johann Wolfgang von Goethe, *Proverbs in Prose* (1819).

Suggestions for Further Reading

Bergeron, Katherine, and Philip V. Bohlman, ed. *Disciplining Music: Musicology and Its Canons*. Chicago: University of Chicago Press, 1992.

Cook, Nicholas. *A Very Short Introduction to Music*. New York: Oxford University Press, 1998.
Eggebrecht, Hans Heinrich. *Understanding Music: The Nature and Limits of Musical Cognition*. Burlington, VT: Ashgate, 2010.
Ferguson, Donald N. *The Why of Music: Dialogues in an Unexplored Region of Appreciation*. Minneapolis: University of Minnesota Press, 1969.
Herbert, Trevor. *Music in Words: A Guide to Researching and Writing about Music*. New York: Oxford University Press, 2009.
Holoman, Kern D. *Writing About Music: A Style Sheet*. Berkeley: University of California Press, 2008.
Jankélévitch, Vladimir. *Music and the Ineffable*. Translated by Carolyn Abbate. Princeton, NJ: Princeton University Press, 2003.
Poultney, David. *Studying Music History: Learning, Reasoning, and Writing About Music History and Literature*. Upper Saddle River, NJ: Prentice Hall, 1996.
Rowell, Lewis. *Thinking About Music: An Introduction to the Philosophy of Music*. Amherst: University of Massachusetts Press, 1984.
Shepherd, John, et al. *Whose Music? A Sociology of Musical Languages*. New Brunswick, NJ: Transaction, 2008.

2
WHAT IS MUSIC?

Conceptions about music are fluid and variable. Music is viewed as an art form and used as a practical tool. In parts of Africa, music cannot be conceived of without dance. Some cultures do not have a word for "music" at all. Music pioneers have stretched the boundaries of tradition and taste with processed sound recordings, extended vocal techniques, computer generated noise, randomly produced electronic signals, field recordings, and more. Identifying music as such involves a complex interplay of cultural, historical, educational, and social considerations. This chapter elucidates the difficulty of defining music, generalized responses to culturally specific sounds, the role of convention in shaping music recognition, and time as the fundamental ingredient of all music.

(Not) Defining Music

A universally applicable definition of music will never be constructed. As an ever-present and ever-malleable aspect of human life, music, it seems, has taken as many forms, shades and variations as humanity itself. A truly objective view of what music is (or can be) would be so inclusive as to be almost useless. Every aspect of the musical entity is open to challenge and reconfiguration: devices used to produce sounds (instruments, found objects, electronic sampling, vocals, etc.); modes of transmission (oral tradition, written notation, live performance, recordings, etc.); means of reception (speakers, headphones, classroom, concert hall, etc.); the sounds themselves (tones, rhythms, consonances, dissonances, etc.).

Yet, at the same time, sources like the *Encyclopædia Britannica* remind us that, while no sound can be described as inherently unmusical, "musicians in each culture have tended to restrict the range of sounds they will admit."[1] Philosopher Lewis Rowell likewise defers to the role of convention: "let *music* signify anything that is normally called *music*."[2] In both cases, monolithism is discarded in favor of relativism: an awareness that ideas about music depend more on one's location and exposure than on sonic properties themselves. And now, with the aid of technology and global connectivity, it is possible to cultivate an ever-expanding musical vocabulary that reaches far beyond one's own cultural milieu.

But, even if we embrace globally diverse musical offerings (or, at minimum, acknowledge that what one culture accepts as music is not the final word), it is still the case that music is a cultural product, and, as such, comes to us through a long and multi-actor process of experimenting, selecting, sculpting, modifying and normalizing. Indeed, while abstract considerations may lead us to abandon hard and fast rules about what constitutes a musical sound, whatever music can be said to be is the result of a cultural process. Music, in other words, is defined for us. (It bears noting that even "rule-breaking" systems like twelve-tone serialism and free jazz draw their raw materials from pre-established tools and conceptions.)

To perhaps state the obvious, we do not begin with the view that music is a loose and inclusive category. Rather, it is the existence of musical variants within and between cultures that forces us to recognize that music is a loose and inclusive category. What we are left with, then, is a formulation that is not entirely satisfactory, but is at least defensible: cultures organize sounds in such a way that they are heard as music.

No Definition

Ambrose Bierce made a name for himself concocting sardonic epigrams. Many of them took the form of witty definitions originally published in the *Wasp*, a satirical San Francisco magazine, and were later compiled as *The Devil's Dictionary*.[3] The name he earned for himself was "Bitter." Each entry divulges the darkness of his humor. For instance, he defined birth as "The first and direst of all disasters," and faith as "Belief without evidence in what is told by one who speaks without knowledge, of things without parallel." Another term Bierce skewered was art, of which he dryly wrote, "This word has no definition."

A more conventional source would describe art as the application of skill and creativity to produce works intended to evoke emotional and/or aesthetic responses. The vagueness in this definition and the total avoidance in Bierce's highlight the difficulty of identifying what constitutes art, as well as the subjectivity of assessment once something has been labeled art. There is a sense that any strict parameter would be unfair, as it would deny options for imaginative excursions and inspired divergences. This is especially true in the wake of the twentieth century, with its envelope pushes, aesthetic challenges, deconstructions, reconstructions, abstractions and distractions. Most of us approach art intuitively: we know it when we see it (or hear it in the case of music). Because this process is personal, there is no guarantee that one person's recognition of something as art will be shared by all. Andres Serrano's *Piss Christ* is an obvious example.

Subjectiveness even extends to things universally accepted as art. Nowhere is this more clear than in the construction of artistic pantheons. Our concept of what constitutes greatness in art is, by and large, determined for us by historians and aficionados. True, the works tend to have some general appeal and strike the obligatory chords of beauty and emotion. But our relationship with art is such that there can be no universal agreement. Art is not just beyond definition. There is also wisdom in the old cliché that there's no accounting for taste.

Take these evaluations of widely admired musical works. Celebrated American violinist Ruggiero Ricci remarked, "A violinist can hide in the Brahms Concerto, where bad taste and musical inadequacies won't show up as easily as they do in Mozart."[4] Nineteenth-century composer Gioachino Rossini quipped, "One can't judge Wagner's opera *Lohengrin* after a first hearing, and I certainly don't intend to hear it a second time."[5] The always-opinionated Igor Stravinsky asked, "Why is it that every time I hear a piece of bad music, it's by Villa-Lobos?" These biting words call to mind Bierce's definition of painting: "The art of protecting flat surfaces from the weather and exposing them to the critic."

The nature of art is the root cause of this diversity of opinion. Both its indefiniteness and its way of triggering emotions expose it to strong and idiosyncratic responses. Tastes vary in every conceivable direction: person to person, group to group, region to region, culture to culture, period to period, life stage to life stage, etc. Behind every like and dislike are innumerable conscious and unconscious reasons. But rather than a weakness, the fact that art invites such individual feelings is perhaps its greatest strength. The freedom of reaction that art affords helps explain our attraction to it, whatever it is.

The Universal Non-Universal Language

A basic premise of ethnomusicological investigation is that music, as a worldwide phenomenon, cannot be subjected to an overarching set of values, standards or expectations. No single conception of what constitutes music is applicable cross-culturally; a definition that satisfies Western principles fails when applied to a non–Western society. Thus, it is argued, each cultural and subcultural manifestation of music should be studied individually and on its own terms. To paraphrase George Herzog, music is a non-universal language that exists in many dialects.[6]

As obvious as this may seem, there was a time, not too long ago, when scholars presumed that music in its varied forms communicated basic emotional information that could be discerned by insiders and outsiders in essentially the same way. But the more they examined the diverse offerings of local music-cultures, the more they came to appreciate the multifariousness of musical expression and the role of social conditioning in shaping musical perception. Like spoken languages, musical languages require a level of fluency to be understood.

Still, a version of the old assumption of universality can be upheld. Our reactions to music may not be uniform, but the types of reactions that music stirs are consistent throughout our species. In other words, while it is unlikely that a song indigenous to one group will evoke the same feelings when played for another, outsiders can at least appreciate the kinds of responses it produces in its native setting. The emotions of a sad or happy song may not resonate beyond a fluency group, but every group has its sad and happy songs.

In this sense, we are all empathetic when it comes to music (except, perhaps, for the roughly four percent who have some form of amusia, which hinders or prevents musical processing). We know emotionally what another experiences in music; we can place ourselves in their musical shoes. Of course, the degree to which music moves us varies from person to person, and shades of response tend to be more sophisticated among musicians. But regardless of how prone we are to emotional outpourings or how developed our musical skills, neurologically intact individuals are born musically sensitive and are predisposed to feeling music as emotion.

We can, then, empathize with another's musical experience irrespective if we feel the music in the same way or with the same level of interest or intensity. Mark Twain, in his characteristically perceptive autobiography, explained why this is so: "The last quarter century of my life has been pretty constantly and faithfully devoted to the study of the human race—that is to say, the study of myself, for in my individual person I am the entire human race compacted together. I have found that there is no ingredient of the race which I do not possess in either a small way or a large way. When it is small, as compared with the same ingredient in somebody else, there is still enough of it for all the purposes of examination. In my contacts with the species I find no one who possesses a quality which I do not possess."[7]

Radical Conventions

Everything we accept as mainstream had a beginning somewhere in the past. It may have sprung from a single source or through gradual development. It may have appeared in dramatic fashion, parting abruptly from ideas, technologies, manners or artistry of the day. Or it may have come with a snail-paced shift in the zeitgeist. Whether or not we know from whence it came, what we now consider normal was not always so.

True, nothing is without precedent. Given the cause-and-effect nature of reality, no entity is absolutely divorced from what came before. There is continuity in the intellectual evolution of our species, even when advancements seem more like mutations than adaptations. And, with enough time and repetition, once-innovative or iconoclastic views can become prevailing norms. Mark Twain put it thus: "The radical of one century is the conservative of the next. The radical invents the views. When he has worn them out, the conservative adopts them."[8]

In the vast universe of music, the transition from radical to conventional transpires in various ways. Two will be examined here, as they seem to be the most common: the appropriation of "far-out" ideas by mainstream musicians, and the discovery of older elements in novel forms.

The first involves convention through indirect channels. A good example is John Cage, hailed as one of the most influential composers of the twentieth century. Cage's legacy is felt more in his ideals than his actual works, which incorporate indeterminacy, spontaneity, expanded use of instruments, and manipulation of electronic and recorded material. Because of his personality, creativity and the experimental ethos of his time, Cage's name became household. But his music never caught on in a popular way. It was and will always remain in the impenetrable realm of avant-garde. Despite this, his conceptions seeped into the musical vernacular by way of Woody Guthrie, John Cale, Sonic Youth, Frank Zappa and Brian Eno, as well as the countless musicians they have inspired.

The second way radical music becomes conventional is through recognition of the past in envelope-pushing sounds. After the initial shock has worn off, new forms and styles are often reframed as unique syntheses of elements culled from a pool of established devices. This is perhaps most prevalent in the jazz community. The innovative playing of Charlie Parker has been reassessed as a fast-paced and intricate rendering of the blues. Eric Dolphy's mold-breaking approach has been described as rhythmically similar to Parker's, but more harmonically developed. The freeform technique of Ornette Coleman has been identified as a rephrasing of old swing patterns. These evaluations help pave the path to convention, where "outsider" sounds inform and are eventually fused with contemporary norms.

Most music is directly influenced by other music. Standards and trends do not arise in an instant or out of nothing, but through a subtle and organic flow that only becomes apparent with the passage of time. Drastic departures can also occur within this linear movement. As things progress, these too can become "normalized," often through secondary influence or reappraisal. Thus, as Twain observed, the radical is made conservative.

The Chronologic Art

Music has been called the chronologic art. In contrast to the plastic arts, which are presented in space and with the impression of completeness, music involves a temporal succession of impulses converging toward an end. The character of a piece—its shape, purpose, temperament, quality, etc.— is divulged gradually through linear progression. Musical information is performed and perceived through the passage of time and the ordering of sound within it.

The idea of music unfolding in time is a staple observation in the philosophy of music. Schopenhauer viewed tempo as the essence of music.[9] Hegel understood music as sound which retains its temporality, but is liberated from the spatial and material.[10] Time, in other words, is as crucial to a musician as canvas to a painter, wood to a carver, stone to a sculptor, paper to a poet. It is the fundamental surface upon which the art is created and experienced.

Music's relationship with time can be thought of in two distinct yet interconnected ways. The first is real or ontological time, which consists of organized elements such as duration, rhythm, meter and tempo. Duration is the length of a note. Rhythm is a regular and repeated pattern of sound. Meter refers to the number of beats and time value assigned to each note in a measure. Tempo involves the rate at which music is performed. These time-centered parts are the basic properties with which music is made.

Music's second temporal component is psychological time, or the listener's perception of music as it is played in real time. How we experience time is not always in accordance with the clock. Engagement in time is shaped by a slew of factors, including but not limited to physical surroundings, inner disposition and momentary circumstances. Feelings such as boredom, excitement, anxiety, anguish, expectation and pleasure set life at different paces. Similarly, moods and sensations derived from music convey temporal movement that seems to exist apart from meter and tempo. The seconds that pass slowly during a dreary piece are the same as those that fly quickly during a scherzo. Their psychological effects create the illusion of independent clocks.

Musical time, then, exists both within and outside of measurable temporal units. The music itself can be divided according to ordered parameters, and is subject to mathematical dissection and scientific analysis. Yet the movement of time becomes less mechanical and more impressionistic as the sounds travel from their source, through the auditory system and into consciousness. Ontological time makes possible and gives way to psychological time.

Notes

1. *The New Encyclopedia Britannica*, vol. 8 (2003), 422.
2. Lewis Rowell, *Thinking About Music: An Introduction to the Philosophy of Music* (Amherst: University of Massachusetts Press, 1983), 1.
3. Ambrose Bierce, *The Collected Works of Ambrose Bierce, vol. VII: The Devil's Dictionary* (New York: Neale, 1911).
4. Galewitz, *Music: A Book of Quotations*, 39.
5. Peter Archer, *The Quotable Intellectual* (Avon, MA: Adams, 2010), 69.
6. George Herzog, "Music's Dialects: A Non-Universal Language," *Independent Journal of Columbia University* 6:10 (1939): 1–2.
7. Mark Twain, *Mark Twain's Own Autobiography: The Chapters from the North American Review* (Madison: University of Wisconsin Press, 1924), 225.
8. Mark Twain, *Mark Twain's Notebook*, ed. Albert Bigelow Paine (New York: Harper, 1935), 355.
9. Arthur Schopenhauer, *Die Welt als Wille und Vorstellung*, cited in Barry Empson, "Schoenberg's Hat: Objects in Musical Space," in *Frameworks, Artworks, Place: The Space of Perception in the Modern World*, ed. Timothy J. Mehigan (Amsterdam: Rodopi, 2008), 85.
10. See Georg Wilhelm Friedrich Hegel, *Aesthetics: Lectures on Fine Art*, trans. T. M. Knox (Oxford: Oxford University Press, 1975).

Suggestions for Further Readings

Alperson, Philip, ed. *What Is Music? An Introduction to the Philosophy of Music*. University Park: Pennsylvania State University Press, 2010.
Cook, Nicholas, and Mark Everis, eds. *Rethinking Music*. New York: Oxford University Press, 1999.

2. What Is Music?

Gracyk, Theodore, and Andrew Kania, eds. *The Routledge Companion to Philosophy of Music.* New York: Routledge, 2011.
Kivy, Peter. *Introduction to a Philosophy of Music.* New York: Clarendon, 2002.
Nettl, Bruno. *The Study of Ethnomusicology: Thirty-One Issues and Concepts.* Champaign: University of Illinois Press, 2005.
Rice, Timothy. *Ethnomusicology: A Very Short Introduction.* New York: Oxford University Press, 2014.
Ridley, Aaron. *The Philosophy of Music: Theme and Variations.* Edinburgh: Edinburgh University Press, 2004.
Robinson, Jennifer, ed. *Music and Meaning.* Ithaca, NY: Cornell University Press, 1997.
Scruton, Robert. *Understanding Music: Philosophy and Interpretation.* New York: Bloomsbury, 2009.
Zbikowski, Lawrence M. *Conceptualizing Music: Cognitive Structure, Theory, and Analysis.* New York: Oxford University Press, 2002.

3

WHERE DOES MUSIC COME FROM?

The observation that we are a musical species is hardly controversial. Confirmation of our musical nature is found in the many and persistent ways we infuse music into our daily lives. Precisely how we became so musical is not as clear. Theories abound, each adding a thought-provoking possibility to the evolutionary discussion. This chapter begins with an overview of the likely stages in musical evolution, and moves on to five specific theories: the likelihood that music predated speech; the Darwinian view of music as a sexually selected courtship display; the notion that music evolved from cohesive rhythmic rituals; the evidence that group singing forges essential bonds; and Steven Pinker's much-discussed proposition that music serves no evolutionary purpose.

The Rudiments of Music

Alfred Einstein, one of the twentieth century's most respected musicologists (and possible fifth cousin of Albert), wrote a daring and enduring book at the age of thirty-seven. *A Short History of Music* first appeared in print in his native German in 1917. The preface to later English editions includes this admission: "[The book] was written in a few weeks, at a time and place that precluded resort to any books of reference."[1] In Einstein's view, this was a help rather than a hindrance. Rather than drown himself (and the reader) in a swamp of names and dates, he attempted a through-composed picture of the development of (Western) music as a whole. Some specialists have pounced on this approach, but the book's resonance among lay readers is attested in the abundance of revised printings in German and English, each amended to include recent data (the last edition I'm aware of was published in 1954).

Naturally, Einstein gave greater attention to the area for which he was the primary authority: sixteenth-century music, especially of Italy. But no period up to his day was overlooked entirely. An intriguing case is the first chapter, which summarizes what was then known about "primitive" music.

Aside from employing that now distasteful term, Einstein's offerings remain the general hypotheses of the field. Indeed, while contemporary interest in the origins of music has produced fascinating details and possibilities, current research mostly complies with broad assumptions made during the first half of the twentieth century.

Einstein included seven hypotheses: (1) Singing has deeper historical roots than speaking (pre-linguistic music); (2) After singing came rhythm and percussion, which were explored in ritual dance (devotional music); (3) Song and rhythm combined to accompany labor (work songs); (4) Notes of definite pitch were used as signals in war (war songs); (5) The "easy" intervals of the fourth and fifth were the first preferred pitches (early scales); (6) Ancient songs were composed of repeated patterns of a few notes (monotony); (7) The rudiments of harmony began with the "unintentional polyphony" of heterophony—what Einstein describes as the "arbitrary ornamentation of the same melody by several performers at the same time" (group song).[2]

As mentioned, these premises are still foundational. Where contemporary studies have expanded upon them is in the aspect of motivation. Advances in anthropology, neuroscience, psychology, evolutionary biology and other fields have added deeper perspectives regarding *why* our species began making music—the dominant theories being mating and cohesion (with variations of the two, like fitness displays, preparing for the hunt, and bonding between mother and child).

Such evolutionary theories, combined with Einstein's strictly musical concerns of many decades ago, help us to ponder not only how the earliest music sounded, but why it was sounded at all. Fortunately, these central questions are currently on the front burners of researchers possessing great skill and imagination. And the more the topic is explored, the more interesting it becomes.

Before Speech

Music and speech are not the same thing. One is abstract and arbitrary; the other is concrete and absolute. One uses sound as its subject matter; the other as a vehicle for logos. The grammar of one is built on pitch, key, rhythm, harmony and technique; the grammar of the other is based on morphemes, phonemes, words, syntax and sentences. One stimulates imprecise affective states; the other imparts precise information. One stems from emotion; the other from reason. Despite these dissimilarities, both music and speech grew from the primal necessity for self-expression.

In the evolution of human communication, wordless vocal music—as distinct from song—is speculated to have preceded structured language. Part of this view is rooted in observation. As anyone familiar with infants knows, our earliest attempts to communicate vocally involve singsong patterns of mostly vowel sounds. Although indefinite, this "naked language" is unmistakable in its desire to relay specific thoughts and needs (often intelligible only to the parent). The result is an emotive sequence of tones approaching, though not identical to, music.

This could lead us to the now-defunct theory of recapitulation (or biogenetic law), popularized by Ernst Haeckel, in which the stages of child development are thought to encompass developmental stages of the species as a whole, which extended over millennia.[3] In that old theory, the infant's progress from nonsense vocables to coherent speech is a repetition of what our prehistoric ancestors went through, only in quick time. Modern biology has dumped this idea into the dustbin of mythology. However, the premise that music-speech predated language-speech has been revived, though in a more limited way.

One intriguing example is Steven Mithen's book, *The Singing Neanderthals*.[4] Mithen, a professor of archaeology at the University of Reading, has traced pseudo-singing to Neanderthals, a Middle to Late Pleistocene species closely related to modern humans. According to Mithen, while Neanderthals lacked the neural circuitry for language, they did have a proto-musical form of communication that incorporated sound and gesture, influenced emotional states and behavior, and was rhythmic, melodic and temporally controlled—that is, "a prelinguistic musical mode of thought and action." He has coined a cumbersome neologism to describe the phenomenon: "Hmmmmm," for <u>h</u>olistic, <u>m</u>ulti-<u>m</u>odal, <u>m</u>anipulative, <u>m</u>usical, and <u>m</u>imetic.

Although the title of the book suggests that Neanderthals "sang," Mithen is careful to state that their vocalization was neither language nor music as we know them today. This implies a more nuanced and complex line of evolution than the earlier simplistic formula of song to speech. Of course, it is impossible to know for sure whether a music-like activity evolved prior to and/or gave rise to language. Without the aid of a time machine, we are reliant on the sophisticated, yet ultimately limited, tools of archaeology, anthropology, psychology and neuroscience. But speculate we can.

Romantic Reverberations

Charles Darwin included this intriguing hypothesis in *The Descent of Man*: "[I]t appears probable that the progenitors of man, either the males or females or both sexes, before acquiring the power of expressing their mutual love in articulate language, endeavored to charm each other with musical notes and rhythm."[5] With this observation, Darwin grouped human beings with other animals whose songs apparently evolved as sexually selected courtship displays. Countless creatures, from spiders and crustaceans to seals and birds, innately distinguish "musical" mating calls from other noises. For Darwin, a trait so pervasive could not be accidental: "unless the females were able to appreciate such sounds and were excited or charmed by them, the persevering efforts of the males and the complex structures often possessed by them alone would be useless; and this it is impossible to believe."[6] Without the function of attracting mates, the instinct for music would not have arisen or persisted.

Of course, the forms and uses of music expanded as human cultures and needs grew in complexity. Unlike most of the animals Darwin studied, human-made music has branched out far beyond mating. Still, it is hard to ignore the enormous quantity of love songs our species has produced. In most societies, songs of romance and sexual longing comprise the largest percentage of musical output. Roughly forty to fifty percent of popular songs recorded in the United States address the topic of romantic love. Like Darwin, many contemporary evolutionary biologists conclude that our unquenchable attraction to love songs—both saccharine-sweet and sorrowful—is a carry-over from the primal epoch when our musical ears perked up at the alluring sounds of potential mates.

Given the apparent sexual origins of music production in all animal species, including our own, it is not surprising that the oldest song scientists have discovered is a song of romance. In February of 2012, British scientists announced that they had reconstructed the simple mating call of a Jurassic-era cricket. Their study, published in the *Proceedings of the National Academy of Sciences*, detailed how they derived the sound from the cricket's pristinely fossilized 72-centemeter wings. The song, which was performed 165 million year ago, was the insect's way of attracting mates in a nighttime forest busy with waterfalls, streams, rustling leaves and scavenging dinosaurs. According to the study's co-author Daniel Robert, an expert in the biomechanics of singing and hearing in insects, this type of tuneful chirping "advertises the presence, location and quality of the singer, a message that females choose to respond to—or not. Using a single tone, the male's call carries further and better, and therefore is likely to serenade more females."[7]

Our ears are tuned to music in much the same way. We hear the melodious ice-cream truck over the roaring engines of a congested street. We notice the piped-in recording over the chatter and clanking dishes of a crowded restaurant. Even when music is incessantly played at a super market or shopping mall, a melodic line or rhythmic hook often catches our ear, inducing us to hum or tap our fingers. Like the calls of the prehistoric cricket and the modern-day songbird, human music pierces through the clamor and din of everyday life.

From an evolutionary perspective, our inborn ability to pick out these sounds stems from the distant days when our ancestors sang songs of courtship. In those long-ago times, hearing love songs through the clutter of nature helped ensure the perpetuation of our species. Though this function was minimized as our intellectual and emotional capacities progressed and diversified—and though we might be ashamed to admit it—we remain instinctively attracted to songs of love.

The Rhythm of Survival

Of all the elements of music, rhythm and tempo are the most fundamental and most attractive to the human senses. Without thinking, we synchronize body movements to beats inferred from sound patterns, and know precisely when to begin, end, speed up or slow down with the music. Regular isochronous pulses effect a variety of physical responses, from toe tapping and hand clapping to marching and dancing. Beat-based rhythm processing, or beat induction, is a cognitive skill we do not share with other primates (and is perhaps only shared with certain parrots). It is the basis of our ability to create and appreciate music, and is among the instincts that make us human.

The urge to synchronize to external rhythm is present from the first stages of human development. A recent study of 120 small children, aged five months to two years, confirms what has long been assumed: we are born with a predisposition to move to musical rhythm. According to University of York psychologist Marcel Zentner, who worked on the study, "it is the beat rather than other features of the music, such as the melody, that produces the response in infants."[8]

Biomusicological reactions occur naturally in small children; they are not learned or imitative behaviors. During the experiment, each child sat on a parent's lap. The parent was instructed to stay still and was given headphones to block out sound. The child, who was fully exposed to the music, freely waved her arms, hands, legs and feet, and swayed her head and torso from side to side. Intriguingly, too, the child responded to the music with greater consistency and enthusiasm than when she was addressed by her parent's voice.

While the study records an innate proclivity for rhythmic incitement, researchers are left to speculate why this tendency evolved. One possibility comes from evolutionary musicologist Joseph Jordania. In his book, *Why Do People Sing?*, Jordania proposes that early human survival was aided by attaining a collective state known as the "battle trance."[9] Our ancestors were too slow, weak and timid to face predators or enemies on their own. They needed to band together, and would do so through ceremonial drumming and dancing. After several hours of ritual performance, participants entered an altered state where they did not know fear, were immune to pain, acted as a single unit and were ready to sacrifice their lives for the community. Repetitive beats and movements brought them to entrainment, wherein self-awareness dissipated into unified thought and collective action.

If Jordania's adroit analysis is correct (either in whole or in part), then the spontaneity with which we react to rhythm can be traced to natural selection. Groups best adept at orchestrating rhythmic rituals had the best chances of survival in a harsh and dangerous world. This impulse eventually became ingrained in our species. Though our existence no longer depends on it, we intuitively move to the beat from cradle to grave.

The Social Basis of Singing

According to Chorus America, a national research and advocacy organization, the United States is home to some 270,000 choruses. A large majority are "church" choirs (217,000), a species that presumably includes non–Christian denominations as well. There are also roughly 41,000 school choirs (K-12) and 12,000 independent community and professional choirs. Nearly a quarter of American households boast one or more choral singers, a figure accounting for an estimated 42.6 million people (32.5 million adults and 10.1 million children). Together with researchers from the National Endowment for the Arts, Chorus America confidently asserts that choral singing is the country's most popular form of performing arts.[10]

Surely, the numbers are too large and too steady to suggest a fad. Choral singing is as ancient as it is popular, and while endowments and advocacy groups can create opportunities for participation, they do not guarantee the participants' dedication. Advertisements help get singers to the audition, but commitment is cultivated through the singing itself.

Author Stacy Horn compares singing to "an infusion of the perfect tranquilizer, the kind that both soothes your nerves and elevates your spirit."[11] This observation is rooted both in anecdotal experience and emerging science that demystifies that experience. The "tranquilizer" effect is partly attributed to two hormones released while singing: endorphins and oxytocin. Endorphins, known as the body's "happy drug," are chemically related to opium-derived narcotics, and induce feelings of pleasure and well-being. Oxytocin acts as a stress and anxiety reliever, as well as an enhancer of trust and bonding.

These latter results—trust and bonding—help explain why group singing is usually felt as the most exhilarating and transformative of song activities. From an evolutionary standpoint, the positive effects of singing can be viewed as a biochemical reward for coming together in cooperation—a social process essential to our species' survival. It is plausible that endorphins and oxytocin were originally released to encourage group cohesion. Indeed, while solitary singing can have a similar effect, the difference in degree is telling. Almost without exception, the benefits are greatly amplified when singing with others.

This premise finds support in a recent study published in the *Journal of Personality and Social Psychology*. In a paper titled "Unraveling the Mystery of Music: Music as an Evolved Group Process," neuroscientists Chris Loersch and Nathan L. Arbuckle suggest a tentative (but potentially once-and-for-all) explanation for our emotional response to music—an occurrence that has long baffled scientists and philosophers.[12] Using seven studies, the researchers establish human musicality as a special form of social cognition, demonstrating that musical-emotional responses are tied to other core social phenomena that bind us together into groups. This evolutionary basis is still extant in the psychological pull of music, which remains linked to the basic social drives underlying our interconnected world. Put simply, music evolved as (and continues to be) a tool of social living.

Concepts like these are not unique in the scope of theories on music's origins. Social conjectures comprise a major area of speculation in the field (the other being sexual selection). What is coming to light is scientific backing for such claims. The benefits have always been felt in choral and other group singing. Now we are beginning to understand why.

Necessary Cheesecake

Literature on the origins of music is dominated by two theories. The first is sexual selection, or the idea that animals develop features that help maximize reproductive success. Charles Darwin introduced the concept in *The Descent of Man*, writing that the human inclination for music came about in much the same way as ornate peacock feathers, lion manes and the antlers of male deer—that is, as sexual enticement. Musical skill, he theorized, stemmed from the biological compulsion to court a mate. Recent scholarship supports this hypothesis, highlighting the performer's dexterity, creativity and mental agility as signs of fitness and desirability. Evolutionary biologist Geoffrey Miller published a study demonstrating a correlation between music-making and the reproductive life of jazz musicians, whose musical output tends to rise after puberty, peak during young adulthood and decline with parenthood and/or advancing age.[13]

The second prevalent view involves group solidarity. In modern experience, music is regularly used to foster and enhance cohesion. This effect likely originated when small bands of people struggled for survival in the precarious prehistoric world. Populations lacking strong ties stood little chance of continuance, and music—especially song and dance—helped keep them intact. Robin Dunbar of Oxford University contends that while music eventually expanded into the area of courtship, it was group selection—not sexual selection—that prompted its emergence.[14]

These theories frame music as basic to the endurance of our species. They assert that music was born of the necessities of reproduction and solidarity, and continues to be a means of sexual attraction and communal togetherness. However compelling, these functional explanations are not immune from criticism. Among the most prominent opponents is Harvard language theorist Steven Pinker.

Pinker devotes just ten pages to music in his massive book, *How the Mind Works*.[15] The quick gloss owes to his assertion that music is not an evolutionary adaptation, but a tangential technology: a human faculty developed and exploited for its own sake. Although musical sounds tickle our requisite capacities for language, auditory scene analysis, emotional calls, habitat selection and motor control, they are, in Pinker's phrase, "auditory cheesecake." Like the decadent dessert, which over-stimulates our biological desire for fat- and sugar-rich foods, music supplies us with an oversupply of sound. An article in *The Economist* likened Pinker's assessment to calling instrumental playing "auditory pornography" and singing "auditory masturbation," both of which sate an appetite that is beyond strict biological need.[16] In other words, if music were to vanish from our species, little else would change.

Although widely disseminated, Pinker's proposition contains at least two faulty assumptions. The first is his argument that music-making is the domain of a small subset of people, and thus not a universal trait essential for survival. This reflects an understanding of music as it exists in the modern

West, where professionalization and music as entertainment have done much to inhibit the participation of large segments of the population—a development unknown for most of human history and in contrast to many places in the world today. The second is his point that music is variable in its complexity from culture to culture, thus indicating an aesthetic rather than fundamental purpose. This may be an accurate comment on the nature of musical diversity, but does not negate the possibility that music production, generally speaking, began as a human need.

Nevertheless, Pinker's analysis is a worthy challenge to the assumed evolutionary significance of music. It could very well be that music is an enhancement rather than a building block of human life. Yet it takes little effort to harmonize the biological theories with Pinker's contrarian view. For instance, it is possible that music originated as a sexually selected feature, developed into a group-selected trait, and over time became an attraction in itself. It began as raw material for survival and, in some ways and in some cases, took on the qualities of "audible cheesecake." Music may no longer be essential for human life, but life's enjoyment would certainly be diminished without it.

Notes

1. Alfred Einstein, Preface to *A Short History of Music* (New York: Alfred A. Knopf, 1954).
2. Ibid., 5.
3. Ernst Haeckel, *The History of Creation, or, The Development of the Earth and Its Inhabitants by the Action of Natural Causes* (New York: D. Appleton, 1892).
4. Steven Mithen, *The Singing Neanderthals: The Origins of Music, Language, Mind and Body* (London: Weidenfeld and Nicolson, 2005).
5. Charles Darwin, *The Descent of Man* (New York: D. Appleton, 1871), 573.
6. Ibid., 598.
7. Daniel Robert, quoted in "Researchers Reconstructed Love Song of Prehistoric Bushcricket," Sci-News.com, February 7, 2012, <http://www.sci-news.com/paleontology/article00173.html>
8. Marcel Zentner, quoted in Richard Alleyne, "Babies Are Born to Dance to the Beat," *The Telegraph*, March 15, 2010, <http://www.telegraph.co.uk/science/science-news/7450560/Babies-are-born-to-dance-to-the-beat.html>
9. Joseph Jordania, *Why Do People Sing?: Music in Human Evolution* (Tbilisi: Logos, 2011).
10. *The Chorus Impact Study: How Children, Adults, and Communities Benefit from Choruses* (Washington, D.C.: Chorus America, 2010).
11. Stacey Horn, "Singing Changes Your Brain," *Time*, August 16, 2013, <http://ideas.time.com/2013/08/16/singing-changes-your-brain/>
12. Chris Loersch and Nathan L. Arbuckle, "Unraveling the Mystery of Music: Music as an Evolved Group Process," *Journal of Personality and Social Psychology* 105 (2013): 777–798.

13. Geoffrey Miller, "Sexual Selection for Cultural Displays," in *The Evolution of Culture: An Interdisciplinary View*, ed. Robin Dunbar, et al. (Edinburgh: Edinburgh University Press, 1999), 71–91.

14. Robin Dunbar, *The Science of Love* (Hoboken, NJ: Wiley, 2012).

15. Steven Pinker, *How the Mind Works* (New York: W. W. Norton, 1997).

16. "Why Music?" *The Economist*, December 18, 2008, <http://www.economist.com/node/12795510>

Suggestions for Further Reading

Bannan, Nicholas, ed. *Music, Language, and Human Evolution*. New York: Oxford University Press, 2012.
Blacking, John. *How Musical is Man?* Seattle: University of Washington Press, 1973
Heline, Corinne. *Music: The Keynote of Human Evolution*. Santa Barbara, CA: J. F. Rowny Press, 1965.
Jordania, Joseph. *Why Do People Sing?: Music in Human Evolution*. Tbilisi: Logos, 2011.
Levitin, Daniel J. *The World in Six Songs: How the Musical Brain Created Human Nature*. New York: Penguin, 2008.
Mithen, Steven J. *The Singing Neanderthals: The Origins of Music, Language, Mind, and Body*. Cambridge, MA: Harvard University Press, 2005.
Morley, Iain. *The Prehistory of Music: Human Evolution, Archaeology, and the Origins of Musicality*. New York: Oxford University Press, 2013.
Schulkin, Jay. *Reflections on the Musical Mind: An Evolutionary Perspective*. Princeton, NJ: Princeton University Press, 2013.
Wallin, Nils Lennart, Björn Merker, and Steven Brown, ed. *The Origins of Music*. Cambridge, MA: MIT Press, 2001.
Zuckerkandl, Victor. *Man the Musician*. Princeton: Princeton University Press, 1976.

4

INNATENESS

Human beings are almost universally equipped with an innate ability to detect, react to, and create musical sounds. This does not mean that everyone is a musician or that all are predisposed to develop musical expertise. Music is both a specialized endeavor and something non-specialists are inclined to appreciate. This chapter delves into the notion of music as an instinct. Among other things, this includes our knack to differentiate between music produced by humans and machines, and our gravitation toward particularly expressive performers. On the other end of the spectrum, we will encounter those for whom music is not especially compelling, and the very few for whom it is an irritant. These outliers will enrich our understanding of what it means to be innately musical.

The Music Instinct

In 1933, fifty-eight-year-old composer Maurice Ravel suffered a stroke while swimming. The ordeal left him with aphasia, which robbed his ability to comprehend or express linguistic symbols. Because music composition, like language, utilizes a written system of signs, aphasia also silenced his creative output. Although Ravel retained musical mentation—the capacity to think musically—he was no longer able to translate musical thoughts into sounds. He could recognize tunes, identify errors in performance, and select a score by patterns represented on the page. But his analytical deciphering disappeared: note naming, sight-reading, dictation.

Contrast this with a more recent story of a sixth grader who was forced to give up sports after sustaining a concussion.[1] The boy's dream of becoming a professional athlete was dashed, but he suddenly discovered a new talent for music. He displayed little aptitude for music prior to the injury, and was even below average when it came to simple functions like matching pitches and predicting phrases. Now a high school student, he plays over a dozen instruments, including guitar, piano, accordion, harmonica and bagpipes—all by ear. It is possible that this talent was dormant before circumstances led to its discovery. But it may also be the result of the brain's rewiring and overcompensating for capabilities lost in the trauma.

Losing or gaining musical genius in the aftermath of a head injury is exceedingly rare. However, these extreme cases do point to the innateness of music in humanity. Ravel, a once expert and meticulous musician, could still conceive of and enjoy music, though he could no longer create or perform it. The student athlete, once indifferent toward music, became musically hyperexpressive. Latent in both was a musical sense that exists in virtually everyone. An underlying musicality was preserved in Ravel, who was reduced to a passive receiver, and magnified in the boy, who was transformed into an active creator.

It is rarely acknowledged that the absence of musical skill or training does not correspond to a lack of musical capacity. Just as one need not be a writer to appreciate a well-written book, one need not be gifted or educated in the musical arts to be moved by a well-executed piece. Likewise, the musically inclined and disinclined benefit from music in essentially identical ways, the difference being one of degree rather than kind. Whatever our talents or limitations—and whether our musical adeptness increases, decreases or stays stagnant over time—we remain musical creatures.

Is It Musical?

British mathematician Alan Turing was among the first to propose that computer programs would someday simulate human creativity.[2] He argued that the hardwiring of computers and human brains were essentially the same, and that the "thought processes" of both could be reduced to mechanical calculations. This concept of disembodied cognition gained enthusiastic support in the initial wake of the computer revolution. Among other things, it spurred predictions that programs would be able to compose pieces and improvise jazz in a way indistinguishable from human musicians. Some even anticipated a machine that would match Bach or Beethoven.

These conjectures failed to recognize the embodied nature of the musical arts. Phrasing is structured on patterns of breathing. Articulation and tone length are imitative of language. The functional morphology of hands informs the range of a musical line. The emotional mind directs melodic movement. Many of us intuitively discern human performances from computer-generated music, even when a digital creation uses samples from live instruments. Our humanity detects the unhumanity of the piece.

Computers cannot, by themselves, generate the musical in music. They may excel at translating a sequence of symbols into audible information, but they do not grasp or communicate structural or affective musical meanings. They produce precision without spirit.

In a similar fashion, human performers can be judged by their musicality, or the feeling they bring to a given piece. As listeners, we make connections between the music we hear and extra-musical images, ideas and sensations, such as drama, poetry and passions. If we do not sense these layers in a performance, we withhold the label of musical. An assiduous player can master instrumental technique and conquer challenging literature. But unless something of that person's interior life is heard, the playing will come across as dull or dry. This is largely what sets impassioned artists like Jascha Heifetz apart from many other skilled musicians.

In contrast, popular singers often lack the dexterity and tone quality typically looked for in Western music. If assessed exclusively for their voices, they would be deemed mediocre or worse. However, they possess what might be called a musical soul. Their innate sense of sound—and their sense of self projected in that sound—is both palpable and seductive. Their instruments may not be conventionally beautiful and their music may not be objectively artful; but their presentation is thoroughly musical. Singers fitting this description include icons such as Bob Dylan, Rod Stewart, Tom Waits, Leonard Cohen and Janis Joplin.

Impressive range and technical acumen do not always amount to musical music. Meticulous performers who convey little emotion are akin to exacting computers: the notes are polished and the passages precise, yet the essence is wanting. In the end, it is difficult to articulate or quantify exactly what this essence is. But we know it when we feel it.

Music Non-Lovers

Aaron Copland wrote a brief and candid article for the music industry magazine *Billboard* in February of 1964. In it, he explained the dilemma of the modern symphonic composer, whose livelihood is built on commissions, royalties and rights collected for public performances. It is a ruthless system that grants few successes, partly because there aren't many places or productions that pay well for original works, and partly because of something Copland was brave enough to admit: "Composers tend to assume that everyone loves music. Surprisingly enough, everyone doesn't."

Sitting through an orchestral performance is not something most people were born to do. Patient reception of drawn-out passages and serene acceptance of slowly developing movements are virtues obtained through discipline, education and cultural training. Even some classical musicians will confess—usually off the record—that lengthy performances can be less than tolerable. Copland found it refreshing whenever people told him they cared little for orchestral fare. He knew that as a composer and music educator, he could drift out of touch with the average listener.

There is one instructive exception to this orchestral rule. Composers have a firm and steady place in movies and television. Anyone who has watched an anxious or action-packed scene with the sound turned off realizes that it is far less anxious or action-packed without the frantic strings, blaring horns and penetrating percussion. The ears are more emotionally attuned than the eyes. Visuals attain their full effect through the aid of the score.

The cinematic example is reflective of how humans have utilized music since the dawn of the species. Music's original and still overwhelming purpose is as an accompaniment to other things: teaching, storytelling, dancing, healing, praying, relaxing, eating, competing, warring, rejoicing, socializing, driving, watching, shopping, napping, waking. Listening to music for its own sake is a recent and largely Western phenomenon, and the amount of people for whom absolute or "for itself" music has any real appeal is so small as to be statistically insignificant.

A multitude of musical functions might be simultaneously present in a given context. For instance, melodies sung and played at a religious service establish sacred time, foster cohesion, encourage introspection, enliven texts, guide choreography, focus concentration, recall memories, inspire sensations, affirm heritage, facilitate moral instruction. The list could go on, and similar lists could be devised for other musically aided events.

It is difficult to imagine just how impoverished a service would be without its musical component. If melody were eradicated, attendance would surely diminish and would probably disappear altogether.

This returns us to Copland's observation. It is certainly the case that not everyone is a music lover. The pure musical experience removed from any practical purpose is a learned and essentially artificial activity. Yet, it is also true that human beings are music "needers." Whether we are conscious of it or not, we rely on musical sounds to support, assist and enhance all sorts of endeavors. This is what Austrian-Jewish musicologist Victor Zuckerkandl meant when he penned these dramatic yet hardly exaggerated words: "man without music is not man and a world without music is not our world."[3]

Pots and Pans

When Ulysses S. Grant was asked what music he liked, he replied: "I know only two tunes. One of them is 'Yankee Doodle'—and the other isn't."[4] At first reading, this seems like a snarky pronouncement of musical stubbornness. Perhaps Grant considered "Yankee Doodle" the apex of musical achievement, and nothing else deserved mention alongside it. This attitude is not uncommon. It is human nature to put certain music on a pedestal and confidently assert that it is better than the rest (though our "pedestal music" is usually more sophisticated than a patriotic ditty). But that was not the meaning of Grant's remark. His words were much more cynical—and much more literal.

From an early age, the great general (and not-so-great president) professed an intense dislike for music. He was extremely tone deaf: he could not hum, recognize or remember even the most popular airs of his day. Perhaps his inability to retain or reproduce music was so frustrating that it spilled over into animosity. Or maybe music truly sounded awful to his ears. Whatever the reason, his was an almost pathological aversion to musical sounds. He never went to concerts, refused to dance and had a particular (and ironic) hatred for military bands.

Grant most likely suffered from congenital amusia, an anomaly that begins at birth and affects roughly four percent of the population. (There is also acquired amusia, which occurs as a result of brain damage.) The primary symptom is a deficit in fine-grained pitch discrimination. Amusics cannot detect pitch changes when the distance between two successive pitches is small, and thus cannot internalize musical scales. This impairs the person's ability to enjoy or respond to melodies, most of which consist of slight interval changes.

However, while amusics typically cannot distinguish one musical selection from the next, they often do recognize a *single* piece, usually one that involves strong rhythms and some sort of fanfare. Many patriotic songs fit this description, with their accompanying parades, flag waving and ritualized gestures. That would explain how Grant could identify "Yankee Doodle" and nothing else.

Music can also be a severe annoyance for some amusics. Their problem is not just a failure of recognition. Music as they hear it is comparable to the banging of pots and pans or some other cacophonous irritant. This also seems to describe Grant's condition.

Nevertheless, Grant was sensitive to how the majority responds music, even as he could not comprehend their enjoyment. After graduating from West Point, he was assigned to duty with the Fourth U.S. Infantry. In those days, regimental bands were paid partly by the government and partly by regimental funds, which were set aside for luxuries such as books, magazines and music. Grant accumulated money for the fund by ordering the Infantry's daily rations in flour instead of bread (at a significant savings), renting a bakery, hiring bakers and selling fresh bread through a contract he arranged with the army's chief commissary. Much of the extra income went to secure a bandleader and competent players, whose music boosted the soldiers' morale (and punished Grant's ears).[5]

Grant's neurological wiring prevented him from being a music lover. In fact, it made him a music hater. He did not process music as music, and could not feel it as most of us do. Yet he was perceptive enough to observe the musical pleasures of others, and gentleman enough to give fellow soldiers the music they yearned for.

Notes

1. "Teen Becomes a Musical Genius," *Mail Online*, November 21, 2013, <http://www.dailymail.co.uk/news/article-2511439/Denver-teen-Lachlan-Connors-musical-genius-suffering-concussion.html>

2. Alan M. Turing, "Computing Machinery and Intelligence," *Mind* 59:236 (1950): 433–460.

3. Victor Zuckerkandl, *Man the Musician* (Princeton: Princeton University Press, 1976), 17.

4. Ulysses S. Grant, quoted in Robert Andrews, ed., *The Concise Columbia Dictionary of Quotations* (New York: Columbia University Press, 1992), 201.

5. Ulysses S. Grant, *Personal Memoirs of Ulysses S. Grant* [1885–1886] (New York: Cosimo, 2007), 65.

Suggestions for Further Reading

Addis, Laird. *Of Mind and Music*. Ithaca, NY: Cornell University Press, 2004.
Ball, Philip. *The Music Instinct: How Music Works and Why We Can't Do Without It*. New York: Oxford University Press, 2010.
Byrne, David. *How Music Works*. San Francisco: McSweeney's, 2012.
Copland, Aaron. *Music and Imagination*. Cambridge, MA: Harvard University Press, 1980.
Deutsch, Diana. *The Psychology of Music*. Waltham, MA: Academic, 2013.
Dissanayake, Ellen. *Homo Aestheticus: Where Art Comes From and Why*. Seattle: University of Washington Press, 1992.
Dutton, Denis. *The Art Instinct: Beauty, Pleasure, and Human Evolution*. New York: Bloomsbury, 2009.
Hallam, Susan, Ian Cross, and Michael Thaut. *Oxford Handbook of Music Psychology*. New York: Oxford University Press, 2008.
Levitin, Daniel J. *This is Your Brain on Music: The Science of a Musical Obsession*. New York: Plume, 2007.
Sacks, Oliver. *Musicophilia: Tales of Music and the Brain*. New York: Vintage, 2008.

5

CHARACTER

Musical literature tends to focus on sound. This makes perfect sense, as music is the intentional organization of sonic ingredients. This chapter looks at music from the opposite direction. While music emanates from external sources and reaches the auditor from the outside, the experience of it derives largely from within. This chapter puts forward diverse ways in which this is so: how we ascribe anthropomorphic qualities to musical sounds; how cultural learning shapes musical impressions; how we respond to the whole of music rather than its constituent parts; how visual aspects of a performance affect our perceptions; and how empathy helps account for musical pleasure.

Sound and Feeling

The raw materials of music include pitch, rhythm, durations, dynamics, texture and timbre. The deliberate ordering of these building blocks of sound and silence produces what we instantly recognize as a musical creation. To be sure, definitions of music vary from rigid to loose, and postmodern requirements are not always as stable or confined as conventional views. But, however far the envelope is stretched and however ambiguous music is made out to be, most of us can agree with seventeenth-century English churchman Thomas Fuller: "Music is nothing else but wild sounds civilized into time and tune."[1]

Understandably, comments on the nature of music usually address its audibility: it is an art form directed at the ears. Our sense of hearing distinguishes between music and the other sounds that constantly bombard us. The very concept of music derives from and depends upon our faculty of perceiving sound. Yet it can be argued that the ears are merely the necessary entry point. As soon as we are made aware of music, it is translated into mood, memory and movement. As poet Wallace Stevens eloquently wrote: "Music is feeling, then, not sound."[2]

The listener's response to specific music will vary in type and intensity. She might feel very hopeful, a little bit sad, extremely calm, slightly anxious, and so on. These reactions may or may not be the intention of the composer or performer, and may change according to when and where the piece is heard. But in almost every instance, human perception converts music into feeling.

Perhaps the clearest evidence of this is how we typically *portray* music. We most often fixate on music's experiential properties, or its "personality." Anthropomorphic qualities are freely projected upon a piece: charming, aggressive, warm, tender, brutish, exuberant, consoling, frustrating, etc. This is partly because of the difficulty of identifying and discussing music's formal properties. But it is mainly because the formal properties are but a means to an end. When we call a composition happy, we are basically saying that it makes us *feel* happy. The resulting emotion is so dominant that it becomes the character of the music. Priority is given to effect over sound.

In some sense, music can be thought of as a delivery system for emotional content. We do not experience music so much as we experience ourselves experiencing music. Our ears funnel the sound to a deeper layer of our being, a layer where sound is made significant. Of course, not all music is equally effective and not every listener is equally moved by musical stimuli. But even the most literate musicians and harshest critics will admit, readily or reluctantly, that music is predominantly about emotions. It only begins as sound.

Musical Characters

Musical expectations are formed at an early age. Infants begin matching pitches by six months. Acquaintance with modal structure occurs by year five or six. Basic harmony is grasped around age seven. Through passive perpetual exposure to musical conventions, culturally specific associations are attached to this or that pitch, sequence, scale or harmonic color. A listener born and raised in the West is accustomed to major and minor scales and their various ascribed connotations. When foreign modalities, say from India, cross the ears of the Westerner, they are heard through the framework and limitations of the familiar system. Thus, while "exotic" music may be enjoyed, it will not stimulate the same responses or convey the same meanings that it does for the native.

In a recent interview, novelist Ron Rash coined a phrase that speaks to this perceptual peculiarity. When asked why his stories take place in his stomping ground of Appalachia, he responded, "Landscape is destiny."[3] Like all of us, the place Rash calls home has an inescapable impact on how he perceives the world. Points of reference, sensory processing, linguistic choices, aesthetic appreciation and so on are largely tied to our environment. For Rash, setting stories in a location with which one is intimate is the best and only true way to write authentically. And, just as the characters in a book tend to derive from the author's encounters and relationships, the perceived character of a musical piece stems from the listener's prior experiences.

In music, character generally refers to the feeling or feelings communicated by a piece. Culturally trained ears are quick to decipher specific moods and nonmusical ideas expressed in familiar music. Listeners of classical music will recognize tranquility in selections exhibiting legato articulation, smooth and easy tempo, balance between bass and treble tones, and an absence of dissonance, dynamic contrast and metric instability. Such pieces will have a different effect on people outside of that music-culture; yet outsiders will find tranquility in music their backgrounds have conditioned them to sense as tranquil.

Detection of musical character occurs almost instantaneously, and subtle changes in one or more aspect of a piece—harmony, speed, volume, etc.—can radically alter our perception of it. A noted case in point comes from E. Janes's classic essay, "The Emotions in Music." As Janes tells it, "an accomplished musician of our acquaintance was once challenged by a distinguished theological professor to make him weep, by the power of music. He soon brought tears to the professor's eyes by a performance upon the piano, which consisted, in reality, of 'Yankee Doodle' in slow time."[4] The manipulation of a single element—tempo—was all that was needed to turn the playful "Yankee Doodle" into a melancholy tune.

On one hand, this is an example of playing *against* musical expectations: the melody is presented in the opposite manner than it is usually performed. On the other hand, it depicts a pianist playing *upon* musical expectations: he exploits the association of slowness with sadness, thereby bringing the professor to tears. The result is an illustrative demonstration of how cultural learning shapes our discernment of musical character. Landscape is destiny.

Acoustic Anatomy

Music is experienced on a macro level. The listener is enveloped in waves of acoustic information, the immediacy of which tends to inhibit real-time analysis. We may recognize pitch-differences in succession (melody), pitch-differences in combination (harmony), rhythmic patterns and basic form, but the elemental makeup remains hidden until it is examined under the microscope of music theory.

This is as it should be. Music is an expression of life. It is a storehouse of memories, a sensory stimulant, a source of pleasure, an igniter of feelings, a conjurer of images, a kinesthetic motivator and so on. More often than not, we embrace the rush of sound on a non-rational level, allowing the force and flow to take us where it will. We encounter it as a complete entity, unaware or unconcerned about the parts that comprise the whole.

However, like a biological organism, a musical selection contains micro and meso structures. Its complexity is determined by the type and amount of these intersecting components. To illustrate the analogy, a nursery rhyme tune might be compared to an earthworm while a drawn-out movement of a symphony might be likened to an elephant.

The micro level of music includes syntactical ingredients like individual notes, rests, durations, intervals, fermatas, ties, slurs and accents. These are the building blocks or atoms with which the piece is composed. Alone, these basic units are identity-less fragments. But when assembled in combination, they constitute the foundation of musical life as we know it.

On the meso level, we find structural segments such as cells and motives. These germinal fragments are molecular in scope. They consist of micro parts, or atoms, bonded together, and represent the smallest identifiable sliver of a musical piece. The cell is a minute and self-contained melodic or rhythmic particle that contributes to thematic content. The motive is a recurring succession of notes that may be separated into more than one cell. It is the smallest subdivision of a phrase or theme that imparts the identity of the piece.

Henry Granger Hanchett, a turn-of-the-twentieth-century organist, inventor and medical doctor, described this biological breakdown in his book, *The Art of the Musician*. He explained, for example, that the motive "contain[s] the germ and life of the product, while the simpler items which unite in its structure are like chemical elements, capable of making up an amorphous mass or even a crystal, but that can never make an organism without first combining to make a cell." In his evaluation, "all great and significant [Western classical] compositions ... are the outgrowths, the organization, so to speak, of one or more recognizable motives which may properly be called the germs of the work."[5]

As listeners, we do not ordinarily take record of these inner workings. We embrace music in its entirety. The same is true when we come across other living beings. We don't usually see or think about their internal organs, connective tissues or skeletal systems—let alone the invisible activity occurring on the atomic level. But without these various interlocking pieces, there would be no organism, animal or musical.

What You See Is What You Hear

Much has been written on the role of paralinguistic gestures in communicating linguistic content. Hand movements, postures, facial expressions and the like give context to spoken words and shade their meaning in significant ways. The non-verbal amplifies the verbal, conveying emotional information that may or may not be overt in the language alone. Something similar occurs in music performance.

Like verbal interaction, musical communication is a complex activity engaging multiple sensory modalities. Listening by itself does not extract all that a performance can disclose. This is especially so with instrumental music, a category of performance unaided by the (usual) clarity of words. No matter how formulaic or accessible, instrumental music is at best an abstract language. Thus, the full message and impact of a performance often relies on accompanying gestures, body movements and other paramusical signals.

It should be noted that research on music and emotions typically falls into three main categories. The most regularly explored is the influence of culture in shaping emotional responses. Schematic expectations and tonal patterns trigger stereotyped reactions among participants in a specific music-culture. The second most widely explored area is the effect of listening conditions. Settings and circumstances in which music is heard, along with the listener's mental and physical states, contribute to how sounds are emotionally received. The third most commonly examined aspect is the impression of movement, form and imagery in musical passages. Such symbolism evokes emotions through mimicry, with slow phrases suggesting lethargy, ascending sequences implying elation, etc.

Visual cues deserve a place beside these conventional explanations. Cognitive studies have exposed the limits of emotional conveyance through strictly auditory features, like vibrato, tempo and dynamics. By itself, aural processing can and does open the pathway to music-induced emotions. However, the strength of music's effect increases considerably and assumes added dimensions when a performance is both heard and seen.

Jane W. Davidson, a musicologist at the University of Western Australia, has examined the extent to which visual communication affects emotional perception.[6] For a 1994 experiment, she had musicians play a piece in three distinct manners: restrained, with little to no physical expression; standard, with natural body and facial movement; and exaggerated, with effusive movement and facial cues. Just listening to the audio of these performances, participants were unable to detect which was played in which fashion. But when the performances were viewed, the intensity of emotional responses was proportional to the amount of gesturing, postural adjustments and facial signals observed. The more demonstrative the playing, the more emotional it seemed. A similar study conducted by Bradley W. Vines et al. concludes that emotional ambiguity in atonal music can likewise be resolved through a player's mannerisms.[7]

Two additional observations deserve mention. The first is that musicians and non-musicians are equally unable to detect changes in performance manner when music is only heard, and are equally swayed by physical displays when performances are both heard and seen. The second is that the less familiar one is with a composition, the more one relies on sight in determining its emotional content. The grand takeaway is this: visuals are an under-appreciated and immensely potent medium for enhancing, complementing and clarifying emotions in music.

Empathy and Art Appreciation

In the *Little Rascals* short, "Mike Fright," several child performers audition for a station manager and a sponsor of a radio station. The Rascals are there as The International Silver String Submarine Band, a rag-tag troupe wielding an assortment of rusty hand-made instruments. The boys wait impatiently as the other acts audition, rudely disrupting the proceedings with their uncultured antics. Leonard, a smug and overconfident trumpeter, has his performance foiled by Little Rascals Tommy and Alvin, who start sucking on lemons while he plays. When Leonard sees the boys, his face puckers involuntarily, making it impossible for him to blow his horn.

This memorable scene depicts the human proclivity for body mapping: an automatic response in which neural representations of perceived motor actions are activated in the viewer's brain and trigger visceral responses. It is the reason we cringe when we see a needle poke someone's arm, or yawn when we see somebody yawning. Similar empathic reactions have been observed in other primates, and the biological mechanisms responsible— mirror neurons, mimicry, and emotional contagion—probably predate the primate order.

Bodily empathy also plays a significant role in aesthetic appreciation.

According to Frans de Waal, director of the Living Links Center at the Yerkes Primate Center in Atlanta, Georgia, a major appeal of ballet, opera or trapeze flying is that, as we watch the performers, we enter their bodies. In his recent book, *The Bonobo and the Atheist*, de Waal explains that when a dancer leaps across the stage, we too are momentarily suspended in air. When the diva sings her dramatic aria, we feel her voice as our own.[8] When we see a painting showing the agony of a human figure, we cannot help but feel that emotion.

Even abstract art can stimulate body channels. De Waal cites an article by Vittorio Gallese, co-discoverer of mirror neurons, and art historian David Freedberg, which describes how observers unconsciously trace movements on a canvas.[9] We sense body motion in the brush marks and put ourselves in the moment of the artist at work. This is like the cellist or pianist who involuntarily moves her fingers while listening to a recording of the instrument.

These examples reinforce the growing scientific view that empathy, while not lacking a cognitive component, begins as a pre-cognitive function propelled by bodily sentiments. This helps paint a bottom-up picture of morality, in which day-to-day interactions stimulate gut motivations that occur before and apart from rationalizations. Such "morality within" is not just a human phenomenon, but appears in other animals (primarily mammals) as well. The associated implications for the arts are equally profound, as empathy accounts largely for the pleasure we derive from them.

Notes

1. Thomas Fuller, *History of the Worthies of England*, vol. 1 (London: Thomas Tegg, 1840), 39
2. Wallace Stevens, "Peter Quince at the Clavier" (1915).
3. Alden Mudge, "Ron Rash: Shaped by the Land, Torn Apart by Intolerance," *BookPage*, April 2012, <http://bookpage.com/interviews/8796-ron-rash#.UznOXihq594>
4. E. Janes, "The Emotions in Music" [1874], in *The Value of Sacred Music: An Anthology of Essential Writings, 1801–1918*, comp. Jonathan L. Friedmann (Jefferson, NC: McFarland, 2009), 95.
5. Henry Granger Hanchett, *The Art of the Musician: A Guide to the Intelligent Appreciation of Music* (New York: Macmillan, 1905), 119.
6. Jane W. Davidson, "What Type of Information is Conveyed in the Body Movements of Solo Musician Performers?" *Journal of Human Movement Studies* 6 (1994): 279–301.
7. Bradley W. Vines et al., "Music to My Eyes: Cross-Modal Interactions in the Perception of Emotions in Musical Performance," *Cognition* 118 (2011): 157–170.
8. Frans de Waal, *The Bonobo and the Atheist: In Search of Humanism Among the Primates* (New York: W. W. Norton, 2013), 133–134.
9. David Freedberg and Vittorio Gallese, "Motion, Emotion and Empathy in Esthetic Experience," *Trends in Cognitive Sciences* 5:197 (2007): 197–203.

Suggestions for Further Reading

Berry, Wallace. *Structural Functions in Music*. New York: Dover, 1987.
Clarke, Eric, and Simon Emmerson, eds. *Music, Mind and Structure* (*Contemporary Music Review* 3:1). New York: Taylor and Francis, 1989.
Cochrane, Tom, Bernardino Fantini, and Klaus R. Scherer, eds. *The Emotional Power of Music: Multidisciplinary Perspectives on Musical Arousal, Expression, and Social Control*. New York: Oxford University Press, 2013.
Davie, Cedric Thorpe. *Musical Structure and Design*. New York: Dover, 1966.
Erickson, Robert. *Sound Structure in Music*. Berkeley: University of California Press, 1975.
Gabrielsson, Alf. *Strong Experiences with Music: Music is Much More Than Just Music*. New York: Oxford University Press, 2011.
Katsh, Shelley, and Carol Merle-Fishman. *The Music Within You*. Gilsum, NH: Barcelona, 1998.
Kivy, Peter. *Authenticities: Philosophical Reflections on Musical Performance*. Ithaca, NY: Cornell University Press, 1995.
Rink, John. *Musical Performance: A Guide to Understanding*. New York: Cambridge University Press, 2002.
Shepherd, Tim, and Anne Leonard, ed. *The Routledge Companion to Music and Visual Culture*. New York: Routledge, 2013.

6

Shape

Much of music's appeal lies in its shape. Across millennia and in cultures spread around the globe, musical forms have evolved to appease and exploit deep-seated human needs. Chief among them are the desires for predictability, stability, catharsis, and affirmation. This chapter elucidates the centrality of repetition in culturally diverse music, and the typical aversion to music that avoids such pleasing patterns. It then proposes that "good" is in some respects "average" music, or music that meets generalized expectations. It also explores how human emotions are sensed in the movement of musical phrases, how we hear our own voices in melodic patterns, and how musical instruments are in some instances valued for their closeness to human singing.

Seeking Patterns

We are pattern-seeking mammals. We are uncomfortable with unanswered questions, and discontent with the apparent randomness of the world around us. We look for familiar images in clouds, stereotype groups of people, categorize things of nature, see faces in inanimate objects, latch on to conspiracy theories, match objects and colors, decode languages, and find comfort in easy resolutions in literature and film. The impulse to locate (and fabricate) order can be traced to the formative stages of humanity. Our ancestors' survival depended greatly on their ability to detect patterns in sense data. Snap judgments of hunters and other tribespeople determined whether they would pursue or flee, explore or hide.

Rather than leaving us, the hunter instinct has expanded into all conceivable areas. Nearly every moment of waking life is spent making quick decisions, classifying information and uncovering (or inventing) structure in observable phenomena. We derive safety and stability from the order we discern, and are attracted to things displaying overt patterns. This is partly why we are drawn to music.

According to science writer Philip Ball, around ninety-four percent of musical selections lasting more than a few seconds contain recurring material—and that only includes verbatim repeats.[1] This calculation applies to music as disparate as electronica and Inuit throat singing. Repetition is among music's most defining elements, and one that helps us to distinguish musical sounds from other audible stimuli. Far from being a source of boredom or irritation, repetitious phrases, relentless rhythms and recurring melodies can be an endless source of enjoyment. They satisfy a primal need.

Pleasing patterns of music have been linked to instincts implanted in us by evolution.[2] As noted, the ability to develop and act upon expectations is fundamental to survival. In all animals, survival rate is proportional to accuracy of anticipation: the more correct the assessment, the more advantageous the response. When accurate, gut feelings lead toward prey and away from danger. We have acquired this mechanism of rewarding good predictions. With patterns comes predictability, and with predictability comes pleasure. Guessing right is utterly gratifying. Musical repetition caters to this tendency.

The fact that repetitious music gives us satisfaction is evidenced in the genres that become popular, as well as those that linger on the margins. In the West and elsewhere, tonal music—in its multitudinous forms—is the most agreeable branch of the art form. It encompasses blues and rock, Baroque and Classical, folksongs and lullabies, ragas and marches. Such genres have almost universal appeal. In contrast, atonal music, avant-garde jazz, noise music and other postmodern approaches reach far smaller audiences. They deliberately dispose of conventions and challenge musical expectations, thereby eliminating most of what attracts the average listener to music in the first place. These styles are not without internal logic or a degree of self-styled repetition; but they do not pander to our evolutionary longings.

It is possible to overstate the delight gained from musical patterns. Pleasure is accentuated or diminished depending on one's affinity, disdain or indifference for specific music. But the general assessment holds: we desire the predictability music provides.

Schoenberg vs. the People

Arnold Schoenberg invented his twelve-tone method to replace normative conceptions of melody. In so doing, he discarded or otherwise obscured the most attractive and enduring elements of music: repetition, anticipation, and predictability. Musical satisfaction derives from our ability to identify phrases, discern tensions, predict resolutions, detect climaxes, perceive suspensions, and recognize other structural features. We are pleased when these expectations are fulfilled and surprised when anticipations are foiled or delayed. The relative unpredictability of Schoenberg's system tosses all of this out.

According to the rules of twelve-tone technique, the chromatic scale must be organized in a tone row wherein no note is sounded more often than another. This eliminates intuitive patterns, annihilates key signatures, and contradicts millennia-old musical tendencies. When the row occurs again, as it does with mathematical regularity, its wide intervals, variation, and turbulent character do little to please the pattern-hungry ears of the average auditor.

Despite its novelty and intellectual intrigue, Schoenberg's method has been called "senseless," "unbearable," "torturous," and worse. In 1930 the *Musical Times* of London declared, "The name of Schoenberg is, as far as the British public is concerned, mud." Two decades later the *Boston Herald* published this invective: "The case of Arnold Schoenberg vs. the people (or vice versa, as the situation may be) is one of the most singular things in the history of music. For here is a composer ... who operates on the theory that if you know how to put a bunch of notes on a piece of score paper you are, presto, a composer."[3]

Witty attacks like these are far too numerous to begin listing here. But are charges of misanthropy warranted? According to psychologist David Huron, Schoenberg's system is less *atonal* (without a tonal center) than it is *contratonal*: it deliberately circumvents tonal implications.[4] If the twelve notes were put into a randomizing computer program, they would occasionally occur in sequences resembling melody as we know it. But Schoenberg and his twentieth-century disciples meticulously avoided even hints of such patterns. As such, they expunged from their music precisely that which human ears have evolved to enjoy.

This does not, of course, mean that twelve-tone serialism is without its admirers, or that Schoenberg's name is unanimously considered "mud." Some of his works even approach accessibility (in their own way), notably *Moses und Aron* and *A Survivor from Warsaw*. But general responses echo those of the *Boston Herald*, which went on to state: "[His music] never touches any emotion save curiosity, never arouses any mood save speculation on how the conductor can conduct it and how the musicians can count the bars."[5]

Hearing Averages

Our field of perception is constantly crammed with tastes, smells, sights, sounds and other intrusions from the outside world. To make sense of this multifarious bombardment, our brains not only choose which stimuli to pay attention to, but also organize that information. The procedure is aided by prototype recognition, or the categorization of perceptions based on the central or average representation of a class. Countless hues enter our vision, but we sort them out based on a finite number of colors—red, blue, green, etc.—with modifying adjectives—light, dark, -ish, etc. The same occurs when deciphering shapes, words, weather conditions, food odors, facial expressions and so forth.

Organizing experiences in this way is highly economical. The brain simplifies reality by placing an enormous variety of information into basic classifications. Virtually everything we perceive is processed in this stereotyping way. Yet, as obvious as this might be, we are less apt to recognize the role of prototypical elements in ascertaining beauty.

In 1990, psychologists Judith H. Langlois and Lori A. Roggman published a study entitled, "Attractive Faces Are Only Average."[6] They asked college students to rank the beauty of human faces in a series of photographs. Their conclusion: faces with features approximating the mathematical average of all faces in a population are the most attractive. On the flipside, the researchers noted, "unattractive faces, because of their minor distortions ... may be perceived as less facelike or as less typical of human faces." We subconsciously reference the prototype of "faceness" when evaluating appearances. Our preference for averages and aversion to extremes is likely rooted in a primal sorting out of genetic regularities from potentially harmful mutations. Normal is safe and safe is beautiful.

Of course, when we go beyond photographs into real life, unconventional faces can be (and often are) judged favorably. In such cases, beauty is said to reside in the "eye of the beholder." However, this very cliché acknowledges a baseline or common appearance of beauty from which an individual departs. (The natural preference for a prototypical face is overridden by extra-facial qualities, like kindness, talent and a sense of humor.)

As it is with faces, so it is with music. Within a given population in a given time and place, certain musical features are normative. These can be likened to the mathematical average of faces, and might include major and minor triads, common chord progressions (e.g., I-V-vi-IV), rising and falling melodies, normal structures (e.g., 8-bar form), and so on. These features comply with expectations and suggest stability—traits also detected in the "normal" face.

Acoustic Analogies

Emotional responses to music have a measure of objectivity. Though the type and intensity of emotions felt are response-dependent, they are not subjective in the sense of being mere projections. Expressiveness is contained in the music itself. As philosopher Stephen Davies has argued, music seems sad or happy because it has the *appearance* of sadness or happiness—that is, we identify characteristics in music analogous to our own experience of those feelings.

Davies calls this "appearance emotionalism," or the resemblance between temporally unfolding music and human behaviors associated with emotional expression.[7] Musical movement is discerned from various motions: high to low pitches, fast to slow tempo, loud to soft volume, harmonic tension and resolution, etc. Like human action, the momentum of music seems purposeful and goal-directed. This perception is part of our broader tendency to personify the things we experience. We are, for example, more likely to notice how weeping willows look like sad people than how they resemble frozen waterfalls. Similarly, we detect in music a dynamic character relating to our own expressive behavior. This is true of all music, be it concrete or abstract, tonal or atonal, formal or informal.

Sounds are instantly anthropomorphized upon reaching our ears. To use a generic illustration, Western music expresses graveness through patterns of unresolved tension, minor tonalities, bass timbre, downward sloping lines and so on. Of course, our responses to music are largely learned: cultural insiders and outsiders are not likely to have identical reactions (nor can we expect all members of a music-culture to react in precisely uniform ways). But once we are trained to associate certain sounds with certain feelings—a process that begins in the womb—our perceptions are more or less set for life.

Appearance emotionalism can also take on a visual dimension. In such cases, not only is music felt as a sensual phenomenon, it is also likened to imagery expressive of that phenomenon. For instance, a song might be heard as a racing antelope, meaning that it exudes excitement. If it is heard as a gathering storm, it inspires trepidation. If it sounds like a rainbow, it stirs a sense of awe. In this respect, stating that music resembles something visible is basically the same as acknowledging that it feels a particular way. And the reason both music and images are so readily compared to emotions is because they exhibit emotive qualities we perceive in ourselves.

This is not to say that we simply project our humanness onto the music. Its emotionalism exists independent of our listening to it. Rather, we are the receivers of music's expressive content. Exactly how this information is interpreted varies from person to person and culture to culture; but it is universally felt as analogous to human emotions.

Feeling Voices

The emotional pull of music is its first, strongest and most ubiquitous effect. It is the primary reason for music's inclusion in a staggering assortment of human activities, and the common denominator for listeners of all levels of education and expertise. If music were divested of its emotional attraction, it would soon fall out of usage. Yet, as widely attested as this observation is, it remains unclear precisely how emotions are musically aroused.

There has been no shortage of proposed explanations. From the moment people began thinking about music, the connection between emotion and sound has been a foremost area of interest. Some older ideas have survived the rigors of modern research and continue to hold sway. One such theory was introduced in the writings of Charles Darwin.

In *The Expression of the Emotions in Man and Animals*, Darwin wrote, "when the voice is used under any strong emotion, it tends to assume, through the principle of association, a musical character."[8] Vocalization patterns change depending on the vocalizer's emotional state. Gloominess is matched by slow and hesitant speech in the lower register. Cheerfulness is partnered with loud and rapid speech in the higher range. Anxiety has its counterpart in uneven spurts of trembling speech. We intuitively recognize underlying moods from the rhythms, timbres and contours present in the expression of these and other states.

Sometime in the distant and unrecorded past, these qualities migrated into the musical vocabulary. Gloomy music mimics the lethargic pace of a downhearted voice. Cheerful music replicates the bright tempo of excited elocution. Anxious music mimics the disjointed phrases of a troubled tongue. The sounds remind us of how we communicate during these states. We detect and respond to vocal patterns in the musical presentation.

Compelling though this analysis may be, it is not uncontested. Some detractors, like philosopher Stephen Davies, argue that music's expressiveness is tied to its replication of physical gestures rather than an essential link to vocal tendencies. Others, like psychologist Vladimir Konečni, contend that music does not directly induce emotions, and that the apparent connection requires more conditioning than Darwin's theory would suggest.

But empirical evidence has mounted since Darwin's day. Researchers have conducted controlled experiments that demonstrate the resemblance between vocal tendencies and musical expression. The titles of several research papers indicate the growing attention: "Voice and Emotion"; "Expression of Emotion in Voice and Music"; "Communication of Emotions in Vocal Expression and Musical Performance."[9] The vocalization theory also resonates on an intuitive level. Once we are made aware of Darwin's statement, it is hard to ignore the presence of vocal patterns in music evocative of various emotions. We realize how basic the connection is.

By itself, the proposition does not definitively or comprehensively solve the puzzle of why music stimulates emotional responses. It cannot account for all instances or why some musical selections are felt more strongly than others. But it is a valuable aid to our understanding.

Imitation of Voice

Musical treatises of late antiquity regularly gave preference to wind instruments over strings. The order was based on the belief that winds imitate the human voice. Since the time of Plato, singing has been placed above instrumental music in both philosophical tomes and popular imagination. This is partly because the vocal instrument is thought to be God-given (*instrumenta naturalis*) rather than human-made (*instrumenta artificialis*), and partly because the voice produces speech as well as song. For writers like Cassiodorus (c. 485–c. 585) and Isidore of Seville (c. 560–636), winds were the closest representation of vocal music, as both operate by sending a column of air through an apparatus controlling vibration and resonation.

From a mechanical standpoint, the similarity between voice and winds is fairly obvious. Blowing and breathing involve the same anatomical tools and physiological processes. But when sound is added to the discussion, comparisons are not always so neat. For instance, the bassoon—a wind instrument—has been likened to a "burping bedpost," whereas the cello—a string instrument—is widely equated with the male singing voice. Similarly, violins are heard to "sing" like a female soprano.

The latter statement was recently put to scientific test. According to Joseph Nagyvary, a biochemist and violin expert, great violinmakers of the seventeenth and eighteenth century designed their instruments to mimic the human voice.[10] In an article comparing Guarneri violins and operatic singing, Nagyvary contends that the instruments produce notes that gravitate toward certain type of vowels, implying the possibility that old masters may have used vowel identification as a means of quality assurance. It is therefore possible that, echoing views from antiquity, the superiority of certain violins derived from their closeness to the vocal instrument. The more humanlike, the more coveted.

For the study, entitled "A Comparative Study of Power Spectra and Vowels in Guarneri Violins and Operatic Singing," Nagyvary compared a series of vowels sung by Metropolitan opera soprano Emily Pulley with a recording of Itzhak Perlman playing a scale on a Guarneri violin. Using high-tech phonetic mapping and analysis, he found that the violin created a number of English and French vowel sounds, along with the Italian "i" and "e."

This suggests that esteemed makers, like Guarneri and Stradivari, strove to replicate the human voice in their violins, and that their success in doing so provided an objective standard for determining the quality and value of the instruments. They may have been inspired by the theological concept of voice as divine instrument, the philosophical assertion of the perfection of nature, or the basic human affinity for things resembling ourselves.

Though philosophers and theologians have long extolled wind instruments for approaching the mechanism of the human voice, the sound of those instruments can fall short of the lofty theories. Alternately, our response to a masterful violin does seem to resemble the pull of a virtuosic soprano. If the value of an instrument can truly be measured by its proximity to the human voice, then the seventeenth- and eighteenth-century violins certainly deserve the millions they sell for. In a manner more than just metaphorical, they speak mellifluously to our ears.

Notes

1. Philip Ball, *The Music Instinct: How Music Works and Why We Can't Do Without It* (New York: Oxford University Press, 2010), 124.
2. David Huron, *Sweet Anticipation: Music and the Psychology of Expectation* (Cambridge, MA: MIT Press, 2006).
3. Nicolas Slonimsky, ed., *Lexicon of Musical Invective: Critical Assaults on Composers Since Beethoven's Time* (Seattle: University of Washington Press, 1965), 162, 165.
4. Huron, *Sweet Anticipation*, 228.
5. Slonimsky, ed., *Lexicon of Musical Invective*, 165.
6. Judith H. Langlois and Lori A. Roggman, "Attractive Faces Are Only Average," *Psychological Science* 1:2 (1990): 115–121.
7. Stephen Davies, *Themes in the Philosophy of Music* (New York: Oxford University Press, 2003).
8. Charles Darwin, *The Expression of the Emotions in Man and Animals* (New York: D. Appelton, 1872), 87.
9. Arvid Kappas, Ursala Hess and Klaus R. Scherer, "Voice and Emotion," in *Fundamental od Nonverbal Behavior*, ed. Robert Stephen Feldman and Bernard Rimé, (New York: Cambridge University Press, 1991), 200–238; Klaus R. Scherer, "Expression of

Emotion in Voice and Music," *Journal of Voice* 9:3 (1995): 235–238; Patrik N. Juslin and Petri Laukka, "Communication of Emotions in Vocal Expression and Musical Performance: Different Channels, Same Code?" *Psychological Bulletin* 129 (2003): 770–814.

10. Joseph Nagyvary, "A Comparative Study of Power Spectra and Vowels in Guarneri Violins and Operatic Singing," *Savart Journal* 1:3 (2013): 1–30.

Suggestions for Further Reading

Brabazon, Tara. *Popular Music: Topics, Trends, and Trajectories*. London: Sage, 2012.
Darwin, Charles. *The Expression of the Emotions in Man and Animals*. New York: D. Appelton, 1872.
Davies, Stephen. *Themes in the Philosophy of Music*. New York: Oxford University Press, 2003.
Frith, Simon. *Performing Rites: On the Value of Popular Music*. Cambridge, MA: Harvard University Press, 1998.
Godøy, Rolf Inge, and Marc Leman, eds. *Musical Gestures: Sound, Movement, and Meaning*. New York: Routledge, 2010.
Huron, David. *Sweet Anticipation: Music and the Psychology of Expectation*. Cambridge, MA: MIT Press, 2006.
Izdebski, Krzysztof. *Emotions in the Human Voice: Foundations*. San Diego, CA: Plural, 2007.
Karpf, Anne. *The Human Voice: The Story of a Remarkable Talent*. New York: Bloomsbury, 2011.
Machin, David. *Analysing Popular Music: Image, Sound and Text*. London: Sage, 2010.
Meyer, Leonard B. *Music, the Arts, and Ideas: Patterns and Predictions in Twentieth-Century Culture*. Chicago: University of Chicago Press, 2010.

7

Transience

Music is an intangible art form. Though it strikes the listener in an intimate and direct manner, it takes no physical form. Because of this, philosophers have long debated whether music—and sound more generally—really exists in the absolute meaning of the term. This chapter investigates a number of issues at the core of this heady topic. It discusses the artificialness of musical recordings, the fleetingness of musical moments, and music's inevitable evaporation into nothingness. It delves into the inadequacies of musical experience and analysis, the limitations of notated music, and the futility of speculating about music that was never made. It concludes by examining the completeness and incompleteness of musical reception, and music's ineffable way of connecting us to our pasts.

Sound in Wax

The earliest wax cylinder phonographs—the first commercial medium for recording and reproducing sound—were entirely mechanical. They were hand-cranked and needed no electrical power. All that was required was a lathe, a waxy surface, a sharp point for a stylus, and a resonating table. To impress sound waves onto wax, the voice or instrument was positioned closely to the large end of a horn. The vibrations moved a needle, which carved a groove on the rotating wax. According to Walter Murch, an acclaimed film editor and sound designer, everything used in these early machines was available to the ancient Greeks and Egyptians.[1] But it took until the middle of the nineteenth century, and the genius of Thomas Edison and his team, to execute the recording process.

Why did it take so long to capture sound? Musician David Byrne has informally speculated that maybe it didn't.[2] Perhaps someone in antiquity invented a similar device and later abandoned it; or perhaps the device itself was simply demolished in the ruins of history. While conceivable on a technological level, this hypothesis is unlikely considering the prevailing ethos of the ancient world. The ephemerality of sound was part of its attraction: it was momentary, mysterious, transient and transcendent. As this fleetingness was highly valued, there was little or no inclination to record. Murch puts it this way: "Poetically, the beauty of music and the human voice was used as a symbol of all that's evanescent. So the idea that you could trap it in any physical medium never occurred to [them]...."[3]

This contrasts with the rush to develop written systems that enshrined language. The ancients recognized that certain things should be documented, like governmental records, priestly decrees, royal chronicles, and philosophical treatises. What these shared in common was a silent beginning: they were soundless thoughts committed to paper (or papyrus or parchment or tablets or wood). Writing gave concrete form to facts and concepts that, while often referencing observable phenomena, had no tangibility of their own. In contrast, sound was understood as being completely formed. It was received sensually, experienced kinesthetically, and processed emotionally. It existed in the moment it was made.

It is worth noting that Edison first thought of wax cylinder recorders as dictation machines. They were to record the owners' ideas and messages and, ideally, preserve the great speeches of the day. This limited purpose reflected the limitations of the early devices: they were too crude and imprecise to capture the nuances of musical performance. True, music recording and playback were in Edison's long-term plan, and they became major functions as the machines advanced. But it is feasible to consider that Edison's initial goal of preserving dictation was—and arguably still is—a worthier and more practical goal than detaining music.

Musicians commonly lament that they are slaves to their own recordings. The version that appears on an album is the version that fans want to hear, and deviations are typically received as imperfections, inaccuracies or unwanted departures from the "authoritative" source. Some improvising musicians even feel obliged to give their audiences note-for-note reproductions of recorded solos. This is not to negate the enormous benefits and incalculable cultural impact of musical recordings. Our understanding of music as a diverse human enterprise owes mightily to the proliferation of recorded sounds, and musical creativity thrives when there is access to other music. But something of music's temporality is lost in recording. Imprinting sound in wax or digital audio creates the illusion of permanence.

The Short Life of Music

Music is concentrated in the present tense. Its lifespan is the length of its performance. It emerges out of nowhere and disappears into nothingness.

7. Transience

It manifests and expires in the same instant. Its two ingredients—sound and silence—evaporate into the hazy ether and the fuzzy recesses of the mind. It leaves no physical traces behind. To the extent that the music existed at all, it occupied the invisible spaces of time and consciousness. It was more energy than mass—more essence than substance.

The preceding eulogy applies to all music. Nothing of the thing lives beyond the act of its creation. Even when meticulously composed and faithfully played, note for note, it is not the same music that was heard before. Its relationship with prior performances is that of a facsimile or reenactment, not a resurrection. Similarly, audio recordings, while capturing data in a replayable format, should not be confused with permanence. What is heard is an impression of performance—however exacting—but not the performance itself. Like light reaching us from a long-extinct star, what enters our ears has already passed away.

The same can be said for musical notation. Though the printed page has material form, the paper is not the music. Jean-Paul Sartre made this point in his book, *L'Imaginaire*.[4] According to Sartre, true existence cannot be claimed for any musical work. Music is not located in the silent symbolism of bar lines, notes, key signatures, dynamics or articulations. Nor is it found in any one performance, since all renditions are fundamentally new and ephemeral creations. In contrast to something empirically real—defined by Sartre as existing in the past, future and present—music disappears as soon as it is heard. Whatever lingering impact it may have in terms of thoughts, images, feelings or earworms, occurs solely in the mind.

This is not always seen as a positive attribute. Indeed, on some level, the desire to record music—both on paper and in audio files—reflects discomfort with the art form's evanescence. As a rule, human beings are averse to impermanence and all the insecurity, unease and futility it implies. But the reality is that nothing lasts forever. From the moment a thing comes into being, it is in a state of decay. So we invent afterlife scenarios and gods that live forever. We think of truth and wisdom as eternal forces. We publish ideas, film events, build monuments and make musical time capsules (notation and recordings). We fabricate fixity for fleeting forms.

The Sound of Zero

The effect of a musical composition is notoriously fleeting. In the moment of listening, the sounds are ear filling, mood shifting, mind absorbing, memory stirring, body infecting. Yet almost as soon as they cease, the impact dissipates. We are possessed and exorcised all within a few minutes. True, a lyric or melodic phrase can repeat in our heads and go on affecting us in a comparatively minor way. But as an ephemeral art form that emerges and vanishes in real-time, music's influence tends to be measured by its duration. It fosters an immediate experience that transitions quickly from profoundness to nothingness.

Philosopher Susanne K. Langer made this observation in her study, *Philosophy in a New Key*. She acknowledged the well-attested interaction of music and heart rate, respiration, concentration and mental state, but noted that none of this outlasts the stimulus itself. There is no real expectation that the music will shape or inform our behavior. Whatever its effect, it tends to be internal rather than manifestational. "On the whole," Langer wrote, "the behavior of concert audiences after even the most thrilling performances makes the traditional magical influence of music on human actions very dubious. Its somatic effects are transient, and its moral hangovers or uplifts seem to be negligible."[5] Again, this does not necessarily apply to songs, which have a greater potential to motivate due to the sway of words and the pathos of the human voice.

The predictability with which music dissolves has a cosmic analogy. In the zero-energy hypothesis, the total amount of energy in the universe is exactly zero. All positive energy, which exists in matter, is canceled out by negative energy, which resides in gravity. The energy exerted as matter separates from other matter is balanced by the gravitational pull that attracts them together. Thus, the universe is made of positive and negative parts that add up to nothing.

If we convert this into a musical metaphor, music can be viewed as matter and its aftermath as gravity. A great deal of energy is expended during a musical performance. Physical maneuvers cause air molecules to vibrate, which make brain waves oscillate, causing thoughts, feelings and physical surges to proliferate. This is the substance of musical matter. But all of this is canceled out in the absence of music that follows. The gravitational pull of silence (or non-musical sounds) nullifies the effect before it transforms into conduct. The experience amounts to nothing.

This is illustrated in a story told of the premiere performance of Beethoven's *Ninth Symphony*. Following the symphony's rousing conclusion, the awestruck audience burst forth into applause. As their cheers reluctantly dwindled away, a child turned to his mother and asked, "What must we do now?" He was compelled to respond to the beauty and force of the music, but was unsure what the appropriate action might be. His mother offered no reply. There was zero to be done.

Object and Motion

The physical universe can be thought of either in terms of objects (substance) or motion (process). When substance is the focus, the universe appears as bundles of photons. When process is emphasized, the universe appears as waves. From the point of view of physics, both perspectives are true. Objects and motion are both made of light: photons are packets of light; waves are undulations of light. It is beyond my purpose (and my ability) to elucidate the finer points of this scientific principle. I wish instead to draw a rough analogy between substance and process as understood in physics, and the general way in which they are used in musical criticism.

Object in music is the final product: the sound recording, the lyric sheet, the notated score (composition or transcription). Process is the performance: the music making, the listening, the audible manifestation. The former is a starting place for (or record of) the latter; the latter is the content of the former. Unlike physicists, music critics tend to perceive object and process as utterly distinct, ignoring the "light" uniting the two. More often than not, one mode of understanding takes over, or is unduly elevated above the other.

For example, John Brownell notes a trend in jazz studies of applying analytical models to improvisation.[6] He takes specific aim at Thomas Owens, who dissected a large number of Charlie Parker's improvisations, cataloging sixty-four melodic devices ranked according to frequency of occurrence. For Brownell, this systematic method is antithetical to the spontaneous purpose and process of improvisation. Brownell is similarly critical of Gunter Schuller's study of Sonny Rollins, which elucidates the saxophonist's "thematic" improvisational approach. Schuller identified hallmarks of a well-crafted composition in Rollins's solos—themes, coherence, deliberation, form—and on that basis claimed that his playing was aesthetically superior. From Brownell's viewpoint, such analytic models have no place in jazz, which is, in essence, a performance practice outside the range of mechanistic tools. He dismisses these attempts as "notism," or the "fixation on the object of analysis rather than on the process from which it springs."

While it is true that aesthetic expectations from one artistic form do not translate appropriately to other forms, the notion that experience and analysis are mutually exclusive is not entirely so. Notation, whether of a written piece or an improvisation notated later, is always and necessarily a shorthand for the real (audible) thing. It is a useful language for understanding music, but it is no substitute for the thing itself. At the same time, a purely experiential appreciation of music, without facility in the written language, is to a certain extent incomplete. It is through listening *and* analytics that music is grasped in its full dimensions.

It is unfortunate that music is often apprehended from an either/or vantage point. Either it is received in the moment of perception, or it is shoved under the microscope. Exclusivity arises in the extremes of experientialism and notism. What is needed is a balanced view, which values both the product and the performance. They are, after all, aspects of the same thing. Returning to the physics analogy, performance (process) is a manipulation of sound, while score (object) is a map of sound.

Score Is Not Territory

William Sharlin was among the twentieth century's most active and innovative composers of synagogue music. A masterful choral writer and self-described "freak" for the canon, Sharlin's music freely crosses stylistic borders and evades conventional limitations and expectations of the worship setting. At its most elegant, his music seamlessly blends melodic modernism, jazz harmonies, Renaissance form and Jewish folk material. And nothing he wrote was ever finished.

Like many artists, Sharlin was never completely satisfied with his output—or, more accurately, ceased being satisfied with it after a short duration. Well into his eighties, he compulsively made changes to vocal lines, expanded harmonic coloring, and added figures to piano accompaniments. Some pieces were left on the brink of indecipherability, while others bear only surface resemblance to their original conceptions. He gave this treatment to published and unpublished pieces alike, and would complain whenever his music was reprinted without his express consent, as he almost certainly had a more recent version.

None of this editing or re-editing was done from a place of frustration. It was the inevitable byproduct of a perspective that saw written notes as temporary suggestions rather than concrete representations. For Sharlin, whatever appeared on the page was but a carefully constructed abstraction (though he was meticulous about how it should be presented). Notation was the model of an artistic reality, not the reality itself.

The above example complements the now widely accepted view of composition as a fluid and potentially unending process. Written notes are performed into existence. They only become music when they are heard. And each interpretation brings something new.

The creative functions of performance and reception cannot be overstressed. A piece is defined and redefined by the tempo, articulations, dynamics, attacks and tone qualities with which it is rendered. No two presentations are precisely the same, and each gives its own character to the composition. (This is clearly demonstrated on jazz albums that include two or more takes of a selection.) Listeners likewise play an active part in the creation of music, as their ears, minds and bodies make meaning of the sundry sound clusters. In this fundamental way, the involvement of performers and audiences, whether the music is live or recorded, is an extension of the compositional process.

The unfolding act of composition expands in cases where the composer continuously modifies his or her work, or leaves us with renditions capturing different stages of critical editing. Each of these versions carries with it unique nuances in addition to those always present among performers and listeners.

The upshot here is that the written note, while central to composed music, should not be confused with the end result. The depiction is not the depicted. Score is not territory.

Art Made and Unmade

Basic to existentialist philosophy is the idea that people are what they make themselves to be. We are born as empty slates and spend a lifetime creating our personas. Who we are is the result of an ongoing series of undertakings and the various thoughts, actions and relationships that comprise those undertakings. We constantly define and redefine ourselves through our dealings in the world. Our nature is not fixed. Critics charge that this view is too harsh, uncertain or arbitrary to be of any positive use. But its proponents see it as the most optimistic of doctrines. It entails that our destinies are within ourselves. Everything we do matters.

The flip side is that unrealized thoughts and unfulfilled potentials are of little or no consequence. Actualizations are what counts. Jean-Paul Sartre put it thus: "A man is involved in life, leaves his impress on it, and outside of that there is nothing."[7] This principle goes for all areas of engagement: there is no love but the love that is felt; there is no skill but the skill that is used; there is no conviction but the conviction that becomes deed.

Sartre gave the example of visual art. An artist's genius is the sum of his or her work. There is no other way to assess it. We cannot discuss the merits of a sculpture that was never sculpted or a concerto that was never composed.

"Nobody can tell what the painting of tomorrow will be," wrote Sartre. "Painting can be judged only after it has a chance to be made."[8] There are no *a priori* aesthetic values: creation precedes evaluation.

This perspective exposes the pointlessness of asking speculative artistic questions. What if Shakespeare had written another play? What if Michelangelo had painted another chapel? What if Plath had not died so young? What if Schubert had finished his eighth symphony? Track records and intentions are not the same as results, and there is no practical use in imagining things that will never be.

Of course, none of this precludes the fact that the artist must begin with a plan. Creations need a conscious creator, and nothing exists prior to the vision or inspiration. Yet if the plan is confined to the vagaries of conception and does not progress beyond them, it will not become art and thus have no impact on the artist's genius.

Existentialists consider this a liberating and motivating concept. Whether the activity is art or something else, it is our efforts that ultimately constitute our identities. We are born without essence and become ourselves through action. Life is what we make of it, and what we make in life is who we are.

Music Complete and Incomplete

Søren Kierkegaard wrote, "Music, like time, is measured but immeasurable, is composed but indivisible."[9] A subject in William James' *The Varieties of Religious Experience* compared a spiritual experience to "the effect of some great orchestra when all the separate notes have melted into the swelling harmony."[10] These quotations speak to the immediate and all-consuming effect of music. While musical elements can be distilled and analyzed through the study of a recording or score, their collective impact defies mechanical examination.

Such is the nature of musical completeness. In an instant too brief to quantify, the entirety of one's being is affected by an indivisible sonic force. The congealed parts of the musical whole—pitches, rhythms, timbres, durations, dynamics—stimulate the inseparable components of the person—mind, body, emotions. It is a holistic experience.

Yet, there is also a sense in which music is incomplete. Both Kierkegaard and James' subject allude to an attribute common to all music: evanescence. Much of music's effect comes from its instantaneous materialization. It tends to enter our perception without warning and manipulate us with or without our permission. However, just as quickly as it enters our awareness, it disappears. Each passing beat, each successive phrase, each fleeting chord evaporates as soon as it is heard. The sounds emerge without physical substance, and leave no physical trace behind. Of course, efforts can be made to transcribe or stipulate a performance with written notation; but this is only an approximation. Every performance is unique.

Something similar occurs with recorded music (and to a lesser degree synthesized music). Though recordings can capture musical occurrences and replay them with near precision, the listener will never hear them the same way twice. Musical perception is influenced by the accumulated experiences leading up to a particular listening, not to mention what the listener is doing, thinking, and feeling when the recording is being played. Thus, permanence is lacking even in the most carefully fossilized music.

Music is, then, both complete and incomplete. In the micro-moment of perception, it is a single, wholly formed, and ineffable force. The listener's response is likewise inclusive, engaging the mental, physical, and emotional realms. But when we zoom out to view the broader phenomenon, this completeness—so viscerally felt by the listener—begins to dissipate. What once seemed absolutely whole becomes fundamentally partial. The image of indivisible notes melting away into an all-embracing harmony is replaced with rapidly appearing and disappearing musical phrases, the effect of which changes in accordance with changes in the listener.

Eternal Song

An issue of the *Animal Man* comic book published in 1990 includes a surreal sequence of panels showing a group of second-rate superheroes in an unusual state of self-reflection. On the brink of being discontinued, these now-irrelevant heroes descend into panic. The story's enigmatic and sometimes-psychedelic writer, Grant Morrison, depicts the anxiety as these characters become aware that their storylines are in peril. One of them shouts forlornly, "If they write me out man, I ain't gonna be seen again!" A more introspective figure consoles the crowd of hapless crusaders: "We can all still be seen. Our lives are replayed every time someone reads us. We can never die. We outlive our creators."[11]

The notion of eternality through revisitation resembles the "eternal return," a theory popularized by religious historian Mircea Eliade.[12] Ritual practices, explained Eliade, return participants to the mythic time in which the events commemorated purportedly took place. A ceremony marking the creation of the world or defeat of an existential enemy, for instance, brings a congregation into that extraordinary moment. In more than just a symbolic sense, each ritual repetition relives the sacred past. Like soon-to-be canceled heroes who achieve immortality on the re-read comic book page, periodic rituals enable myths to outlive the civilizations that produced them. They procure an eternal life transcending the constraints of linear time.

It is debated whether this cyclical idea of time should be viewed literally or as an inflated conception of nostalgia. Bernard Lewis, for one, has warned us of the human tendency to creatively remember, recover and reinvent our cultural heritages.[13] Whatever the case, there is a powerful "as if" in play during ritual repetition, perhaps best articulated in the Passover *seder* when Jews of every era proclaim, "We were slaves in the land of Egypt."

This takes place as well in (non-improvised) music, especially when replayed on recordings or replicated with reasonable precision in live performances. Songs often transport us to where we first heard them or to a phase of life when they held an important place. Old feelings, old relationships, old situations are resurrected and made present through sound. As long as we continue to hear those songs—and each time we do—that bygone period is restored to vibrant immediacy.

Time-tested music also serves as an intergenerational pathway, promoting a real or imagined sense of continuity between past and present. Songs known (or thought) to be deeply woven into the societal fabric bring us face to face with long-dead ancestors and with a world we did not inhabit but feel viscerally connected to.

This is not the extent of how music connects us to eternal time. Further reflection would yield further indications of this effect. And it bears reiterating that these musical sensations are not experienced simply as emotional memories, but as the past made present once more. On a practical level, this explains the regularity with which recurring repertoires are affixed to communal rituals, both religious and secular. Such music helps tie participants to the activity itself and to the flow of history in which similar activities have already occurred and will occur again. Succinctly put, eternal myths are made eternal in part through eternal tones.

Although this discussion of return implies endlessness, it is not a static process. As we have learned from countless time travel tales of popular fiction, inserting ourselves into events that have already taken place invariably introduces new elements and causes new variations, subtle and not-so-subtle. So it is with time relived on the pages of comic books, retold in rituals and contained in repeated songs. Each of us is a constantly changing accumulation of thoughts, feelings and experiences, and every time we return to the familiar—the eternal—we approach it from a different vantage point.

Far from discrediting the notion of timelessness, the changes precipitated when our current selves encounter the perpetual past can be understood as the dynamic anatomy of eternity. Without this potential for freshness, the eternal return would hardly be longed for.

Notes

1. Walter Murch, "Hyser Memorial Lecture" (paper presented at the Audio Engineering Society 117th Convention, San Francisco, October 30, 2004).
2. David Byrne, *How Music Works* (San Francisco: McSweeney's, 2012), 77.
3. Murch, "Hyser Memorial Lecture."
4. Jean-Paul Sartre, *L'Imaginaire* (Paris: Gallimard, 1940), 243–245.
5. Susanne K. Langer, *Philosophy in a New Key: A Study in the Symbolism of Reason, Rite, and Art* (New York: Mentor, 1964), 181.
6. John Brownell, "Analytical Modes of Jazz Improvisation," *Jazzforchung/Jazz Research* 26 (1994): 9–29.
7. Jean-Paul Sartre, "Humanism and Existentialism," in *Essays on Existentialism* (New York: Citadel, 1965), 48.
8. Ibid., 55.
9. Søren Kierkegaard, *Either-Or*, trans. Water Lowrie (Princeton, NJ: Princeton University Press, 1974), 67.
10. William James, *The Varieties of Religious Experience* (London: Longmans, Green, 1905), 66.
11. Grant Morrison, *Animal Man: Deus Ex Machina* (New York: DC Comics, 2003), 171.
12. Mircea Eliade, *The Myth of the Eternal Return* (Princeton, NJ: Princeton University Press, 1991), 12.
13. Bernard Lewis, *History: Remembered, Recovered, Invented* (New York: Simon & Schuster, 1987).

Suggestions for Further Reading

Brady, Erica. *A Spiral Way: How the Phonograph Changed Ethnography*. Jackson: University Press of Mississippi, 1999.
Chanan, Michael. *Repeated Takes: A Short History of Recording and Its Effects on Music*. New York: Verso, 1995.
Cook, Nicholas. *Beyond the Score: Music as Performance*. New York: Oxford University Press, 2014.
Davies, Stephen. *Musical Works and Performances: A Philosophical Exploration*. New York: Oxford University Press, 2001.
Dickreiter, Michael. *Score Reading: A Key to the Music Experience*. New York: Hal Leonard, 2000.
Gordon, Edwin. *The Aural/Visual Experience of Music Literacy: Reading and Writing Music Notation*. Chicago, GIA: 2004.

Langer, Susanne K. *Philosophy in a New Key: A Study in the Symbolism of Reason, Rite, and Art*. New York: Mentor, 1964.
Philip, Robert. *Performing Music in the Age of Recording*. New Haven, CT: Yale University Press, 2004.
Sartre, Jean-Paul. *L'Imaginaire*. Paris: Gallimard, 1940.
Zuckerkandl, Victor. *Sound and Symbol: Music and the External World*. New Haven, CT: Princeton University Press, 1969.

8

Language

Music is often compared to language. This comparison usually involves recognition of music's communicative qualities, and its ability to convey things rarely achieved in written or spoken words. The present chapter examines the "language-ness" of music, beginning with the widely held assertion that musical communication exists on a higher plane than the ordinary or materialistic realm of linguistic expression. Next we investigate the belief that music expresses something beyond the capability of words to impart. Lastly, we turn to songs—words set to music—and their unique ability to add clarity and directness to thoughts, feelings, and ideas.

Above Noise

Aldous Huxley authored one of the most widely cited statements on music: "After silence, that which comes nearest to expressing the inexpressible is music."[1] The popularity of this maxim has long outlasted any general interest in the collection of essays from which it originated, *Music at Night*. That the phrase resonates with many readers is evidenced by its frequent and usually context-less appearance on websites and books devoted to useful quotations. Some might reverse the hierarchy, placing music before silence, but the substance of Huxley's comment remains the same: these acoustic phenomena communicate something beyond the limits of language.

It is fruitless to venture an elucidation of what Huxley meant by "inexpressible." As the term indicates, the things expressed cannot be justly or fully described. Nevertheless, we can presume it refers to a category of experience variously called emotional, non-rational or spiritual. These ineffable sensations, while universally desirable, are not arrived at easily in our noise-saturated world.

Huxley's thoughts on the subject are fleshed out in *The Perennial Philosophy*, a compendium of mystical insights from sages of the world's religions. In his chapter on silence, Huxley includes instructive excerpts from the writings of religious figures like Lao Tzu and William Law. His own remarks are hardly reserved.

The first barrier to silence he identifies is frivolous speech: "Unrestrained and indiscriminate talk is morally evil and spiritually dangerous."[2] Huxley claims that most words thought or spoken during the course of the day fall into three main groups: "words inspired by malice and uncharitableness towards our neighbors; words inspired by greed, sensuality and self-love; words inspired by pure imbecility and uttered without rhyme or reason, but merely for the sake of making a distracting noise."[3]

The other impediment to silence Huxley cites is incessant ambient noise. Writing toward the middle of the twentieth century, he diagnosed a reality that has only been exacerbated in the intervening years. As Huxley astutely notes, "the resources of our almost miraculous technology have been thrown into the current assault against silence." Most damaging from his perspective is the still-ubiquitous radio, which "penetrates the mind, filling it with a babel of distractions—news items, mutually irrelevant bits of information, blasts of corybantic or sentimental music, continually repeated doses of drama that bring no catharsis, but merely create a craving for daily or even hourly emotional enemas."[4]

As is apparent from the passages above, Huxley's praise for the non-material rewards of silence is matched by his disdain for unfiltered and unrewarding sounds—whether of our own making or mechanically produced. Quietness of mind and environment is, for him, the most effective path to emotional ease, psychological calm and spiritual awakening. Next on his list is music, which cuts through jumbled noises, diverts distractions and communicates directly with the realm of affections. Music combats noise not by eliminating it, but by organizing it. In this respect, Huxley would likely give preference to instrumental music, which is free of the potential contamination of linguistic assertions (like of the "sentimental music" he condemns).

For Huxley and the many admirers of his famous phrase, expressing the inexpressible is a lofty and virtuous aspiration. It implies reaching a level of awareness obscured by the trappings of ordinary existence. In the materialistic landscape of the modern world, meaningless words and noisy devices are among the obstacles blocking our way to a deeper experience. And for the reasons discussed, silence and music are perhaps the best antidotes.

Expressing Expression

The popular appreciation of music as a language beyond words has origins in nineteenth-century German Romanticism and its unrestrained obsession with the expressiveness of musical sound. While composers of the genre were busy expanding the emotional dimensions of their craft, poets were writing about music with equal sentimental effusiveness. The expression heard in the works of Schubert, Schumann and Brahms inspired poets like Tieck, Schlegel and Heine to pour out laudatory verses proclaiming music's unsurpassed ability to convey true feeling. To the poets, music was the embodiment of expression itself—their most venerated aesthetic principle—and they regularly infused their poems with musical references in hopes of harnessing that emotive power. Their ethos is captured in a quote from E. T. A. Hoffmann: "Music is the most romantic of all the arts—one might say the only purely romantic one."[5]

The view of music as a transmitter of emotions spread throughout Europe and influenced other fields. Herbert Spencer, the English philosopher and biologist, concluded that "primitives" developed the capacity for music specifically as a means of communicating their state of being.[6] This anthropological assumption, while a product of its time, had many antecedents. The ancient Greeks, for instance, devised a musical system consisting of modes intended to evoke or intensify particular reactions. Other societies past and present possess a similar (if not as systematic) awareness of music's potential to penetrate and manipulate our inner lives. Nonetheless, the exuberance with which Romantic-era writers emphasized and exalted music's expressiveness has not been equaled.

As an example, here are some of Hoffmann's comments on Beethoven: "Thus Beethoven's instrumental music opens us to the monstrous and immeasurable. Glowing rays shoot through the deep night of this realm, and we sense giant shadows surging to and fro, closing in on us until they destroy us, but not the pain of unending longing in which every desire that has risen quickly in joyful tones sinks and expires. Only with this pain of love, hope, joy—which consumes but does not destroy, which would burst asunder our breasts with a mightily impassioned chord—we live on, enchanted seers of the ghostly world!"[7]

Embedded in this characteristically verbose appraisal is the contradictory concession that music is "immeasurable" and thus incapable of being justly described in words. Goethe said it best: "Music begins where words end."[8] Try as they might to explain the sounds and effects, the poets freely admitted that their verse—like other art forms—could only approximate the purity of emotional transmission they felt in music. Theirs was an era when composers and performers greatly expanded the range and intensity of dynamics, phrasing, articulation, tempo, harmony and all manner of musical coloration. Sympathetic feelings aroused in audiences reached unprecedented levels, and it was widely held that the soul of music made contact with the soul of the listener. All of this put music outside the grasp of language.

It is not necessary to adopt the often-exaggerated stance of the Romantics to value music's emotional impact. Nor must one agree with the view of post-modern detractors, who argue that feelings induced by music are illusory, to acknowledge the limits of musical expression. Still, it is easy to accept the basic Romantic assertion: our emotional responses to music, real or imaged, account largely for our interest in the art form.

The Limits of Language

"Where words fail, music speaks."[9] This saying, attributed to Hans Christian Andersen, has been restated in one way or another in numerous sources. A random survey of musical quotations yields endless similar remarks, including one from Victor Hugo: "Music expresses that which cannot be said and on which it is impossible to be silent."[10] Pulitzer-Prize winning composer Ned Rorem opines, "If music could be translated into human speech, it would no longer need to exist."[11] Charles William Wendte, a renowned Unitarian minister of the early 1900s, expanded on the theme: "When words fail to express the exalted sentiments and finer emotions of the human heart, music becomes the sublimated language of the soul, the divine instrumentality for its higher utterance."[12]

An assemblage of like statements from notable personalities could fill an entire volume. The frequency and eloquence with which the sentiment is repeated is a testament to its accepted truth. Without need for deep reflection or the parsing of meaning, such comments just seem to ring true. The sense that musical expression picks up where language leaves off is an inference made by luminaries and laypeople alike. Music, in its various manifestations, is felt to communicate something that exceeds the conceptual limits of vocabulary.

Exactly what this information is can only be hinted at. The fact that music's impact occurs outside the bounds of language means that language is inadequate to describe it. Our conversations with music occur in the realm of emotions, and insights we glean from that experience are no less (and can be more) significant than that which is gained from reading or speaking.

This assessment is hardly novel. As mentioned, it is alluded to or expressly made in all sorts of literature. Still, it is striking that the observation usually comes from people of words: poets, novelists, philosophers, theologians and the like. It seems the more fluent one is with language, the more one recognizes its insufficiencies. For reasons more intuitive than intellectual, music is reached for as the next level of expression. It can be assumed that authors arrive at this point independently; but similarities between their articulations reflect a common process and shared epiphany.

Among the clearest examples of a wordsmith turning to music is Augustine of Hippo (354–430), whose theological output includes one hundred separate titles. His writings span apologetics, exegesis, letters, sermons, polemics, personal confessions and doctrinal teachings. But even Augustine, arguably the most prolific Latin writer, admitted instances when music is a better communicator than words.

This is especially apparent in his commentary on Psalm 33:3: "sing Him a new song; play sweetly with shouts of joy." Augustine asked, "What does singing in jubilation signify?" His answer: "It is to realize that words cannot communicate the song of the heart." This inner-song—which, again, is more intuitive than intellectual—is best sung as *jubilus*: a spontaneous and wordless musical divulgence. "In this way," he wrote, "the heart rejoices without words and the boundless expanse of rapture is not circumscribed by syllables."[13]

Whether the writer is religious or secular and whether the medium is literary or philosophical, the assertion is the same: music conveys that which words cannot. It is a reality easier to acknowledge than to explain, but a powerful reality nonetheless.

Scripted Thoughts

A song consists of words set to music for the purpose of being sung. This definition is so basic that it hardly needs mention. What is perhaps less obvious is the power that language exerts on the music to which it is set. Lyrics give musical sounds a specific character, turning a notoriously abstract medium into a delivery system for potential crystal clarity—*potential* because, depending on the subject's accessibility and the intelligibility of the language, a song can approach a level of directness rarely achieved in other modalities.

To be sure, lyrics can at times seem superfluous, regardless of how poorly or finely crafted they are, or how well or badly they merge with the music. For some people, the words are merely a doorway into a musical experience, and have little attraction in and of themselves (I tend to fall in this camp). Songs are also multidimensional artifacts, saturated with cultural assumptions, subject to critical judgment, and filtered through personal lenses. Moreover, each individual has heard songs wearing different sets of ears, sometimes gravitating toward the words and other times not. Still, despite this diversity of engagement, the greatest strength of song remains its potential for clarity.

Lyrics have a distinct advantage over other types of linguistic expression. The placement of words in musical confinement yields many clarifying constraints and devices, including: metered stanzas that regulate the number of syllables; recurring phrases that eliminate ambiguity; familiar idioms and clichés that provide instant messages; choruses that reiterate central themes; poetic tools like rhyme, assonance and alliteration, which help weed out extraneous language. Of course, some songs employ these elements better than others, and there is room for nuance and creativity (and miscommunication), even with these controls. But, taken as a whole, songs are uniquely adept at compressing, containing and conveying streamlined concepts.

This unclutteredness runs counter to the human condition, which condemns our minds to ceaseless and often-disjointed thoughts. True, most of us can steer ourselves into clear thinking when needed; but it is impossible to harness the mechanism at all times. The thought motor is always running, even in our sleep.

I'm reminded of a scene in Kurt Vonnegut's *Cat's Cradle*, when Mrs. Pefko complains to Dr. Breed, "You scientists *think* too much." "I think you'll find," replied Dr. Breed, "that everybody does about the same amount of thinking. Scientists simply think about things one way, and other people think about things in others."[14] This is the blessing and burden of our species.

Songs embody the elusive ideal of lucidity. They are neatly packed containers, carefully arranged and efficiently delivered. They are, in short, the opposite of wandering words.

Notes

1. Aldous Huxley, "The Rest is Silence," in *Music at Night and Other Essays* (Leipzig: Albatross, 1931), 19.
2. Aldous Huxley, *The Perennial Philosophy* (New York: Harper, 1940), 216.
3. Ibid., 217.
4. Ibid., 218.
5. David Charlton, ed., *E. T. A. Hoffmann's Musical Writings: Kreisleriana, the Poet and the Composer, Music Criticism* (New York: Cambridge University Press, 1989), 96.
6. Herbert Spencer, "The Origin and Function of Music" [1857], in *Essays: Scientific, Political, and Speculative*, vol. 2 (London: Williams and Norgato, 1891).
7. E. T. A. Hoffmann, *Werke*, ed. Georg Ellinger (Berlin: Deutsches, 1900), 42.
8. Johann Wolfgang von Goethe, quoted in Crofton and Fraser, *A Dictionary of Musical Quotations*, 159.
9. Lorin F. Deland, ed., *The Musical Record: A Journal of Music, Art, Literature* (May 1895): 15.

10. Victor Hugo, *William Shakespeare* (London: Hauteville, 1864), 73.
11. Ned Rorem, *Music from Inside Out* (New York: George Braziller, 1967), 95.
12. Charles William Wendte, quoted in Helen Granat, *Wisdom Through the Ages: A Collection of Favorite Quotations* (Victoria, BC, Canada: Miklen, 1998), 17.
13. Augustine, *St. Augustine on the Psalms* (New York: Newman, 1961), 2:111–112.
14. Kurt Vonnegut, *Cat's Cradle: A Novel* (New York: Random House, 2009), 33.

Suggestions for Further Reading

Goldsmith, Mike. *Discord: The History of Noise*. New York: Oxford University Press, 2012.
Hendy, David. *Noise: A Human History of Sound and Listening*. New York: HarperCollins, 2013.
Higgins, Kathleen Marie. *The Music Between Us: Is Music a Universal Language?* Chicago: University of Chicago Press, 2012.
Lussy, Mathis. *Musical Expression, Accents, Nuances, and Tempo, in Vocal and Instrumental Music*. Stockbridge, MA: Hard Press, 2012.
Patel, Aniruddh D. *Music, Language, and the Brain*. New York: Oxford University Press, 2010.
Rebuschat, Patrick, ed. *Language and Music as Cognitive Systems*. New York: Oxford University Press, 2012.
Rorem, Ned. *Music from Inside Out*. New York: George Braziller, 1967.
Thomson, Virgil. *Music with Words: A Composer's View*. New Haven, CT: Yale University Press, 1989.
Vandercook, H. A. *Expression in Music*. New York: Hal Leonard, 1989.
Williamson, John, ed. *Words and Music*. Liverpool: Liverpool University Press, 2005.

9
NATURE

The natural world provided the earliest inspiration for musical expression. Natural sonic phenomena motivated our ancient ancestors to create their own demonstrative sounds. An echo of this natural history is present in the "gravity" of melodic phrases, and the (usually unconscious) influence of environmental sounds on musical concoctions. As time progressed and music developed into a recognizable cultural form, it became a self-referential art, imitative of itself rather than its primitive sources. Recently, researchers have been drawn back to the wild in search of musical possibilities. Some are convinced that, contrary to popular opinion, human beings are not the only musical species on the planet. Others note that certain animals react to human music in very human ways.

The Rise and Fall of Melody

Music exhibits the human propensity to imitate nature and the delight we take in that imitation. Rhythm is a stylization of natural motion. Beating hearts, falling rain, rustling leaves, prancing animals and other organic patterns inspire rhythmic mimesis. Birdsong has influenced musicians throughout history, from indigenous folk singers to classical composers like Mahler and Messiaen. Harmonic dissonances and consonances are unconsciously sensed as simulations of human passions. Since the beginning, natural forces have molded and been woven into music's very essence.

The bond between music and nature did not escape Italian Renaissance composer and music theorist Franchinus Gaffurius. A noted humanist and personal friend of Leonardo da Vinci, Gaffurius was keenly interested in how people derive musical sounds from their environment and utilize those sounds to achieve specific aims. Among his contributions to the naturalistic conception of music is the notion of "musical gravity," which he introduced in his major treatise *Practica musicae*: "A descent from high to low causes a greater sense of repose."[1] With this simple statement, Gaffurius encapsulated the instinct of tonal music to resolve in a cadence to the tonic, or first scale degree.

This movement is imitative in two important ways. First, the downward movement of the musical line resembles forces that regulate motion in the natural world. The descending pull reinforces our orientation toward the tonic and causes us to feel as though we have arrived at the ground level. Second, it simulates a sense of emotional resolution or closure. By bringing us back to the home or tonic note, melody gives a sensation of gratifying release.

Acknowledging the tendency of musical phrases to descend and rest at the tonic, composers of tonal music employ various methods to protract the time leading to the inevitable conclusion. What often results is a series of ascensions, which generate tension and energy, followed by the much-anticipated resolution, which bestows satisfaction proportional to the duration the listener has waited for it.

Music theorists since Aristotle have recognized tension as one of music's fundamental properties. Like a coiled spring that is pushed and pulled, musical passages portray a cyclic dance, passing through increases and decreases in intensity on their way to a resting position. Human beings seem hardwired to perceive this musical interplay. We feel musical tension on a primal level, as if it were a visceral or kinesthetic experience. When musical suspense reaches its height, our muscles tighten, and with musical resolution, our muscles relax. Of course, no tone, interval, or harmony is intrinsically tense. The impression of tension stems from culturally derived expectations, which may differ from place to place. But, regardless of cultural variation, musical gravity almost universally wields its power on melodic structure, alleviating tension through downward movement.

The mutually reinforcing elements of musical gravity and tension and release go a long way toward explaining our affinity for melody. These forces are an imitation of nature, both in terms of mimicking the rise and fall of objects and in terms of replicating emotional life. Moreover, the usual melodic path toward repose appeases our longing for closure. Through a succession of notes, melody creates and resolves drama in a clean and logical manner that is a human ideal.

Civilizing Soundscapes

Suggestions of music are present everywhere in nature. The rustling of leaves, the babbling of brooks, the pattering of rain, the howling of wolves, the singing of birds, the chirping of crickets. Such sounds may be the original impetus for human musical creativity. They are not yet compositions, but hints of musical form, whispers of motifs, invitations for sonic expansion. The receptive ear recognizes and collects them. The brain organizes, imitates and embellishes them. The imagination combines them with other tonal elements. They are made into music.

This natural history of music is a dominant narrative in the theoretical literature. Mark Changizi, an evolutionary neurobiologist, paints a compelling portrait in *Harnessed*,[2] and Bernie Krause, a prolific archivist of natural soundscapes, shares decades of meticulous research in *The Great Animal Orchestra*.[3] In addition to tracing musical inclinations to the non-human environment, these and related studies confirm the broader instinct of human beings to turn nature into culture.

Culture is prepared more than it is created. Available materials are manipulated to fit our needs, fashioned to meet our tastes, adapted to serve our ends. In the process, we carve a place for ourselves on the planet and gain a semblance of control over our surroundings. What Claude Lévi-Strauss famously wrote about food preparation applies to all aspects of human civilization: it is the continuous effort of transforming the raw into the cooked.[4] Nature provides, we construct.

The culinary view of culture is particularly apt when the subject is music. Musicians sometimes call their influences a stew, composers cook up new works, improvisatory players sizzle, musical choices are likened to a buffet. Implicit in these gastronomical comparisons is recognition that, like meals made from scratch, music involves measuring, mixing and preparing ingredients.

Of course, as cultures advance and humanity increasingly separates itself from the untamed world, pure sonic resources are harder to come by. Music becomes less an imitation of nature and more an imitation of other music. But we nevertheless remain susceptible to natural influences. Just as the landscape offers up an array of edible material, so does the soundscape offer audible material waiting to become music. Musical potential is detected in the many-voiced environment; musical possibilities exist in the listener's mind. The organic substance is harvested, organized and repackaged in endless ways for human expression, reception and appreciation. Sounds are made civilized.

From Source to Self-Reference

There was a time in our distant past when sounds emanating from non-human animals were a major source of musical inspiration. Our ancient ancestors were completely absorbed in their wild habitats. Their ears perked at the calls and songs of birds and other animals. They mimicked those sounds in their own voices, adding a human signature to the dense and varied biophonic soundscape. Over time and through waves of experimentation, replication, manipulation and refinement, human sounds developed their own logic and conventions. The sequences became more and more complex and yielded increasingly numerous varieties. Found and handcrafted instruments were added to the acoustic mixture. At some point, probably early on, their efforts came to resemble what we call music: nonlinguistic and conscious control of sound exhibiting structure and intent.

The above hypothesis is consistent with what is known about the development of human culture. Biological evolution does not achieve adaptations by concocting novel mechanisms, but by modifying what is already in place. New skills and behaviors are not the result of radical blueprints, but of re-configuring existing capacities and apparatuses. Quoting neurophilosopher Patricia S. Churchland, evolution's *modus operandi* is "tinkering-opportunistically rather than redesigning-from-scratch."[5] Likely, then, music is an outgrowth of our biological predispositions for language, sensuality, motor control, dexterity, emotionality and, perhaps most importantly, imitation.

Imitation is the hallmark and foundation of human culture. We innately transmit information and pass on practices from person to person and generation to generation. We learn from, add to, and carry forward this imitative process. Elements are preserved and gradually upgraded, culminating in culture: an assortment of behaviors, customs, skills, methods, standards, norms and expectations.

Cultural evolution occurs at a far quicker pace than biological evolution. Modification of tendencies is much more fluid than the extremely slow process of adaptation that brought about those tendencies. Of course, the speed of change within a society tends to be self-regulated, hinging on things like access to resources and social outlook (conservative, progressive or something in between).

Musically, this helps explain how the urge to add human sounds to the biophony (animal soundscape) developed relatively rapidly from imitation of natural sounds to musical invention. This process occurred in three generalized stages (accounting for thousands of years and inclusive of untold variations): (1) The human capacities for language, emotionality, etc., set the conditions for nonlinguistic sound production; (2) These capacities combined with the inclination to mimic, making environmental sounds the fodder for musical production; (3) Human beings began imitating each other's music, thereby distancing themselves from nature (in degrees relative to the group's physical distance from a natural setting).

The third stage has particular relevance for music in the West. As Western culture has separated itself incrementally from the natural world, its music has followed suit. Sounds become further and further detached from organic sources and more and more abstract. The progressive distancing from nature is perceptible in the timeline of musical periods. Instead of drawing inspiration from wild landscapes, we base our music on other music, our instruments on other instruments, our techniques on other techniques.

We have reached a point where musical iterations and innovations occur in an almost purely human domain. True, a few composers have replicated birdsong in Western form or sampled field recordings from native habitats; but these are novelties and not the norm. Western music is millennia removed from its feral origins. It is a self-referential art.

Music in Wild Places

When George Berkeley posed the question, "If a tree falls in the forest and no one is around to hear it, does it make a sound?"[6] he apparently assumed that humans are the only sentient beings capable of hearing. Given the perpetual popularity of this eighteenth-century hypothetical, many are still convinced that audible events can only be confirmed in human ears. This anthropocentric view is often coupled with an equally condescending assumption that acoustic behaviors of birds, fish, insects and non-human mammals have just two basic functions: mating and territory. Aside from being psychologically reassuring—providing much-desired, yet difficult-to-substantiate, solace that the gap between human beings and "mere" creatures is unbridgeably wide—these beliefs betray our musical ignorance. As naturalist and musician Bernie Krause warns us, "When it comes to natural sounds, there are few rules."[7]

For forty-plus years, Krause has traveled the world recording and analyzing wild soundscapes. His archive includes over 4,000 hours of sound from more than 15,000 species. Captured at undisturbed locations, these chronicles reveal an aural aspect of natural selection. Contrary to what the untrained listener might suspect, the vast array of biological sounds did not come about arbitrarily. Rather, Krause explains, "each resident species acquires its own preferred sonic bandwidth—to blend or contrast—much in the way that violins, woodwinds, trumpets, and percussion instruments stake out acoustic territory in an orchestral arrangement."[8] Krause calls this the "niche hypothesis," or a partitioning process in which voices of a biome form unique sonic signatures that serve as terrestrial voiceprints or sound-marks. The nuanced audibles of each species accomplish specific functions: mating, protecting territory, capturing food, group defense, social contact, emotional cues, play, etc. From Krause's vantage point, such sounds can be considered "musical" in the broad sense of being controlled patterns that exhibit structure and intent and are organized vertically (texture and layering) and horizontally (over time).

The impulse to find a niche may have also been a driving force of human music. Our forest-dwelling ancestors paid close attention to their native soundscapes, listening for signals in the rich textures of their habitats, finding distinct bandwidths to communicate with one another, and imitating the sounds of other species, both for play and practical purposes (like the hunt). From there, human cultures gradually developed the diverse sounds and sundry uses that comprise what we know as music.

Krause also opens our awareness to the multiplicity of sound sources on our planet. He proposes three distinct categories. The oldest is *geophony*: natural sounds springing from non-biological phenomena, such as wind, rainfall and bodies of water. All acoustically sensitive animals—including humans—evolved to accommodate the *geophony*, as "each had to establish a bandwidth in which its clicks, breaths, hisses, roars, songs, or calls could stand out in relation to nonbiological natural sounds."[9] Animal sounds come in two types: *biophony*, or sounds emanating from nonhuman biological entities; and *anthrophony*, or human-generated sounds (physiological, controlled, electromechanical and incidental).

One of the implications of Krause's work is that it can help evaluate the health of a biome. Not only can studying the acoustic community demonstrate the intrusion of foreign elements—i.e., human-made noise and the audible response of native creatures (silence, restlessness or alarm calls)—it can also indicate the diversity and vibrancy of the wildlife, or the absence thereof. Sadly, over a half of the wild habitats Krause has recorded no longer exist due to human encroachment—a reality discerned in part from the silencing of *biophonic* activity and the rise of *anthrophonic* noise.

Funktionslust, Birdsong and Beauty

Ethology, the biological study of animal behavior, concerns itself primarily with uncovering survival advantages in animal activities. Balancing a desire to find purpose in animal behavior and avoid the sin of anthropomorphism, ethologists refrain from ascribing emotions or extraneous pleasures to non-human species. What appears to the untrained observer as a creative act or outpouring of feeling is reduced to a survival impulse or an instinctive behavior. It is, of course, wise to keep from seeing too much of ourselves in other animals. Our tendency to anthropomorphize everything around us says less about reality than it does about ourselves. Yet strict adherence to the ethologist's code can create undue distance. As Jeffrey Moussaieff Masson asks in his controversial bestseller, *When Elephants Weep*: "If humans are subject to evolution but have feelings that are inexplicable in survival terms, if they are prone to emotions that do not seem to confer any advantage, why should we suppose that animals act on genetic investment alone?"[10]

This question is all the more penetrating given the impressive spectacles exhibited by many species. A gibbon swinging fervently from branch to branch, a dolphin thrusting itself out of the water, a cat hunting backyard critters for sport. The German language has a word for such behavior: *funktionslust*, meaning "pleasure taken in doing what one does best." This, too, is thought to be adaptive. Pleasure derived from an activity increases an animal's proneness to pursue it, thus increasing the likelihood of survival. A gibbon who spends extra time swinging in the trees is better fit to flee leopards and snakes when they attack.

But is that all there is to it? Masson points out that a loving animal (again, a controversial concept) may leave more offspring, making lovingness a survival trait. But the same animal may also provide excessive care to a disabled (and therefore doomed) offspring, exposing itself to hazards in the process.

The presumed practicality of *funktionslust* is further challenged by the performance of songbirds: the roughly 4,000 species of perching birds capable of producing varied and elaborate song patterns. To the standard scientist, the sounds these birds produce—no matter how inventive—serve the basic purposes of establishing territory and advertising fitness to potential mates. But some researchers argue that survival alone cannot account for the amount or variety of imitation, improvisation and near-composition evident in birdsong, nor the seemingly arbitrary times and circumstances in which the songs are often heard.

David Rothenberg and other birdsong experts see this music-making as approaching *pure funktionslust*, or pleasure derived from a native ability exceeding any evolutionary purpose. In his book *Why Birds Sing*, Rothenberg proposes that songbird patterns rival human music in terms of structure, aesthetics, expressiveness, interactiveness and extra-practical life enhancement.[11] A philosopher and jazz clarinetist who "jams" with songbirds in the wild, Rothenberg has been accused of the double infractions of anthropomorphism and evaluating birdsong with the bias of a musician. In his defense, he concedes that birds, not people, are the arbiters of their own songs, and only they can know what their repertoires mean to other birds. But he calls it art nonetheless, quoting Wallace Craig: "Art *is* a fact and after all it would be rather ridiculous from our evolutionistic ideology to deny the possibility that something similar may occur in other species."[12]

Following this argument, we might deduce that songbirds experience beauty in their songs. This proposition harmonizes with the work of Denis Dutton, a philosopher of art who posits an evolutionary basis for the human perception of artistic beauty.[13] Dutton identifies Acheulean hand axes as the earliest hominid artwork. Prevalent from 500,000 to 1.2 million years ago, these teardrop carvings have been located in the thousands throughout Asia, Africa and Europe. This sheer number and the lack of wear on their delicate blades suggest they were not used for butchering, but for aesthetic enjoyment. Indeed, they remain beautiful even to our modern eyes. The reason for this, explains Dutton, is that we find beauty in something done well. We are attracted to the meticulousness and skill evident in the axes. They satisfy our innate taste for virtuosic displays in the same way as well-executed concertos, paintings and ballets. Beauty is in the expertise.

If this attraction existed among our prehistoric ancestors, why not in songbirds? Taking *funktionslust* in a logical direction, might we assume that songbirds sing for the joy of it, and that their skilled displays feed aesthetic yearnings of other songbirds? These questions point to a possible compromise, in which animal behavior retains its evolutionary explanation and art finds evolutionary justification outside of the drive to survive.

Music and Animals

Music has always been thought of in human terms. We detect and respond to certain sounds as music. We set aesthetic parameters within which those sounds are assessed. We decide where to place the sounds on the spectrum of genres. We determine which sounds we like and which ones we do not. This process is unconscious and automatic: we naturally distinguish musical from other sounds and label them as this or that quality and type. From an anthropological perspective, humans are the only creatures capable of this brand of discernment. We have convinced ourselves that of all the animals on the planet, we are the musical judges.

Semiologist Jean-Jacques Nattiez summed up the conventional view: "[I]t is a human being who decides what is and is not musical, even when the sound is not of human origin. If we acknowledge that sound is not organized and conceptualized (that is, made to form music) merely by its producer, but by the mind that perceives it, then music is uniquely human."[14] Thus, even when we hear music in a cricket's chirp or rustling leaves, it is us—not the phenomenon itself—that makes music out of the sounds. There is, however, a growing body of research that challenges this basic assumption.

Music can be defined as the purposeful arrangement of sounds with relation to pitch, rhythm and tonality. The organization and appreciation of this information are widely held as human capacities. But animals such as whales emit songs displaying human-equivalent rhythms, phrase lengths and compositional form; and birdsongs include pitch variances and rhythmic patterns compatible with human musical expression.

Scientists have long presumed that these and other non-human animal sounds serve only biological functions, such as mating, and are not received as art. It is through our ears that they are anthropomorphized into music. Yet some experts, like Cornell neurobiologist Ronald R. Hoy, are inclined to consider that animals experience music the way we do.[15]

There is a minor field of science called zoomusicology, which studies the musical sounds and perceptions of animals. In addition to discovering what appears to be an aesthetic attraction to species-specific sonic stimuli, researchers have shown that certain animals have clear reactions to human-made music. For instance, one study found that java sparrows prefer Bach versus Schoenberg.[16] An experiment with carps suggests that they enjoy Baroque music more than the songs of John Lee Hooker.[17] Work done with lab rats indicates that classical pieces that are "rodentized" (sped up and adjusted to the hearing range of rodents) have an enriching effect on their behavior.[18]

The most provocative implication of this research is that animals respond to human music in remarkably human ways. Or, more accurately, that there is something about musical stimulation that is so universal as to include beings beyond the human. The main indicator of humanity's musicalness is not our music-making skills, which vary from unrefined and rudimentary to pristine and virtuosic. Rather, it is our innate ability to recognize and respond to music. If this ability is present in animals, as zoomusicologists contend, then musical processing is not just a human venture.

Notes

1. Franchinus Gaffurius, *Practica musicae*, Book 1, Chapter 8 (Millan: 1496).
2. Mark Changizi, *Harnessed: How Language and Music Mimicked Nature and Transformed Ape to Man* (Dallas, TX: BenBella, 2011).
3. Bernie Krause, *The Great Animal Orchestra: Finding the Origins of Music in the World's Wild Places* (New York: Little, Brown, and Co., 2012).

4. Claude Lévi-Strauss, *The Raw and the Cooked*, trans. John and Doreen Weightman (New York: Harper and Row, 1969).
5. Patricia S. Churchland, *Braintrust: What Neuroscience Tells Us About Morality* (Princeton, NJ: Princeton University Press, 2011), 98.
6. George Berkeley, *A Treatise Concerning the Principles of Human Knowledge* [1710] (Whitefish, MT: Kessinger, 2004).
7. Krause, *The Great Animal Orchestra*, 59.
8. Ibid., 97.
9. Ibid., 39.
10. Jeffrey Moussaieff Masson and Susan McCarthy, *When Elephants Weep: The Emotional Lives of Animals* (New York: Random House, 1995), 15.
11. David Rothenberg, *Why Birds Sing: A Journey into the Mystery of Bird Song* (New York: Basic Books, 2006).
12. Wallace Craig, "The Song of the Wood Peewee" (1943), quoted in Ibid., 127.
13. Denis Dutton, *The Art Instinct: Beauty, Pleasure, and Human Evolution* (New York: Bloomsbury, 2009).
14. Jean-Jacques Nattiez, *Music and Discourse: Toward a Semiology of Music* (Princeton, NJ: Princeton University Press, 1990), 58.
15. See, for instance, Ronald R. Hoy, "Acute as a Bug's Ear: An Informal Discussion of Hearing in Insects," in *Comparative Hearing: Insects*, eds., Ronald R. Hoy, Arthur N. Popper and Richard R. Fray (New York: Springer, 1998), 11–17.
16. Shigeru Watanabe and Katsufumi Sato, "Discriminative Stimulus Properties of Music in Java Sparrows," *Behavioural Processes* 47:1 (1999): 53–57.
17. Ava R. Chase, "Music Discriminations by Carp (Cyprinus Carpio)," *Animal Learning & Behavior* 29:4 (2001): 336–353.
18. S. Fekete, C. Winding and T. Rülicke, "Effect of Human as Well as Rodentized Mozart and Bach Music on the Open-Field Activity of BALB/c Mice" (paper presented at the CEELA-II Triannual Conference, Budapest, 2012).

Suggestions for Further Reading

Changizi, Mark. *Harnessed: How Language and Music Mimicked Nature and Transformed Ape to Man*. Dallas, TX: BenBella, 2011.
Crocker, Richard L. *A History of Musical Style*. New York: Dover, 1986.
Krause, Bernie. *The Great Animal Orchestra: Finding the Origins of Music in the World's Wild Places*. New York: Little, Brown, and Co., 2012.
_____. *Wild Soundscapes: Discovering the Voice of the Natural World*. Berkeley: Wilderness, 2002.
Marler, Peter R., and Hans Slabbekoorn. *Nature's Music: The Science of Birdsong*. San Diego, CA: Academic, 2004.
Martinelli, Dario. *Of Birds, Whales, and Other Musicians: An Introduction to Zoomusicology*. Scranton, PA: University of Scranton Press, 2009.
Nattiez, Jean-Jacques. *Music and Discourse: Toward a Semiology of Music*. Princeton, NJ: Princeton University Press, 1990.
Rothenberg, David. *Bug Music: How Insects Gave Us Rhythm and Noise*. New York: Macmillan, 2013.
_____. *Why Birds Sing: A Journey into the Mystery of Bird Song*. New York: Basic Books, 2006.
_____, and Marta Ulvaeus, eds. *The Book of Music and Nature: An Anthology of Sounds, Words, Thoughts*. Middleton, CT: Wesleyan University Press, 2013.

10

Folk Music

The use of music as entertainment is a late a relatively rare practice in human history. Rather than an end in itself, music most often serves as an aid to other objectives and an enhancement of everyday life. This chapter focuses on "ordinary" music, commonly known as "folk music" or "music of the people." It begins by framing creativity as a common trait of our species, and looks at how the creative drive manifests in folklore. From there, we turn to the cultural processes that give rise to folk music, and probe various meanings of that musical category. Lastly, the chapter highlights the crucial role of anonymous individuals and cultural forces in shaping the music of the "greats."

Creativity Within

Western music history attempts a straight line connecting the "greats," whose biographies demarcate the beginnings and endings of musical periods (Medieval, Renaissance, Baroque, Classical, Romantic, Modern, Contemporary). Like any effort to construct a palatable narrative from multitudinous ingredients, this image of music's march through the ages sweeps over outliers, ignores "lesser lights," overlooks ambiguities, excludes styles, and defines and focuses on centers rather than peripheries. Sniffing out deficiencies in this approach is nothing new. Ethnomusicologists, for instance, strive for an inclusive and holistic appreciation of "music as culture," which embraces music of all sorts (and of all sorts of people) as group-specific repositories of information, identification, social cues, and symbolism.

The Western outline of music history also presumes that creativity "progresses" or "improves" with time. For example, it is held that Medieval music was harmonically inferior to the complex techniques of later centuries. But it can just as well be claimed that intricate harmonies simply didn't work in Medieval social and spatial contexts. Similarly, the excessive orchestration and emotionalism of the Romantics are regarded as more evolved than the refinement and gentility of Classical composers. But, again, music that works in one setting typically doesn't work in another. The same applies to folk and popular musics, which should be recognized as group-centric and purpose-serving cultural containers, rather than artifacts to be placed on an evolutionary continuum.

This revised conception resonates with the work of Ellen Dissanayake, who puts aesthetic creativity in anthropological perspective. In her convincing analysis, presented in *Homo Aestheticus*, Dissanayake argues that an artistic drive was key to the emergence, survival and adaptation of early humans.[1] Departing from the dominant view of aesthetics as a tangential feature, Dissanayake illustrates how art grew from an innate impulse to mark certain objects and activities as "special," thereby ensuring their perpetuation.

It is no coincidence that art—in the form of song, dance, poetry, jewelry, painting, sculpture, engraving, costume, piercing, decoration, etc.—developed around occasions and practices crucial for group survival. These include but are not limited to: birth, rites of passage, marriage, mourning, hunting, food production, warfare, peacemaking, and religious ceremonials. Art can thus be understood as both a behavioral predisposition and a human necessity (like language and lovemaking).

This view puts into question the notion of creative progress. Creativity is an innate human trait, part and parcel of the artistic drive. Cultural conditions, social expectations, and technological advancements steer this tendency into diverse manifestations, all of which satisfy basic human needs. To be sure, some individuals are encouraged and excel in this tendency more than others; but it is present in us all. If artistic displays observable across cultures and throughout history tell us anything, it is this: creativity is a constant.

Heart Song

The heart and mind are in some ways theoretical constructs. Though both can be located within physical space—the chest and cranial cavities respectively—they have deeper significance in metaphysical discourse. The heart is not just a vital organ pumping blood around the body. In Western and some non-Western cultures, it is the seat of passion, empathy, love, conviction, intuition and emotional impulses. The mind is not just the locus of high-level cognitive activity—consciousness, perception, memory, etc. It is viewed as somehow separate from the brain (and physical existence in general). In popular usage, the mind represents self-awareness and intellect, which are considered distinct from the emotion-based attributes assigned to the heart.

Whether rational and emotional states can truly be separated is a subject of ongoing debate. Judgments, convictions, sensations and decision-making derive from a mixture of thoughts and sentiments. Feelings inform cognition; cognition informs feelings. Nevertheless, the heart and mind remain useful (and inescapable) metaphors for a complex entanglement of functions and traits.

A case in point comes from Zoltán Kodály, an influential twentieth-century composer, ethnomusicologist and educator. Kodály spent his early career on the Hungarian countryside collecting phonograph cylinder recordings. From that experience, he concluded that human beings have two native tongues. One is the language spoken at home. The other is folk music. Verbal communication is the language of the mind: the principle medium of thought and sensory processing. Folk music is the vocabulary of the heart: a storehouse of emotions and longings.

Rather than getting bogged down in ambiguities surrounding what is and what is not folk music, we can broaden Kodály's observation to include all music that is "indigenous" to an individual. Most of us possess an assortment of musical selections that are folk-like: they capture our spirit, embody our history and encapsulate our identities. Hearing or performing them helps ground us in our pasts, situate us in our surroundings and remind us of who we are. To use a symbolic term somewhat analogous to the heart, a personal soundtrack is the record of one's soul. In a pre-rational yet undeniable way, it puts us in contact with our interior selves.

Of course, the impact of such music is not purely emotional or otherwise ineffable. It stirs memories, images and ideas—things usually ascribed to the mind. This demonstrates the difficulty of demarcating between feelings and thoughts (heart and mind). The notions, imagery and recollections aroused by our favorite music tend to be feeling-laden: they are attached to sentimental moments in our lives, and inspire emotionally infused concepts and mental pictures.

This brings us back to Kodály's observation. Whatever standards are used to identify music as "folk," the qualifying sounds typically evoke regional and/or ethnic pride, rich communal associations, and the shared sentiments and experiences of a specific population. All of this constitutes a multi-layered heart—one consisting of nuanced and particularistic feelings. It is not an unthinking seat of emotions; it has an identity. These aspects are easily adapted to individual playlists. Like the "people's music" of a culture or subculture, personally meaningful pieces forge a connecting line to one's inner life. They speak the language of the heart.

That's All Folk

Louis Armstrong once remarked to the *New York Times*, "All music is folk music; I ain't never heard no horse sing a song."[2] This quotable quip suggests that music-making is among the creative behaviors that set human beings apart from the instinct-driven animals of nature. This supposition has been challenged with some success in recent years. There is growing recognition of intentional sonic production (read: music) among nonhuman species from rodents to whales. Armstrong's point reflects the conventional view that humanity's claim to distinction—which is ever diminishing in light of evolutionary theory—is somehow proven by our musical imagination.

Although the notion of a song-less horse may be faulty, the first part of the phrase jives with the deconstructive tendencies of the postmodern age. All human music is, in a sense, folk music—or at least has the potential of achieving that distinction. This is true not only in the literal sense Armstrong implied—folk is a synonym for people—but also in the technical sense that folk music, as a category, has become less amenable to definition and more inclusive of kaleidoscopic sounds.

Folk music first entered the nomenclature in the nineteenth century, alongside other cultural elements somewhat derogatorily identified as folklore. Words like simple, savage, unsophisticated, primitive, rough and unschooled were common in those early writings. As the designation proliferated in the musical literature, its meaning expanded at a corresponding rate. A casual review of its usage over the past century and a half reveals an array of imperfect, oft-chauvinistic and non-binding definitions: music passed on orally; music of indigenous peoples; music of the lower classes; music with unknown composers; music with collective origin; music interwoven with a national culture; music long associated with an event; non-commercial music; music that comes to identify a people in one way or another.

Any one of these meanings is susceptible to collapse under closer inspection, and contradictions arise when they are placed side by side. For instance, cherished songs of unknown authorship are commonly packaged for consumers as art songs, recordings, concert performances and other profit-seeking ventures. Does this eliminate their folk-ness? Oftentimes, too, melodies identified as folk can be traced to known composers and may have been extracted from more elaborate works written with commercial aims. This is the origin of many "traditional" melodies of the church and synagogue, and describes how show tunes and other popular idioms find their way into the nursery, where they pass from the mouths of one generation to the next.

While matching a presumed-anonymous tune with its true composer is admirable and responsible, it does nothing to change its folk status. The same can be said for similar investigative pursuits. This is because folk music is a process, not a thing (we might dub it "folkalization"). Almost any music of almost any origin can become folk through widespread circulation, continuous use, accumulated associations and its role as an identity marker for an affinity group.

In his instructive book, *Folk Music*, musicologist Mark Slobin concedes that the term folk music is so widely applied and has so many nuanced meanings as to evade simple summary. He stresses that it is a fluid amalgam of sounds that constantly adapts as it travels from person to person, location to location, and age to age, and that it is best to identify it using the practical, though unscientific, measurement of "we know it when we hear it." One of Slobin's key points is that folk music is not a body of fossilized tunes but the record of a *living* experience, which is subject to shift depending on cultural trends, courses of events, a performer's whim, etc. As he relates: "Every group has a stock of tunes and texts that have come together so skillfully that they have no past and which expand into an unlimited future."[3]

With all of the sentiments, convictions, disputes and controversies a discussion like this entails, the best we can do is scratch the surface. The topic is endless. Yet despite the uncertainties, speculations and counter-speculations folk music has and will provoke, it is increasingly apparent that Louis Armstrong was, perhaps unintentionally, on to something.

Sound Stories

Scottish historian and essayist Thomas Carlyle observed, "History is the essence of innumerable biographies."[4] The biographies he had in mind were not those of famous men and women, but the lives of anonymous individuals who constitute the real spirit of a nation. The notion of regular folk as history makers was almost unheard of in Carlyle's day. And although some modern historians focus on ordinary people and groups long neglected—like women and indigenous populations—our awareness of history is overwhelmingly shaped by profiles of the "greats."

Understandably, writers of history are drawn to high profile players, dra-

10. Folk Music

matic episodes and popular places. In order to map out and find patterns in the sweep of time, dots are connected between a handful of carefully selected people and events. What the writer chooses to include or exclude is shaped by biases and pet interests. The story presented invariably favors certain views, parties and locations. However, while this process is faulty and subject to revision, it is essential for reducing the immensity of human experience into a comprehensible snapshot.

Music history is similarly conceived of as a linear path punctuated by luminaries. The annals of historical musicology—the study of musical composition, performance and reception over time—are filled with anecdotes and analyses of the lives and works of big-name composers. In the West, the periodization of music is centered on famous figures, both representative and transitional. Mozart, for instance, is seen as a quintessential Classical composer, while Beethoven is considered a bridge between the Classical and Romantic periods.

That the musical timeline is organized around emblematic personalities is perfectly logical. Music is a human invention and those who make it determine its course. Yet, while we can trace stylistic developments by linking one famous composer to the next, this neat (and in some ways necessary) construction not only obscures less prominent musicians, but also ignores multifarious influences that inform each piece along the way.

It is no secret that major composers inspire other major composers, either through friendship, study, admiration or a master-disciple relationship. The inspiration is sometimes acknowledged by the composers, and other times gleaned from their compositions. But musical information does not pass on exclusively through masters and masterworks.

The ear of the composer is alert and sensitive to all sorts of sounds, some of which are consciously or unconsciously recalled during the act of composition. The sources of these sounds may be famous, folk or forgotten, but their imprint is indelible. No piece of music is an island. Whether conventional, groundbreaking or somewhere in between, music involves the absorption and manipulation of existing sonic material. Even the most innovative composition is built upon previous efforts. And the more musical access a composer has, the more eclectic and plentiful the influences.

The potential complexity of this musical picture is captured in a reminiscence from trumpeter Frank London: "We studied [at the New England Conservatory] a mixture of classical and jazz, as well as lots of other stuff—pop, folk, and ethnic musics—while developing a particular philosophy that still guides my own musical life and that of many of my peers. The idea is that one can study and assimilate the elements of any musical style, form, or tradition by ear. You listen over and over to a Charlie Parker solo or a Peruvian flute player and learn to replicate what you hear.... We became cultural consumers. No music was off limits."[5]

The history of a single piece contains the histories of many other pieces, which are themselves built on the histories of other pieces, and on and on. Thus, as Carlyle might conclude, music is the "essence of innumerable biographies."

Notes

1. Ellen Dissanayake, *Homo Aestheticus: Where Art Comes From and Why* (Seattle: University of Washington Press, 1992).
2. Louis Armstrong, quoted in *New York Times*, July 7, 1971, 41.
3. Mark Slobin, *Folk Music: A Very Short Introduction* (New York: Oxford University Press, 2011), 8.
4. Thomas Carlyle, *Works*, vol. 27 (New York: Charles Scribner's Sons, 1904), 86.
5. Frank London, "An Insider's View: How We Traveled from Obscurity to the Klezmer Establishment in Twenty Years," in *American Klezmer: Its Roots and Offshoots*, ed. Mark Slobin (Berkeley: University of California Press, 2002), 206. 206–210.

Suggestions for Further Reading

Alves, William. *Music of the Peoples of the World*. Belmont, CA: Cengage, 2012.
Bohlman, Philip V. *The Study of Folk Music in the Modern World*. Bloomington: Indiana University Press, 1988.
Cahn, William L. *Creative Music Making*. New York: Psychology, 2005.
Cohen, Ronald D. *Folk Music: The Basics*. New York: Routledge, 2006.
DeNora, Tia. *Music in Everyday Life*. New York: Cambridge University Press, 2000.
Gelbart, Matthew. *The Invention of Folk Music and Art Music: Emerging Categories from Ossian to Wagner*. New York: Cambridge University Press, 2007.
Govaner, Alan B. *Everyday Music: Exploring Sounds and Cultures*. College Station: Texas A&M University Press, 2012.
Legdin, Stephanie P. *Discovering Folk Music*. Santa Barbara, CA: ABC-CLIO, 2010.
Slobin, Mark. *Folk Music: A Very Short Introduction*. New York: Oxford University Press, 2011.
Titon, Jeff, et al. *Worlds of Music: An Introduction to the Music of the World's Peoples*. Belmont, CA: Thomson.

11

Art Music

"Art" as something set apart from the rest of life is a construct of the modern West. Since prehistoric times, humanity has exhibited an aesthetic impulse that has given rise to the various art forms we know today. Although not every culture sees these beautifying adornments and artifacts as art, they all fit into branches of that modern category: painting, jewelry, makeup, sculpture, architecture, poetry, music, etc. This chapter posits that beneath the enormous surface variety, all cultures share artistic forms, including music. It looks at how "art" as a separate construct developed in the West, and challenges the notion of "absolute" music, or music for its own sake. It argues that artistic elements are present in music of every kind, and outlines the problem of thinking of musical creations as "works." The chapter closes with the claim that broad musical judgments, like "good" and "bad," owe more to functionality than to objective values.

Art Everywhere

Some assert that it is a fallacy to compare cultural elements cross-culturally. Sometimes called the "incommensurability thesis," this position posits that because objects, concepts and behaviors tend to have very specific meanings for the groups that produce them, they must therefore be utterly unique. Variety negates universality. Basically a version of cultural relativism, this attitude emanates from three circles (or, rather, minorities within three circles): philosophers who attack commonalities in human experience; critics who over-emphasize outlier phenomena in order to challenge conventional assumptions; and ethnographers who argue for the absolute uniqueness of the populations they study, in part to elevate their own stature as privileged experts. Yet, just because human activities take heterogeneous forms does not eliminate the possibility of shared motivations.

Steven Pinker argues this point as it relates to the human capacity for language. He concludes in *The Language Instinct*: "Knowing about the ubiquity of complex language across individuals and cultures and the single mental design underlying them all, no speech seems foreign to me, even if I cannot understand a word."[1] This observation seems indisputable: language is a biological characteristic of the human species.

Philosopher of art Denis Dutton expands on Pinker's claim in *The Art Instinct*. He asks: "Is it also true that, even though we might not receive a pleasurable, or even immediately intelligible, experience from art of other cultures, still, beneath the vast surface variety, all human beings have essentially the same art?"[2] Dutton contends that, like language, artistic behaviors have spontaneously appeared throughout recorded human history. Almost always, observers across cultures recognize these behaviors as artistic, and there is enough commonality between them that they can be placed within tidy categories: painting, jewelry, dance, sculpture, music, drama, architecture, etc. To Dutton, this suggests that the arts, again like language, possess a general omnipresent structure beneath the varied grammar and vocabulary.

It should be noted that Pinker himself has elsewhere challenged this assumption. Most famously, he dubbed music "auditory cheesecake," or a non-adaptive by-product (of language, pattern recognition, emotional calls, etc.) that serves no fundamental role in human evolution.[3] It is not my intention here to place that hypothesis under a microscope or investigate the many arguments against it. (Perhaps, being a linguist, Pinker sees language as a sort of holy ground that mustn't be stepped on by "lesser" human activities.) Wherever the evolutionary debates travel and whatever clues or counterclues they accumulate, one thing is convincing: art appears rooted in universal human psychology.

The Invention of "Art"

Marxist philosopher Paul Mattick, Jr., once remarked that "art" has only been around since the eighteenth century.[4] On the surface, this audacious claim seems to dismiss the creative impulse evident in hominids since the cave-painting days and probably before. But, really, the idea of art as something abstract or "for itself" is a Western construct with roots in the Enlightenment. That era gave rise to the notion of "the aesthetic" as a stand-alone experience, as well as individuals and institutions that actively removed artistic creation from organic contexts: critics, art dealers, academics, galleries, museums, journals, etc. Terms previously used in other areas, like "creativity," "self-expression," "genius" and "imagination," were re-designated almost exclusively as "art words."

Prior to that period (and still today in most non–European cultures) art was not a thing apart, but an integral and integrated aspect of human life. Sculpture, painting, ceramics, woodwork, weaving, poetry, music, dance, and other expressive mediums were more than mere aesthetic excursions. They beautified utensils, adorned abodes, demarcated rituals, told stories, and generally made things special. Skill and ornamentation were not valued for their own sake, but for their ability to draw attention to and enhance extra-artistic objects and activities.

Eighteenth-century Europe witnessed the extraction of art from its functionalistic origins. It was segregated from everyday life and displayed as something of intrinsic worth. With this program came the panoply of now-familiar buzzwords: commodity, ownership, property, specialization, high culture, popular culture, entertainment, etc.

In the world of music, the contrivance of "absolute art" is even more recent. As *New Yorker* music critic Alex Ross explains, the "atmosphere of high seriousness" that characterizes classical concerts—with the expectation of attentive listening and quiet between movements—did not take hold until the early twentieth century.[5] When public concerts first became widespread, sometime after 1800, they were eclectic events featuring a sloppy mix of excerpts from larger works and a miscellany of styles. Attendees chatted, shouted, scuffled, moseyed about, clanked dishes, and yes, even applauded (or booed) between (or during) movements. The performance was less a centerpiece than an excuse for a social happening.

As concert going morphed into a refined, bourgeoisie affair, the rigid format we are now acquainted with became the norm. Hushed and immobilized audiences sat in specially designed symphony halls and opera houses, which allowed composers to explore dynamic extremes hitherto impossible. "When Beethoven began his Ninth Symphony [1824] with ten bars of otherworldly pianissimo," writes Ross, "he was defying the norms of his time, essentially imagining a new world in which the audience would await the music in an expectant hush. Soon enough, that world came into being."[6]

The impact of this development was wide-ranging. In no small way, it signaled the birth of music as an attraction in and of itself—a brand-new conception in the history of human culture. Like other artistic tendencies filtered through the Western consciousness, music was artificially detached from activities with which it had always co-existed. The radical break paved the way for the more general phenomenon of "music as entertainment" (highbrow, lowbrow and in between), and the commercialization and professionalization that came with it.

Absolutely Not

German Romantic authors introduced the concept of "pure" music, or music without extra-musical meaning. They conceived of instrumental music as the language of a higher realm—a language transcending anything that could be said about it and any link that could be made between it and the things of this world. Richard Wagner was an early critic of their proposition. To him, music without signification was as impossible to create as it was worthless to consume (he coined the term "absolute" music to mock the very idea). Even when devoid of words, subject matter and programmatic purpose, music is intertwined with the environment in which it is heard and the images and feelings it induces. Its message might be abstract and open to interpretation, but it is not absent.

Life occurs in context. Being alive means being engaged in a perpetual and usually unconscious process of amassing observational input, experiential data and sensory information. Nothing that we taste, touch, smell, hear, see or think can be divorced from prior experiences, and all of it is present when we encounter new stimuli. We cannot help but make connections between incidents current and past, and the lens through which we perceive reality is modified with each passing moment. We are swimming in a stream of constant accumulation.

Our relationship with music exists in this perceptual complex. Aesthetic tastes and artistic meanings are influenced by factors like culture, environment, schooling, philosophy and politics, not to mention the settings and situations in which listening takes place. It is possible in a lab or study hall to reduce music to an organized composite of pitches, intervals, alignments and values. But music is not received in this mathematical manner. It comes to us as a container brimming with associations, the contents of which are the by-product of our unique life experiences. It triggers a varied assortment of memories, visuals, sensations and sentiments. In short, we derive meaning from it whether we intend to or not.

The same is true for the music's creator. Composers tend to work within inherited rules and conventions, or actively reject those norms. Either way, they situate themselves in relation to other composers or styles, and cannot escape the connotations they carry. As much as they might desire to write music for its own sake, it will always be about something. Absolute music—

or, better, music that pretends to be absolute—may be vague in purpose; but neither the composer nor audience hears it as purposeless.

This discussion is summed up in the words of musicologist Nicholas Cook: "Pure music, it seems, is the aesthetician's (and music theorist's) fiction."[7] Music is never just sound. It is everything the sound evokes.

Always Art

The designation "art music" has come under fire in recent years. As a synonym for "legitimate music," "serious music" and other labels rife with elitism, the term generally refers to notated music composed with advanced structural frameworks and theoretical tools. It is regarded as distinct from "lesser" types of music, which are commonly heaped into two overcrowded categories: folk and popular. Many contemporary scholars and performers refrain from applying these distinctions, and those who do tend to be critical of the old assumptions they carry.

The objections center on two main issues. First is the notion that only Western classical music (in the various ways that descriptor is used) is sophisticated enough to qualify as "art." There are numerous examples from rock, jazz, soul and other sources that display a level of complexity exceeding that of the usual fare. Second is the belief that technical refinement and difficultness are prerequisites for artistry. This view ignores the dignity intrinsic to all kinds of music—no matter how simplistic from an analytical standpoint—and creates an artificial hierarchy in which complicated means superior.

To these criticisms can be added a third. If we take "art" to mean works of human skill and imagination that express beauty and emotional power, then no music should be considered artless. Whatever guise it takes or genre it fills, music is designed with and directed toward aesthetic sensibilities. In this basic way, it is inaccurate (and disingenuous) to identify certain music as artistic and other types as something else. Doing so reveals more about one's biases than it does about the music itself.

Part of the problem is that when it comes to music, art is understood in terms of style and substance rather than attraction and effect. For those set on distinguishing art music from the rest, things like intricacy, instrumentation and theoretical considerations are the deciding factors. However, none of this makes the music automatically more beautiful or emotionally potent than a simple folk tune or popular hit. In fact, the opposite is often the case. It is as though the parts comprising music—harmonic progressions, tonal variety, colorations, etc.—are of greater significance than how listeners respond. By these standards, the most artful music is that which is most advanced with respect to performance demands, occurrences of modulation, number of notes and the like. It is almost a plus if the music has limited audience appeal—a sign that it is artistic in the most elitist sense of the word.

This is not meant to suggest that all music is of equal quality or that classification serves no purpose. There are objective measurements by which musical creations can be judged and categorized, especially when examining structure, range, meter and other compositional elements. The point here is that music, in all its incalculable manifestations, has the potential to move listeners in profound ways, regardless of the box it fits or doesn't fit into. From a results-based view of art, in which art is something that *happens* when a person is touched aesthetically, virtually no music can escape the label.

Music as Work

A musical "work" is the axiomatic unit of measurement in Western concert music. Like a book, play or painting, a musical work is conceived of as a clearly defined entity with hard edges and a fixed identity. This sense of concreteness stems from the assumption that the music a composer writes is the same thing that performers play, audiences hear and musicologists study. Thus, only that music which is written down (and has the appearance of "art") is given the status of a work. The history of Western music is paved with these presumably self-contained artifacts, and its periodization relies on their firm borders.

While it would be a mistake to abandon "work" as a taxonomic category, its implied immutability, reliance on written notation, and dominance in conventional hierarchies of music have generated much criticism. British musicologist Michael Talbot brought focus to these objections at a symposium entitled "Musical Work: Reality or Invention?" (University of Liverpool, 1998).[8] Among other things, participants argued that a musical work is a historically and culturally conditioned construct of relatively recent lineage. Ethnomusicologists and popular music scholars noted that musical works provide only one possible way of understanding music-cultures, and have little analogy in global contexts. Avant-garde and improvisational musicians disputed the fixity implicit in the concept, showing how spontaneous input exists within the fuzzy edges of their music. Technologists pointed out that computers offer new and evolving ways of encoding and producing music that bypass the written page. What these challenges propose is that work is not only a limited concept, but also undeserving of the legitimacy it is typically given *vis-á-vis* other types of music.

Still, it is possible to retrieve the idea of work and apply it to all music—not just pieces in the classical mold. Such an approach requires looking at the term from the opposite direction, wherein fixity is replaced with action and stability with fluidity. Instead of seeing work as a final product, we can understand it as effort exerted toward a result.

Viewing work as a tightly constructed end product obscures the activeness of music. Musical performance is labor-intensive. Whether scripted or unscripted, premeditated or unplanned, music unfolds in real-time. Musicians actively perform it, listeners actively receive it, and the participation of both parties actively shapes the musical outcome. If there happens to be sheet music, it is a blueprint rather than a culmination of the composer's vision. In order to become music, the notes must be decoded by musicians, who bring their own experiences to bear, and interpreted by listeners, who bring their experiences to bear as well. The composer sets the musical process in motion, but the music itself is recreated each time it is performed.

Scholars are becoming increasingly aware of music's global diversity, the artistic value of popular forms, and new avenues of musical thought and practice. These realities, along with an aversion to ethnocentrism, have contributed to growing dissatisfaction with "work" as a high and reliable measurement of music. Its implied changelessness and reliance on written notation make it obsolete in many instances. But if we take work to mean an activity involving efforts and outcomes, then all music is work.

Is All Music Functional?

The role function plays in determining aesthetic qualities is far greater than we might intuit. Responses to artistic creations and performances are largely rooted in perceived levels of functionality. "I like it" or "I don't like it" are, in essence, statements about whether or not the artistic object left us moved and, if so, whether it moved us to a desirable or undesirable outcome. If the goal is to be sent into a state of awe or a flood of tears, does it happen or not? When we dial through the radio on a highway drive, does the music aid the journey or not? If the artwork accomplishes the task and/or meets certain expectations, it is "good"; if it fails, it is "bad."

Along with this observation come two sub-points: (1) No creative display satisfies everyone's tastes (which are, more accurately, needs); (2) Evaluation of the art's effectiveness (the foundation of aesthetic judgment) varies depending on the setting, season, activity, momentary mood, and so on. As such, phrases like "It does it for me" and "It doesn't do it for me" are closer to the functional-aesthetic mark.

If we travel along this line of thinking, we might conclude that aesthetics are utterly arbitrary. This may or may not be so. (The adverb "utterly," in any case, gives too strong a sense of certainty.) External conditions constantly and subconsciously inform our sense of beauty, including cultural norms and evolutionary adaptations. What the functional lens brings into focus is the *active* nature of aesthetics—that is, the degree to which deciding that something is pretty, repulsive, profound, trite, pleasant, disturbing, inspiring, bland, touching or cold is shaped by what we're doing and what we're looking for while we're doing it.

Turning to music specifically, we find explicit and implicit ways in which functionalism is linked to appraisal. The explicit group includes all music that is overtly functional, or music made for an extra-musical purpose (the majority of music in the history of music-making). A holiday concert, a commercial jingle, a nursery rhyme, a military march, a movie soundtrack. These and countless other situational sounds either work—and earn positive assessments—or do not work—and collect harsh critiques.

Here, associations are key. If a particular genre or manner of performance is generally or personally associated with a context other than the one for which it is presented, it is likely to be called "bad." Stylized renditions of "The Star-Spangled Banner" and identifiably secular styles in religious services are common illustrations of this. Yet, the mere fact that a performance location is odd or unusual does not automatically make it bad. If the person sitting next to the grumpy critic is fond of the associations the music connotes, then the opposite reaction will take place. The music works for her, therefore it is "good."

Implicit functional music is music that is not overtly attached to a purpose. Pop music, for instance, is not designed for or heard within a single designated setting. It is accessible virtually anywhere and at virtually any time. If it supports, synchronizes with, or in any way resonates with what one is doing in the listening moment (including "just" listening), then it is positively labeled. If the opposite occurs, then an opposite label occurs too.

Again, this appraisal is prone to fluctuate depending on the circumstances: something heard as lousy in one situation may be heard as lovely in another. And even our aversion to certain styles or songs can serve the beneficial function of reminding us of who we are, which is almost synonymous with what we do or do not like.

All music can be placed in either the explicit or implicit functional categories. Thus, by simple extension of the argument, all music can be viewed as functional. More important, the functional efficacy or inefficacy of a given piece of music (or any artwork) contributes mightily to our judgment of it. A simple formula: what works is "good," what doesn't work is "bad."

Notes

1. Steven Pinker, *The Language Instinct* (New York: W. Morrow, 1994), 480.
2. Dutton, *The Art Instinct*, 29.
3. Pinker, *How the Mind Works*, 534.
4. Paul Mattick, "The Institutions of Art" (paper presented at the Forty-Seventh Annual Meeting of the American Society for Aesthetics, New York City, October 25, 1989.
5. Alex Ross, "Why So Serious? How the Classical Concert Took Shape," *The New Yorker*, September 8, 2008, <http://www.newyorker.com/arts/critics/musical/2008/09/08/080908crmu_music_ross?currentPage=all>
6. Ibid.
7. Nicholas Cook, *A Guide to Musical Analysis* (New York: Oxford University Press, 1987), 1.
8. Michael Talbot, ed., *Musical Work: Reality or Invention?* (Liverpool, UK: University of Liverpool Press, 2000).

Suggestions for Further Reading

Chua, Daniel K. L. *Absolute Music and the Construction of Meaning.* New York: University of Cambridge Press, 1999.
Dahlhaus, Carl. *Esthetics of Music.* New York: Cambridge University Press, 1982.
_____. *The Idea of Absolute Music.* Chicago: University of Chicago Press, 1991.
Danto, Arthur C. *What Art Is.* New Haven, CT: Yale University Press, 2013.
Gracyk, Theodore. *Listening to Popular Music, Or, How I Learned to Stop Worrying and Love Led Zeppelin.* Ann Arbor: University of Michigan Press, 2007.
_____. *On Music.* New York: Routledge, 2013.
Ingarden, Roman. *The Work of Music and the Problem of Its Identity.* Berkeley: University of California Press, 1986.
Scruton, Robert. *Beauty: A Very Short Introduction.* New York: Oxford University Press, 2011.
Talbot, Michael, ed. *Musical Work: Reality or Invention?* Liverpool, UK: University of Liverpool Press, 2000.
Van der Braembussche, A. A. *Thinking Art: An Introduction to Philosophy of Art.* New York: Springer, 2009.

12

Consumer Music

Music is made to be heard. The way it sounds, the manner in which it is presented, the success it enjoys—all of these are determined or shaped by the interplay of creator(s) and audience. This chapter explores the process of musical reception. It analyzes the sensation of boredom in music, and what it can teach us about ourselves. It surveys the development and effectiveness of the three-minute norm of popular songs. It espouses the appropriateness of calling listeners "consumers." And it explains how listening to the same music on multiple occasions can yield different reactions.

Useful Boredom

Conventional wisdom has it that boredom is of two main types. The first occurs when stimuli or circumstances are too simple, as when the gifted child finds herself in a remedial classroom. The second is when sensory input is so complex as to lull the mind into a quasi-vegetative state. This accounts for the general avoidance of subjects like philosophy and math. Musically, these species of boredom are embodied in the overly simplistic pop song on the one hand, and the overly orchestrated concert work on the other. The former is boring because it poses no challenges and offers no surprises. The latter is boring because its multitude of interacting tones and timbres require more concentration than most are willing to dedicate. In this binary view, the culprits reside at the poles: underload and overload.

On the surface, this analysis might seem uncontestable. But there is a sense in which it derives from and supports an elitist view of music appreciation. Pop music is labeled as such because its style, structure and conventions appeal to the general public. Whether a selection is fairly or unfairly painted as "simple" has little impact on the audience's acceptance of it. In fact, its obviousness can be gratifying, as it satisfies a primal desire for predictability. In contrast, it is not always the case that education or exposure causes one to derive pleasure from a drawn-out classical piece. There are many classically trained musicians who find it difficult to sit through a symphony performance (myself included)—a reality that dispels the assumption that understanding eliminates boredom. The typical abundance of valleys and paucity of peaks make for a tedious experience, regardless of the subtleties and layers aficionados detect and convince themselves to enjoy.

It is fair to blame symphonic fatigue on the music itself and not the listener. If we do so, we can begin to see the value this sort of boredom holds. As Bertrand Russell reminded us in *The Conquest of Happiness*, the rhythm of nature is slow. The human body has evolved and adapted according to the leisurely pace of the seasons. The ultra-fast speed of modernity and the quest for convenience have numbed our patience and obscured the virtue of stagnancy. The boringness in classical music can help us to retrieve our long-forgotten tolerance for life's unexciting moments, and discover in those moments opportunities for fruitful contemplation.

Russell made this point with the following illustration. Imagine a modern publisher receiving the Hebrew Bible as a new and never-before seen manuscript. It is not difficult to imagine the response: "My dear sir, this chapter [in Genesis] lacks pep; you can't expect your reader to be interested in a mere string of proper names of persons about whom you tell him so little. You have begun your story, I will admit, in fine style, and at first I was very favorably impressed, but you have altogether too much wish to tell it all. Pick out the high lights take out the superfluous matter, and bring me back your manuscript when you have reduced it to a reasonable length."[1]

In a similar way, classical music exposes the difficulty most of us have engaging in "superfluous matter." But instead of taking the common path of frustration or the snobbish approach of elevating musical lulls into something more than they are, we should accept boring passages as boring, and embrace the stillness they can invite within us. After all, if everything were exciting or immediately appealing, nothing would be.

The Three-Minute Rule

Most popular songs heard on the radio run about three minutes. This convention has roots in the 1920s, when the 10-inch 78 rpm gramophone disc was the industry norm. The crude groove cutting and thick needle limited each side of a disc to roughly three minutes. This engineering constraint forced songwriters and musicians to compress their creative expression into three-minute singles. The habit persisted despite the introduction of microgroove recording (LP, or 33⅓ rpm) in the 1950s and the possibility of longer durations. Even in our boundless world of digital technology, the three-minute song remains the archetype.

To be sure, there are successful exceptions to the three-minute rule, such as Don McLean's "American Pie," Queen's "Bohemian Rhapsody" and Guns N' Roses' "November Rain," which run between six and nine minutes. But there is something universally satisfying about the radio standard.

This owes to a mixture of conditioning and natural inclination. From the beginning, three-minute songs proved to be both practical and highly profitable. Radio stations earned money by airing advertisements, and shorter songs meant more space for commercials. Producers also turned a better profit from short songs than long recordings, which were more expensive to press. As a result, listeners were fed a steady diet of time-restricted tunes, and were culturally trained to expect and derive pleasure from them.

It is also thought that the three-minute length caters perfectly to the attention span of young people, the primary consumers of popular music. The duration fits comfortably within their threshold of patience, which averages five minutes or so. And most people's ability to concentrate on music does not increase much after youth, save for those accustomed to drawn-out classical works, jazz improvisations and other expanded forms.

Moreover, three minutes seems an optimal timeframe for the delivery of music's emotional and informational content. Anything more risks dissolving into tedium. Of course, there are short pieces that bore quickly and longer pieces that retain interest. But, as a general rule, our tolerance for musical intake peaks at the radio play limit.

Igor Stravinsky is quoted as saying, "Too many pieces of music finish too long after the end."[2] The comment was directed at his compositional colleagues and forbearers, and could be applied to a few of his works as well. Yet it is not exclusive to the orchestral realm. Many pieces in many genres could benefit from some trimming. And we do not need Stravinsky's knowledge or experience to recognize when endings come too late. A combination of musical exposure and musical intuition signals whether a piece has overstepped its temporal maximum. It is the same instinct that attracts us to three-minute songs.

For Human Consumption

There are two basic modes of musical transmission: direct and indirect. Direct transmission consists of live performers and auditors in relatively close proximity with one another, while indirect transmission involves the emission of prerecorded music through speakers. In the first, performers are visible, identifiable and capable of interacting with listeners. In the second, listeners have no immediate or real-time connection with the music, other than the spontaneity with which sounds are processed in the brain. As populations grow in size and technological sophistication, the main route of musical transmission shifts from direct to indirect. Performances are increasingly replaced by phonograms, and music becomes a commodity.

In small-scale societies, where technology is limited and participation is the norm, senders and receivers of music tend to be the same people. The entire community is involved in all aspects of the musical happening: singing, dancing, playing and listening. In large-scale mechanized societies, where music is given to specialists and indirect transmission is the dominant modality, there exists a separation between producers and listeners. Rather than an integrative and cooperative means of expression, music is packaged as a purchasable item.

Fittingly, those who receive music through indirect transmission are called "consumers." Like other products in the marketplace, music can be obtained for personal use, and buying trends dictate the sorts of new music that are made available. Because of its collective pocketbook, the general listenership retains an active role in the musical experience. But the part it plays is distant compared to the community-based music-making typical of tribal and other small-scale societies.

Yet, even as cultural observers stress distinctions between direct and indirect modes of transmission, "consumer" is being used more and more to refer to all listeners of music, regardless of the modality. This equal application is partly meant to downplay tendencies to raise one mode above the other (namely, direct above indirect). Both types of musical experience are genuine to the participants, well suited for their social settings and serve the basic needs of the respective listeners. Additionally, the term highlights the reality that everyone consumes music, regardless of the activeness or passiveness of our musical involvement.

Interaction with music goes deeper than simply hearing, a sensory perception localized in the ears. Listening is a holistic activity incorporating a variety of physical, cognitive and emotional processes. We consume music in a way similar to how we consume food. It enters the ears (ingestion) and is distilled into perceptible material (mastication). From there it travels to processing centers (swallowing), where it is further broken down (digestion), and useful substances are extracted from it (absorption).

It is no coincidence that eating-related words are routinely used to depict musical listening. We drink in sounds, chew on musical passages, digest phrases, absorb musical input, and so forth. Plus, we talk about musical preferences in terms of taste. In this elemental sense, music is made for human consumption, and each of us is a musical consumer.

Never Heard Twice

Heraclitus of Ephesus (c. 535–475 BCE) coined one of the most well-known aphorisms of Western philosophy: "You can never put your foot in the same river twice." Nothing in the universe remains the same; everything is in perpetual motion. This principle is equally applicable to physical phenomena and our recollections of them. Not only does each moment differ from those that precede and follow it, but memories of things past and thoughts of the future are also in constant flux. History changes, technology changes, fashion changes, etiquette changes. Relationships change, religions change, demographics change, social mores change. To list everything that changes is to list everything. And once the list is finished, it too must change.

Critics of Heraclitus argue that, while appearances certainly alter, the underlying reality is steady. Our minds and senses are faulty, but the things we perceive are rooted in something eternal. However, any "underlying reality" is, in the end, a theoretical property, and thus subject to revision, interpretation, elaboration, imagination and other unstable processes of the intellect. Even things that are ostensibly unwavering, like recorded music and motion pictures, are subtly transformed with each experience, both perceptually and materially (physical and chemical deterioration occurs in discs, reels, tapes and other storage formats).

Philosopher-composer Leonard B. Meyer made this point in *Emotion and Meaning in Music*. He wrote that repetition in music never "exists psychologically," since our mindset and store of experiences are different each time we listen to a piece. Thus, while the musical substance may be fixed (or as fixed as anything can be said to be), it is never received through identical ears. Consistency is demonstrated in sound specifications, but the thoughts and feelings conjured differ depending on when the music is heard. Meyer explained it this way: "The fact that as we listen to music we are constantly revising our opinions of what has happened in the past in the light of present events is important because it means that we are constantly altering our expectations."[3]

This truism applies to repetition within a musical selection as well. Repeated patterns of rhythm, melody, and harmony are prominent in all sorts of music. According to Meyer, this internal repetition—which is relentless in minimalist compositions, Sufi *qawwali* and other genres—generates changes in meaning as the music pushes forward. Take the example of the classical sonata form, with its exposition, development and recapitulation. When the listener hears the recapitulation of the opening section, the meaning is very different from that communicated in the original statement. The same occurs with the verse-chorus form of popular music and other such musical structures.

Like everything known and unknown, observed and learned, music is ever changing. It is always experienced in the non-replicable present tense. To adapt Heraclitus' famous maxim, "The same music is never heard twice."

Notes

1. Bertrand Russell, *The Conquest of Happiness* [1930] (New York: Routledge, 2006), 39.
2. Igor Stravinsky, quoted in Galewitz, *Music*, 49.
3. Leonard B. Meyer, *Emotion and Meaning in Music* (Chicago: University of Chicago Press, 1956), 49.

Suggestions for Further Reading

Appell, Glenn, and David Hemphill. *American Popular Music: A Multicultural History*. Belmont, CA: Cengage, 2010.
Clarke, Donald. *The Rise and Fall of Popular Music*. New York: St. Martin's Griffen, 1995.
Gronow, Pekka, and Ilpo Saunio. *International History of the Recording Industry*. New York: Bloomsbury, 1999.
Hull, Geoffrey P., Thomas William Hutchison, and Richard Strasser. *The Music Business and Recording Industry: Delivering Music in the 21st Century*. New York: Taylor and Francis, 2011.
Inglis, Ian. *Performance and Popular Music: History, Place and Time*. Burlington, VT: Ashgate, 2013.
Meyer, Leonard D. *Emotion and Meaning in Music*. Chicago: University of Chicago Press, 1956.
Neer, Richard. *FM: The Rise and Fall of Rock Radio*. New York: Random House, 2001.
O'Hara, Kenton, and Barry Brown. *Consuming Music Together: Social and Collaborative Aspects of Music Consumption Technologies*. New York: Springer, 2006.
Weisbard, Eric. *Listen Again: A Momentary History of Pop Music*. Durham, NC: Duke University Press, 2007.
Williams, Andrew. *Portable Music and Its Functions*. New York: Peter Lang, 2007.

13

Creativity

Musical creation is often explained as a mysterious or supernatural event. The elusiveness and intangibility of the creative act lends itself to otherworldly explanations. This chapter chips away at these romantic assertions. In place of a divinely gifted composer or performer, we find a person devoted to education and practice, and unfazed by errors and setbacks. Additionally, the inspiration for a musical offering is more often found in outside conditions and circumstances than strictly inward impulses. What all of this implies is that inborn talent can only take one so far: training and persistence are necessary factors. The chapter concludes with current research into walking as a creativity nurturing exercise.

From Thin Air

The genesis of musical creativity has long been perplexing. As a medium composed of the invisible properties of silence and sound, music seems to emerge from and return to thin air. Its substance and impact defy pictorial and linguistic descriptions, and the experience of it is beyond the grasp of notated scores and mathematical graphs. Of all the arts, music is both the most mysterious and the most intimate. It is intangible and transient, yet deeply affects the interior of our being.

Because music-making is so difficult to unravel, many cultures have arrived at supernatural explanations. These range from calling musical genius a "gift from heaven" to more involved mythologies. An extreme example is found among the Suyá, a tribe of about three hundred located at the headwaters of the Xingu River in Mato Grosso, Brazil. The Suyá maintain that all new music originates outside of their dwellings. The composer's spirit is sent to a village of animal spirits, where it listens to and learns different songs. When the spirit returns, the composer transmits the songs to the people.

The Suyá also believe that the spirits of tribespeople are linked with particular animal spirits. This has musical implications, as the spirit of one person may travel to the spirit village of fish, while the spirit of another might go to a community of deer spirits. The former will return with fish songs, the latter with deer songs. According to Anthony Seeger, an anthropologist and author of *Why Suyá Sing*, about thirty percent of Suyá men and women in a generation claim to have spirits that acquire new songs.[1]

However fantastical this and other beliefs about musical creativity may be, they do illustrate the enigma of the process. Musical inspiration is difficult to pinpoint, as it is often spontaneous and rarely perceptible by sight or other senses. Cultural factors naturally shape the details of the musical stories. A monotheistic group places its deity at the inspirational center, animistic tribes locate music with animals, polytheistic societies assign the role of muse to a god or two, and so on.

Whatever form a myth takes, its impetus is the mysteriousness of musical creation. While a painter begins with paints and a sculptor starts with stone, the composer commences with seemingly nothing but air. Of course, on a technical level, all of the available notes, durations, and articulations are already present in nature, and the organization of these sounds can be distilled, mapped, and analyzed with precision. But music-making may be as close to *creatio ex nihilo* as we can approach.

The materials of music differ from materials in the physical sense. Most creative activities involve selecting, arranging and shaping pre-existing external matter, or *creatio ex materio*. But music, while played on instruments and within mechanical parameters, seems to reside in a spiritual or otherwise inexplicable realm. As a result, musical creativity lends itself to supernatural storytelling.

The Myth of the Gift

A person exhibiting talent in the arts is often said to possess a "gift." Though usually said with kind or neutral intentions, this phrase can have a negative impact on both the "gifted" and the less impressive majority. For the owner of artistic talent, the term "gift" is, at best, a reminder of the role of heredity in creative excellence. Darwin set the framework for this now-obvious observation, surmising that his daughter Annie's aptitude for the piano was passed on from her musical mother.[2] True, inborn capacities and innate dispositions can pre-condition people for imaginative exploration. But this is a relatively small ingredient. As any prodigious artist will attest, time, energy, passion and practice play a far greater role than mere genes. To overlook all of that work (10,000 hours worth by one popular estimation[3]) and reduce it to a "gift" is tantamount to an insult. The impact is compounded when aptitude is identified as "God-given"—a label that erases human agency, hereditary or otherwise, from the equation.

This (mis)conception can also be discouraging for those who admire the über talented and don't feel particularly talented themselves. If they have not been blessed, then why bother with artistic pursuits? Again, this places too much focus on native talent, which is, in the strictest sense, an impossible concept. Whatever influence genetic factors have in determining one's artistic aptitude, artistry is not something one can excel at without having to learn it. Finely honed skills and effortless performances are the product of copious study, instruction, refinement and repetition. This is equally true for the highly educated and informally seasoned, whose learning process is called, perhaps overstatedly, "self-teaching."

Recent studies in psychology show that even "super-skills," like perfect pitch and lightening-fast manual dexterity, are not inherited advantages, but the result of training. The myth of the gift crumbles further. According to psychologist K. Anders Ericsson, author of landmark papers on this topic, people thought of as "gifted" share three distinguishing traits: They balance practice and rest over long periods of time; their practicing is driven by deep passion and interest; they redirect adversity into success.[4]

The last point is easy to overlook. A finished product does not reveal what took place behind the scenes. For every masterful painting, virtuosic performance or architectural marvel, there are countless failed visions and discarded projects. But, rather than insignificant inevitabilities, these failures, false starts and dashed ideas are the foundation upon which great creations arise. Quality comes from quantity.

Master author Ray Bradbury, no stranger to trial an error, put it thus: "A great surgeon dissects and re-dissects a thousand, ten thousand bodies, tissues, organs, preparing thus by quantity the time when quality will count—with a living creature under the knife. An athlete may run ten thousand miles in order to prepare for one hundred yards. Quantity gives experience. From experience alone can quality come. All arts, big and small, are the elimination of waste motion in favor of the concise declaration."[5]

Practical Creativity

Creativity is conventionally defined as the use of imagination for the purpose of achieving something novel. The Romantics understood it as a supernal gift bestowed upon a select and superior few. In the present day, "creative genius" is generously recognized in almost anyone involved in an artistic or quasi-artistic pursuit. Whether framed as a rarified possession or a universal property, creativity is made out to be a disembodied quality, appearing in a flash of insight and removed from everyday matters. Forgotten in all of this is the utilitarian proverb: "Necessity is the mother of invention."

This saying reverberates throughout music history. The acoustic demands and tolerances of a music-making venue—forest, cave, hut, chapel, cathedral, club, concert hall, amphitheater, stadium, living room—have done more to shape musical styles, instruments and ensemble configurations than any other single factor. Technological advances in the 1920s gave us the 10-inch 78 rpm gramophone disc, which played for just three minutes on each side and forced songwriters to invent the three-minute popular song form—still the industry norm. Architects of worship music often keep track of changing tastes of the general public, adjusting devotional sounds accordingly in hopes of filling the pews. Even jazz improvisation had a practical beginning. People wanted to continue dancing after the melodies were exhausted, so the musicians accommodated them by jamming over chord changes to stretch out their playing.

These and countless other musical developments were born of necessity. Their inspiration was more contextual than spiritual, more pragmatic than epiphanic. Like everything else, musical innovation is motivated by and responsive to perpetual forces: cause and effect, need and satiation, transition and mutation, problems and solutions. It is, then, better to think of creativity as an adaptive awareness than as something emerging from mythical nothingness.

Music is a living art. It is guided by evolutionary pressures. The survival of music in any of its myriad genres and forms requires that elements be modified and redirected to fit the social, physical and acoustic environment. When conditions are relatively static, music undergoes few and subtle alterations. When circumstances shift, musical creativity shifts along with them. These adaptive traits—technical, instrumental, presentational and other—are further tweaked as settings continue to morph. With the passage of time, and the technological advancements, trends and counter-trends that come along with it, some of these features persist and are absorbed into new mixtures, while others are rejected and replaced with new adaptations. And so it goes, down through the ages.

Need creates an opening for artistic maneuvering. Thus, at the risk of over-simplification, we might re-define creativity as the practical confrontation with necessity.

Musical Motivation

Motivation to compose music is often portrayed in spiritual terms. A flash of inspiration consumes an abnormally gifted individual. A supernaturally selected musician channels a mysterious surge of energy. A person becomes possessed by cosmic sounds, which find their way onto the manuscript page. Melodramatic depictions like these were promulgated during the eighteenth and nineteenth centuries, and continue to influence how we think of the music-writing process. Composition is viewed as an inaccessible and unlearnable art. It is the endeavor of a chosen few, who have been blessed by fate and deemed worthy by the heavens above.

In case these characterizations seem exaggerated, let us look at a couple of actual examples. Music critic and theoretician Heinrich Schenker wrote this of a compositional moment: "The lightning flash of a thought suddenly crashed down, at once illuminating and creating the entire work in the most dazzling light. Such works were conceived and received in one stroke."[6] Arnold Schoenberg perpetuated this sensational image, stating that musical inspiration can well up as "a subconsciously received gift from the Supreme Commander."[7]

Such statements are faulty for at least four reasons. First, they imagine music as materializing out of nowhere. Without preparation or hesitation, the composer sits at the piano and lets the opus pour forth. But anyone who has improvised music or jotted down a melody knows that it involves practice, forethought and trial and error. Moreover, most composers write within generative musical systems, which provide structures and formulas to draw upon. Their motivation is exposure and experience, not divine direction.

A second and related issue is the false notion that composition cannot be taught, learned or acquired. Romantics and their ideological inheritors willfully ignore that composition has many prerequisites: listening, studying, performing, reading, etc. Rather than a skill bestowed at birth or received through revelation, music writing is available to anyone who has the desire, discipline and determination to do it.

Third is the elitism implicit in the mystical view. Almost without exception, writings about the inspirational muse involve composers of Western art music. It is their music that cannot be replicated. Classically trained musicians like Schenker and Schoenberg acknowledged that folk music and other popular forms exist in wide variety. But, for them, the homegrown-ness and abundance of such music indicated its worldly origins, and made it less than the rarified creations of "high culture." The bias of this view is too obvious to warrant comment.

Fourth, most of the world's music has practical aims. The impulse to compose is more likely to come from necessity than artistic urge. The many functions of music range from instruction and storytelling to work and exercise. These "mundane" motivations have proven strong enough to generate the majority of music ever heard.

And then there's the revealing statement from Cole Porter. When asked what stimulates him to write, he responded: "My sole inspiration is a telephone call from a producer."[8]

Creativity's Conditions

Creativity in any enterprise is spurred on by some perceived need, the type and magnitude of which are usually proportional to the issue being addressed and the field in which the innovation is taking place. Anthropologists point to a slew of social and environmental factors that determine the presence and rate of innovation in a given society. Among them are population density, area of inhabitance, natural resources, inter-group interaction and societal organization (bands, tribes, chiefdoms and states). Certain combinations of factors encourage invention, while others do not. As Jared Diamond writes in *Guns, Germs, and Steel*: "All human societies contain inventive people. It's just that some environments provide more starting materials, and more favorable conditions for utilizing inventiveness, than do other environments."[9]

This rule applies equally to inventions that are practical, artistic or a combination of the two. Where necessity is absent, so is ingenuity. This is why, for example, slow technological development is a hallmark of indigenous hunter-gatherers, while rapid advancements characterize post-industrial societies. Hunter-gatherers are continually on the move, following the animals on which they depend and migrating to where the plants they use are available. These small and mobile populations lack the motivating circumstances to devise new and potentially cumbersome tools, and have little of the downtime necessary to experiment with technologies. In contrast, producing new ideas is the main way to grow the diverse, globally connected, information-rich and service-based economies of the post-industrial world.

Musical innovation follows a similar pattern. Societies that are small, isolated and relatively uniform generally do not demand fresh musical styles or forms. Their music is almost entirely of a functional sort, serving practical aims such as warfare, ritual and storytelling. There is room for improvisation, but musical customs tend to be conservative, operating within longstanding and typically limited musicways. In other words, their music is consistent with the rest of their lifestyle.

The opposite occurs in first-world societies, where everything seems in constant flux and there is seemingly unlimited access to the world's music library. With endless musical influences comes virtually endless musical possibilities, particularly in (sub)cultures that demand continuous output. Moreover, larger populations produce larger numbers of musical innovators, as well as larger audiences to appreciate the innovations.

The crucial role of human and natural environments in musical creativity is not just evident when we compare radically divergent populations, like hunter-gatherers and denizens of an American metropolis. Historically and cross-culturally, those climates most conducive to musical creativity have yielded the greatest inventive flourishes. It is no coincidence that chronological lists of famous Western composers are heavily represented by a few countries, or that certain performers living in certain places are more popular and prolific than others stationed in similar societies elsewhere on the globe.

This discussion and its supporting examples could go on and on. The specific ingredients favorable for musical creativity or non-creativity vary from cultural setting to cultural setting. However, there is a simple formula that can be used to make the broader point: Creativity has conditions; innovation has inducements.

Walk Like a Composer

Beethoven's daily routine included vigorous walks with a pencil and sheets of music paper. Robert Schumann's regular walks were punctuated with poetry writing and drawing sketches. Tchaikovsky took two walks per day: a brisk stroll in the morning and a two-hour hike after lunch. Benjamin Britten had company on his walks, during which he talked about music and after which he wrote it down. The list of strolling composers could go on and on. More than just mundane details of famous biographies, these examples give credence to Nietzsche's overstated but still compelling aphorism: "All truly great thoughts are conceived by walking."[10]

The link between walking and creativity is apparent across disciplines. Celebrated cases include John Milton, Jane Austen, Charles Dickens, Immanuel Kant, Sigmund Freud, and Eric Hoffer. Again, the list could stretch on without end. A skeptic might note that walking is a natural human activity: it is something that creative and not-so-creative people share in common.

But this is walking of an intentional and recreational kind, not the humdrum mode of moving the body from place to place.

Until now, connections between walking and novel idea generation have come from historical and personal anecdotes. Britten working out a musical passage on a leisurely jaunt has parallel in the average person working out an average problem on a stroll around the neighborhood. Perhaps the benefits are so apparent that scientific confirmation is not needed. Be that as it may, the emerging science provides intriguing confirmation.

A recent paper in the *Journal of Experimental Psychology* outlines preliminary findings of four walking experiments. "Give Your Ideas Some Legs: The Positive Effect of Walking on Creative Thinking" (a highly technical study with a deceptively inviting title) shows that walking not only increases formation of creative ideas in real-time, but also for a period afterward.[11] Without going into depth here, the experiments, conducted by Marily Oppezzo and Daniel L. Schwartz of Stanford University, record thought processes of people in various combinations of seating and walking. Not surprisingly, walking resulted in substantial creative boosts, with outdoor walking producing thought patterns of the highest quality and novelty.

Without jumping to premature conclusions, the authors predict that the walk-thought mechanism "will eventually [be shown to] comprise a complex causal pathway that extends from the physical act of walking to physiological changes to the proximal processes."[12] This is something we could have learned from Brahms, who was often seen walking around Vienna with hands folded behind his back. He gave this advice to Gustav Jenner, his only formal composition student: "When ideas come to you, go for a walk; then you will discover that the thing you thought was a complete thought was actually only the beginning of one."[13]

Notes

1. Anthony Seeger, *Why Suyá Sing: A Musical Anthropology of an Amazonian People* (Urbana: University of Illinois Press, 2004), 55.
2. Darwin, *The Descent of Man*, 477.
3. Malcolm Gladwell, *Outliers: The Story of Success* (New York: Hachette, 2008).
4. See K. Anders Ericsson, ed., *The Road to Excellence: The Acquisition of Expert Performance in the Arts and Sciences, Sports, and Games* (New York: Psychology, 2014).
5. Ray Bradbury, *Zen in the Art of Writing* (New York: Bantam, 1992), 131.
6. Heinrich Schenker, "Eugen d'Albert," *Die Zukunft* 9 (1894): 33.
7. Arnold Schoenberg, *Style and Idea: Selected Writings*, ed. Leonard Stein, trans. Leo Black (Berkeley: University of California Press, 2010), 222.
8. Galewitz, *Music: A Book of Quotations*, 38.

9. Jared Diamond, *Guns, Germs, and Steel: The Fates of Human Societies* (New York: W. W. Norton, 1999), 408.
10. Saying widely attributed to Friedrich Nietzsche.
11. Marily Oppezzo and Daniel L. Schwartz, "Give Your Ideas Some Legs: The Positive Effect of Walking on Creative Thinking," *Journal of Experimental Psychology* (2014): 1–11.
12. Ibid., 7.
13. Gustav Jenner, "Johannes Brahms as Man, Teacher, and Artist," in *Brahms and His World*, ed. Walter Frisch and Kevin C. Karnes (Princeton, NJ: Princeton University Press, 2009), 404.

Suggestions for Further Reading

Beeching, Angela Myles. *Beyond Talent: Creating a Successful Career in Music*. New York: Oxford University Press, 2005.

Deliège, Irène, and Geraint A. Wiggins, ed. *Musical Creativity: Multidisciplinary Research in Theory and Practice*. New York: Psychology, 2006.

Donovan, Siobhán, and Robin Elliott, ed. *Music and Literature in German Romanticism*. Rochester, NY: Camden House, 2004.

Ericsson, K. Anders, ed. *The Road to Excellence: The Acquisition of Expert Performance in the Arts and Sciences, Sports, and Games*. New York: Psychology, 2014.

Lippman, Edward A. *Musical Aesthetics: The Nineteenth Century*. New York: Pendragon, 1986.

Mazzola, Guerino, Joomi Park, and Florian Thalmann. *Musical Creativity: Strategies and Tools in Composition and Improvisation*. New York: Springer, 2011.

Odena, Oscar, ed. *Musical Creativity: Insights from Music Education Research*. Burlington, VT: Ashgate, 2013.

Prager, Brad. *Aesthetic Vision and German Romanticism: Writing Images*. New York: Camden House, 2007.

Schoenberg, Arnold. *Style and Idea: Selected Writings*. Edited by Leonard Stein, and translated by Leo Black. Berkeley: University of California Press, 2010.

Seeger, Anthony. *Why Suyá Sing: A Musical Anthropology of an Amazonian People*. Urbana: University of Illinois Press, 2004.

14

Music-Making

Music does not make itself. It emanates from the talents and imaginations of human beings, especially the subspecies known as musicians. This chapter peers into the musician's mind, searching for what makes it tick and how it perceives the world. Topics include how finite musical elements yield unlimited possibilities, what it is like to be in the musician's "zone," why some musicians feel they are in constant contact with the sacred, what musical displays teach us about human potential, and the importance of silence in musicians' lives.

The Art of Tune

"In battle, there are not more than two methods of attack—the direct and indirect; yet these two in combination give rise to an endless series of maneuvers."[1] This truism, taken from the classic tome *The Art of War*, speaks to the almost inexhaustible possibilities that can arise from limited choices. Like much of the treatise, attributed to Chinese general Sun Tzu (c. 544–496 B.C.E.), this aphorism has been applied to areas outside of warfare where slight tactical changes can have an enormous impact. It is especially apt for competitive entities like sports teams and marketing firms, which are constrained by conventions and regulations, yet find sometimes-subtle ways to out-smart and out-play their opponents.

Sun Tzu (or whoever wrote *The Art of War*) was aware of the book's multiple applications, as he frequently used non-military examples to illustrate battlefield insights. In the sentences leading to the words quoted above, several comparisons are made to non-combative life pursuits. The possibilities arising from direct and indirect attacks are likened to the five primary colors (blue, yellow, white, red, black), which in combination "produce more hues than can ever be seen," and to the five tastes (sour, acrid, salt, sweet, bitter), which in combination "yield more flavors than can ever be tasted." The author cites a musical analogy as well, explaining that the five tones of his native pentatonic scale "give rise to more melodies than can ever be heard."[2]

The inclusion of these examples in *The Art of War* shows the diversity of painting, food and music known in China at the time. When we add the rest of the world and the centuries that have passed since the treatise was written, the amount of creations made from finite raw materials is staggering. And new mixtures are being concocted each day.

This becomes apparent when we consider the variety of potential melodic phrases. A widely cited article posted at the collaborative website Everything2 computes the number of one-measure melodies possible within a Western octave.[3] Assembling the twelve notes in their various values (whole, half, quarter, eighth, sixteenth and thirty-second) gives us a figure thirty-six digits long—a theoretical integer far exceeding our comprehension. Actual melodies are much less numerous, partly because they are subject to restrictive forces like taste and cultural expectation. Even so, music that has and will be composed borders on endless.

Similar observations could be made about visual, culinary and other art forms. The drive to invent through combination is a peculiar trademark of our species. It may, in fact, be the only type of creativity we are actually capable of. Whether the activity is battle, artistic expression or something else, minor gradations and small manipulations can make a significant difference.

The Musician's Mentality

Legendary jazz musician Nina Simone once remarked, "Music is my God. The structure, the cleanliness, the tone, the nuances, the implications, the silences, the dynamics ... all having to do with sound and music. It is as close to God as I know."[4] These words echo the feelings of many musicians. The experience of making music can (and regularly does) bring one into a spiritual zone: a state of being in which cognitive functions, emotional highs, sensory perceptions and creative energies fuse into a transcendental whole. There is no need for theology in such a state. Holiness becomes a sensation rather than an idea.

Of course, there are devout musicians who contextualize musical sensations in the language of their faith. The God they encounter in music is the same one they read about in holy writ. (They might agree with Luther: "Apart from theology, music is God's greatest gift. It has much in common with theology because it heals the soul and raises the spirits."[5]) But countless others feel as Simone did.

Her position is supported by the long list of prominent atheist musicians, including such luminaries as Hector Berlioz, Georges Bizet, Giuseppe Verdi, Béla Bartók, Ralph Vaughan Williams and Frederick Delius. These composers were in contact with their inner-nature and explored the recesses of the human mind and spirit. Music provided them with the sort of spiritual nourishment commonly sought in religious concepts and practices.

A glimpse into this aspect of the musician's psychology is found in *Music as an Asset to Spirituality*, an enigmatic book written by Laura J. Richards. The origins and ideology of this old book are difficult to decipher, and nothing is available of the author's biography. In truth, it is an almost incomprehensible work of pseudo-science and pseudo-mysticism, and probably deserves less attention than it is getting here. A random sampling exposes its baffling content: "How to cultivate a musical feeling is a very difficult subject. It takes many centuries for the musician to come to this state of perfection"; "What is mind? It is the soul functioning perfectly according to the laws of nature"; "Winds are nature's entities to destroy the impure forces that cause the vibrations to intermingle."[6]

The bulk of the text reads in this fashion. Like other theosophical writings, its sentences can be poetic and may on the surface seem profound; but when we pierce through the flowery language, we discover jumbled thoughts that offer nothing of substance. Richards' clumsy esotericism and happy disregard for reason are typical of early twentieth-century spiritual literature, and persist in some contemporary New Age publications.

Even so, there are moments when Richards is coherent and insightful— as long as her exaggerations are read as metaphors. One such instance is her section on the musician's mentality. She notes that musicians are often misunderstood "because their organism is created of an entirely different material than other individuals." There is no literal or scientific validity to this claim: we are all made of the same matter. But the "material" she refers to is dispositional, not elemental. One who is perpetually engaged in musical activities can, as it were, lose touch with the ordinary. Musicians familiar with the upper reaches of human consciousness can effortlessly drift into a heightened, spiritual or transcendent state (whichever terminology one prefers). "Consequently," writes Richards, "the material world is very difficult for them to endure."[7]

Music-making is a sacred act: it is removed from the mundane and hints at something deeper than the physical. This has made it a helpful aid to religion and prayer. However, music is just as readily experienced as an equivalent to (or a substitute for) theological concepts. For the musician, music can be God enough.

Art and Apartness

Art is a sacred endeavor. Not in a theological or ideological sense—which is clouded by intellectualism and socio-religious determinations—but in the purer and more experiential sense of apartness. The primary aim and impetus of art is connection with the "beyond-the-ordinary": a sensation of transcending the confines and occurrences of the mundane world. The artist who labors undisturbed in the creative process occupies a separate and all-consuming sphere of consciousness.

This explains the casual observation that artists are rarely drawn to the usual aspects of religious life: regulated rituals, group affiliation and formalistic prayers. Without having statistics to support this perception, it nevertheless seems that utterly artistic people—those who exist in an almost perpetual state of inward reflection and inspired invention—live the ideals that religion strives to impart through texts and structured practices. The artist is intimately familiar with transformation and elevation, making religion's attempt to manufacture these qualities superfluous or even disruptive.

This does not mean that artists cannot be religious in the normative sense. The same variations of religiosity and non-religiosity are found among artists and the general population. Obviously, too, numerous artworks have been created for and commissioned by religious institutions, and many performing artists (mainly musicians) find steady employment in houses of worship. Even so, artists need not rely on public rituals or religious calendars to tell them how or when to encounter otherness.

From a humanistic perspective, religion, in all its forms and modes of engagement, is but a particularistic means toward a universal goal. The aspiration for transcendence is present within every human being. It is built into our biology. The fact that religions emerged at all in the course of human evolution is proof of this inborn longing of our species. Those who do not find sacred peaks in the everyday often turn to religious events (or pseudo-religious events, such as sports or concerts) in order to be pushed into that experience.

William Sharlin, a cantor-composer who found ecstasy alone at the piano and transmitted ecstasy through liturgical singing, included this remark in a lecture on the topic of art and the sacred: "The non-artist at best may strive for the occasional moment of transcendence and therefore may need the help of worship to separate himself from the ordinary."[8] Not so the artist.

Beauty and Human Potential

Beauty is chiefly understood as a matter of the senses rather than of the intellect. Familiar phrases like "in the eye of the beholder" and "there's no accounting for taste" stress the role of individual perceptions and gut reactions in arriving at aesthetic conclusions. More than an absolute law, beauty is typically described as a feeling, emotion, passion or sentiment. From one point of view, this removes aesthetic judgments from the plane of rational discourse, essentially eliminating the possibility of an empirical framework for measuring gradients of beauty. However, aesthetics remains an active area of philosophy concerned with principles of attractiveness and taste. Even liberal humanism, that branch of philosophy that champions the dignity of personal values and opinions, has put forward criteria for evaluating beauty.

A particularly lucid formulation comes from Rabbi Daniel Friedman, one of the founders of the Society for Humanistic Judaism. In "Art and Nature: Beauty and Spirituality," a philosophical sketch originally presented at the 2001 Colloquium of the International Institute for Secular Humanistic Judaism, Friedman offers some yardsticks for aesthetic determination that approach objectivity (as much as such a thing is possible).[9] Friedman contends that beauty is not a property of nature, but a concept formed in the mind. As human beings, we extract and infuse purpose, meaning and value in our experiences and observations. Judging something as beautiful is fundamentally a conceptualization of feelings evoked inside of us: serenity, wonder, elation, awe, satisfaction, etc. Aesthetics is thus an internal process. It is idiosyncratically derived.

Yet, according to Friedman, this does not relegate beauty to an arbitrary decision or a relativistic whim. While the assessment takes place internally and is ultimately shaped by forces like culture and biography, the object or phenomenon itself remains outside of us. It is in that realm of creation— rather than perception—that objective standards can be applied, however imperfectly. Specifically, Friedman argues that higher and lower worth can be assigned to human artworks based on how much and to what degree they utilize distinctly human qualities.

He gives the example of comparing Mozart to elevator music (presumably meaning easy-listening instrumentals with simple and unobtrusively looped melodies). A Mozart composition is aesthetically superior, Friedman claims, because it uses more and better-refined human capacities, including reason, intellect, imagination, discipline, education and talent. It demands deeper understanding and appreciation from both the composer/performer(s) and the listener. It requires more of our humanity, and is thus more beautiful.

The obvious flaw in this comparison is a confusion of kind: it is improper to apply the same criteria or expectations to two selections from disparate musical spheres. Mozart should be compared to other composers of the Classical period, just as bluegrass should be judged against other bluegrass and yodeling against other yodeling. (It also follows that all elevator music should not be lumped together—some elevator music exhibits more and fuller human qualities.) Nevertheless, Friedman's proposal—the measurement of beauty by degrees—is consistent with the broader thrust of humanism, which celebrates the exploration of human potential as the highest goal one can strive for. In art or anything else, the more of our potential we use and the further we push ourselves toward that end, the more worthy the outcome.

The Musician's Burden

"Maybe due to my involvement in it, I feel I have to either listen intently or tune it out."[10] This statement by Talking Heads front man David Byrne speaks for many who make a living in the musical arts. It is an expression of the professional's burden: an inability to subdue the analytical impulse when confronted with the subject of expertise. Total immersion in a craft or line of work—be it music, medicine, gardening, or child rearing—makes casual experiences in that area hard to achieve. The more time and energy one spends in a field, the less that field invites frolicking. For the musician, this leaves the two polar options Byrne suggests: conscious listening—which invariably involves critical assessment—or conscious distancing—which, in his words, makes music "an annoying sonic layer that just adds to the background noise."

This might seem counterintuitive. Musicians are obviously music lovers, and their profession is largely a pursuit of that love. But theirs is usually a refined affection rather than a wild passion. As skills are honed and knowledge sharpened, so are opinions deepened and judgments polished. Nuances of performance and details of construction are ever apparent to the learned listener; it is difficult to readjust the ear for "just" listening. True, such a state is more easily attained when listening to music of a type or culture other than one's own. Yet, because the brain still recognizes those foreign sounds as music, it may instinctively launch into assessment mode, whether or not it is justified in doing so.

This is not to diminish the value of music appreciation courses and other programs of cultural enrichment. The premise of such enterprises is undoubtedly valid, namely, that listening is enhanced through greater understanding of musical styles, materials, and techniques. However, a line tends to be crossed when avocation becomes vocation, when amateur infatuation becomes professional discipline. Enjoyment is no longer the primary goal or foremost outcome. Music—all music—becomes work.

Of course, this condition is not universal. Some musicians have more success than others dividing musical labor from musical play. A rare and enviable few can even derive endless pleasure from listening. But most are more selective and methodical in picking their musical spots. Again quoting Byrne: "I listen to music at very specific times. When I go to hear it live, most obviously. When I'm cooking or doing the dishes I put on music, and sometimes other people are present. When I'm jogging or cycling to and from work down New York's West Side bike path, or if I'm in a rented car on the rare occasions I have to drive somewhere, I listen alone. And when I'm writing and recording music, I listen to what I'm working on. But that's it."[11]

Notes

1. Sun Tzu, *The Art of War*, trans. Lionel Giles (Radford, VA: Wilder, 2008), 15.
2. Ibid.
3. "How Many Melodies Are There in the Universe?" Everything2, <http://everything2.com/title/How+many+melodies+are+there+in+the+universe percent253F>
4. Nina Simone, *Live at Ronnie Scott's*, DVD (MVD Music Video).
5. Martin Luther, quoted in Heiko Augustinus Oberman, *Luther: Man Between God and the Devil* (New Haven, CT: Yale University Press, 2006), 310.
6. Laura J. Richards, *Music as an Asset to Spirituality* [1928] (Whitefish, MT: Kessinger, 2011).
7. Ibid., 51.
8. William Sharlin, "The 'Artist' and the Sacred," undated/unpublished lecture.
9. Daniel Friedman, "Art and Nature: Beauty and Spirituality," in *Secular Spirituality: Passionate Journey to a Rational Judaism*, ed. M. Bonnie Cousens (Farmington Hills, MI: Milan, 2003), 101–108.
10. Byrne, *How Music Works*, 136.
11. Ibid.

Suggestions for Further Reading

Berkowitz, Aaron. *The Improvising Mind: Cognition and Creativity in the Musical Moment.* New york: Oxford University Press, 2010.
Blanning, T. C. W. *The Triumph of Music: The Rise of Composers, Musicians and Their Art.* Cambridge, MA: Harvard University Press, 2008.

Boardman, Eunice, ed. *Dimensions of Musical Thinking*. New York: Rowman and Littlefield, 1989.
Clarke, Eric, Nicola Dibben, and Stephanie Pitts. *Music and Mind in Everyday Life*. New York: Oxford University Press, 2010.
Howard, Vernon Alfred. *Charm and Speed: Virtuosity in the Performing Arts*. New York: Peter Lang, 2008.
Klickstein, Gerald. *The Musician's Way: A Guide to Practice, Performance, and Wellness*. New York: Oxford University Press, 2009.
Lehmann, Andreas C., John A. Sloboda, and Robert H. Woody. *Psychology for Musicians: Understanding and Acquiring the Skills*. New York: Oxford University Press, 2007.
McAllister, Lesley Sisterhen. *The Balanced Musician: Integrating Mind and Body for Peak Performance*. New York: Rowman and Littlefield, 2012.
Rothko, Mark. *The Artist's Reality: Philosophies of Art*. New Haven, CT: Yale University Press, 2006.
Wade, Bonnie C. *Thinking Musically: Experiencing Music, Expressing Culture*. New York: Oxford University Press, 2013.

15

Mind

Musicians are not the only active participants in the musical experience. Much of the process falls on the ears that receive the sounds and the minds that interpret them. True, composers and performers often imbue their music with certain meanings, but their intentions do not always determine how the music will be understood. This chapter investigates the role of perception in creating musical meaning. This includes the "inside information" contained in group-specific melodies, the memories and associations housed in music of personal importance, the role of the auditor in completing the formation of music, the listener's ability (or inability) to separate the artist from his or her art, and the fluidity and malleability of musical essence.

Economy of Notes

Jean-Paul Sartre posed the following scenario: Imagine listening to a raw recording of everyday conversations transpiring in a foreign time and place. They begin mid-sentence, jump organically from topic to topic and come with no guidelines or commentary.[1] Even if we could understand the language, much of the substance of the dialogue would be lost. The words would be laden with subtleties, references and turns of phrase natural to the speakers' environment and experiences, but alien to our own. Context would be a matter of conjecture, as people generally avoid dwelling on the details of their surroundings or the larger conditions in which their discussions are taking place. Extraneous and unnecessary information is left out without conscious consideration. The actors simply know who they are, where they are and what they're talking about. They intuitively favor an economy of language.

Sartre saw a parallel between such conversations and literature written in and about a given culture. Native readers do not require lengthy descriptions, meticulous word-pictures or fleshed-out narratives. As Sartre wrote:

"[P]eople of a same period and collectivity, who have lived through the same events, who have raised or avoided the same questions, have the same taste in their mouth; they have the same complicity, and there are the same corpses among them. That is why it is not necessary to write so much; there are keywords."[2] But when their stories and ideas are told to an outside audience, many pages are needed to introduce history, outline customs, explain prejudices, chronicle social tensions, describe economic conditions and so on.

Something similar occurs in music. Like the direct language of everyday speech and the concision of certain time- and space-specific writings, music is able to communicate an abundance of information with minimal material. A brief melodic sequence, stylistic signature or pithy phrase can capture the ethos of the group or subgroup from which the music sprang and to which it is addressed. Its sound—and, in the case of song, its subject matter—encapsulates collective experiences, consolidates common concerns, addresses ubiquitous feelings, accentuates shared fondnesses and enfolds many layers of cultural expression.

Group-defining music is like a time capsule, gathering together tastes, struggles, longings, tendencies, aspirations and other particulars. Take the American baby boomer who nods knowingly to a Bob Dylan record, or the Yoruba of West Africa who understand the messages and milieu of their talking drums. Each time the music is played, its contents are spilled out. The insider knows precisely what it means; she is overtaken by a flood of familiar associations. For that person and others of her background and heritage, the music is an instant and unmistakable identity marker. It is history, memory, emotion, spirit, essence and conviction rolled into a sonic container.

This is partly why we are attracted to the music that attracts us: it is *our* music in a deep sense of the term. But it also accounts for why outsiders often have difficulty relating to or fully appreciating the music of others. For those who lived the stories and know the references, the music is a constant source of meaning and identification. Yet those unfamiliar with the music and its context can find it dated, irrelevant, uninteresting, unimportant, unapproachable or worse. And when an outsider desires to learn what the music recalls and represents, he needs the sort of informational and analytical framework insiders happily do without.

Listening to Ourselves

Linguist Dwight L. Bolinger included this observation in his classic book, *The Symbolism of Music*: "Repetition, or return to the familiar, to the learned, is more striking in music than elsewhere—a very good book may be read twice, a masterpiece of literature three or four times, a poem a dozen times; but in no other art-form could we expect the literally hundreds of repetitions to go on pleasing us."[3] Three things are especially striking about this statement. First is that it came from a professor of Romance languages—a man whose passion for linguistic form, function and meaning far surpassed the norm. Despite his personal and professional proclivities, Bolinger acknowledged the superiority of music in the crucial area of pleasure-making. Second, the type of music he refers to is the "favorite": a song or piece that a person elevates above others and has a special attachment to. Third, Bolinger alludes to the essential contribution of musical favorites to the human experience. Favorites are valuable to us precisely because they are a reliable and potentially boundless source of satisfaction.

It seems a human instinct to isolate, accumulate and curate a personal pantheon of greatest hits. The content of these customized collections is informed by interwoven forces, such as cultural conditioning, personality type, life experience, peer group, social station, education, exposure and heritage. Virtually everyone gravitates toward and snatches up favorites that (almost) never grow dull and often become more fulfilling with the passage of time. Counter to rational expectation and contrary to our relationship with literary works, musical favorites are heard (or performed) on countless occasions without the decrease in interest normally associated with repetition.

What accounts for this persistent gratification? The answer boils down to a simple proposition: when we listen to our favorites we are listening to ourselves. To understand this, it is best to think of music extra-musically—that is, in terms of what it does and stands for. Although certain and varied musical qualities make a piece attractive to certain and varied people, it is mainly what the music connotes that will make it a favorite.

Familiar music is a storehouse of personal information. It brings us into instant and powerful contact with emotional memories, nostalgic feelings, significant events, past and present relationships, group affiliations, intellectual leanings and other vivid reminders of who we are. To use an analogy from the computer age, musical favorites are data storage devices. They are a repository of cognitive and sentimental associations that flash into consciousness each time we hear them. They are, in short, externalized portals to our inner selves. And since identity and meaning derive largely from the data housed in this music, its repetition is a kind of self-reinforcement.

Among other things, this discussion helps us understand the affinity for recurring prayer-songs in worship services. Few ritual changes stir as much controversy as the introduction of new melodies. Musical innovations in church and synagogue have long encountered fervent objections from the people in the pews. This is conventionally attributed to factors like the religious impulse for preservation, the comfort of routine and the perceived holiness of long-established tunes. These are certainly important forces. However, if we apply the above analysis to the worship setting, we begin to appreciate that replacing cherished melodies with unfamiliar settings is, for many people, tantamount to an identity crisis. For this reason in particular, it must be handled with care.

The Role of the Listener

In *The Role of the Reader*, Umberto Eco carefully elucidates "the cooperative role of the addressee in interpreting messages."[4] When processing a text, the reader derives meaning(s) based on his or her linguistic and cultural competencies. Eco explains that the text itself is never a finished or enclosed product. Its essence is incomplete until it meets the readers' eyes. And each time it does so, it assumes a new and person-specific character.

This observation fits into Eco's wider theory of interpretative semiotics, in which words and other signs do not disclose a full range of meaning, but invite readers to construct signification from them. As Eco writes elsewhere, "Every text, after all, is a lazy machine asking the reader to do some of its work. What a problem it would be if a text were to say everything the receiver is to understand—it would never end."[5] Among the types of signs open to individualized interpretation are natural languages, secret codes, formalized languages, aesthetic codes, olfactory signs, cultural codes, tactile communication and visual input.

Eco distinguishes these systems from music (or "musical codes"), which he considers to be resolutely indeterminate. In his view, there is no depth to the semantic levels produced by musical syntax. A musical line, even when conventional, reveals no real baseline or essential undercurrent for the interpretive process. Virtually everything we extract from the listening experience is culturally conditioned and subjectively filtered. To be sure, this issue is less indicative of song, which is actually a species of text, or "music with a message."

The abstractness of music is evident whenever an instrumental piece is performed. Take, for example, Vivaldi's "Spring." Though it is programmatic—linked by title to a seasonal theme—its Baroque pleasantries can inspire an endless slew of associations, even for listeners familiar with the intended subject matter. It can conjure images of horseback riding, a morning cup of coffee, aristocratic tea parties, falling snowflakes, frolicking dinosaurs, a tray of cupcakes, a journey to Mars. Along with these representations are companion feelings, such as relaxation, invigoration, exhilaration and boredom. The possibilities are as numerous as the individuals who hear it. And, because music is a living and continuously unfolding art, any future listening can evoke an assortment of different connotations.

The vagaries of music make the listener's role even more crucial than that of the reader (or the receiver of other semiotic stimuli). Not only is musical meaning absent without someone to derive it, but music's very existence depends on ears to detect it. Operating in the amorphous medium of sound and traveling through the invisible element of air, it needs sensory organs to hear it, bodies to feel it and imaginations to engage it. It has no material form; it takes shape inside the listener. And it is in that materialization that meaning is born.

Art Is Not Artist

Biographies and backstories can taint our perception of artistic creations. The more that is known of the life and views of the artist, the more potentially challenging it is to embrace the art. Classic examples include the bigoted composer, the abusive author, the misogynistic painter, the egotistical architect, the politically opinionated actor. Without providing names, these epithets likely bring specific individuals to mind—a fact that itself shows the difficulty of separating the art from the artist. Because human minds and human hands are the imaginative and actualizing forces behind the art, the artist's personality is, it would seem, inextricably woven into the work.

It hardly needs mention that the foregoing dilemma is specific to controversial creators. The upright artist is outside of this discussion, as is the one we know little about. It is also true that the nature and severity of a negative trait will determine our ability or inability to excuse a less-than-noble artist. Still, the reality remains: as soon as we learn of something incriminating or offensive (universally or personally) about an artist, the experience of his or her art is irreparably influenced.

Although this judgment is natural and perhaps unavoidable, there are three ways in which it is unfair to both artist and audience. First, like any human being, the artist is composed of an assortment of qualities, some good, some bad, some neutral. Artists may differ from "ordinary" people in areas such as talent, training, creativity and vision, but they have flaws and virtues like everyone else. Indeed, the inner complexity of the artist is popularly thought to exceed that of others—a stereotype that should, at the very least, caution us from reducing the artist to his or her blemishes.

Second, artistic expression is an indicator of higher attributes. That things of beauty can emerge from someone possessing a despicable quirk is proof of an internal coexistence of dark and light. It should not be forgotten that Beethoven, whose compositions are among the outstanding achievements of Western culture, practiced his craft in a pigsty apartment, replete with piles of garbage, un-emptied chamber pots, and a stew of foul odors. These physical conditions were an extension of Beethoven's psychological condition; but just as his music transcended the filth in which it was written, so did it rise above the smudge in his mind.

Third, a work of art is but a stage in a larger process. The creative offering—whether a piece of music or a building—is made to be perceived. Art is not fully formed unless and until it enters the consciousness of someone other than the artist. It has no absolute identity apart from the perceiver's interaction with it. Reception is, in a sense, the completion of creation. Our own personalities—our characteristics, inclinations and experiences—actively shape what we perceive, thereby nullifying (or mitigating) whatever trace of the creator's persona is present in the work.

The key is to preserve our initial response to art, which occurs on a pre-rational and pre-interpretational level. It is only when the analytical mind kicks in that gut reactions are obscured by thoughts of the artist and other reflections. To avoid such second-level impediments, it is helpful to remember that art is not artist.

Essence and Non-Essence

The absence of essentialism is a recurring motif in postmodern philosophy. In that line of thinking, there are no foundational or inherent characteristics that distinguish one entity, object or idea from another. Whatever essence or defining substance there appears to be is an illusion shaped in the mind of the perceiver. Even the concept of human nature comes into question. Without confidence in our suppositions or in data derived from reason and observation, there cannot be a stable or set core of human characteristics. Our personalities become a malleable matrix of personal and socially constructed thoughts, perceptions and experiences.

The notion that we are the product of dispositions and circumstances can be overstated. Physical and elemental properties, scientific laws, genetic encoding and other measurable aspects of the material world inform who we are and what we know. Still, the practice of critical self-reflection—the "postmodern pause"—does help us confront tendencies, proclivities and prejudices we unknowingly possess, and realize the degree to which the beliefs we hold are grounded in subjective consciousness. Whatever the limits of the postmodern position, it does force us to examine and re-examine our assumptions.

This is particularly valuable for subjects rooted in aesthetics, such as music. For the strict postmodernist, music has no essence defining its fundamental nature. Rather, it exists in boundless varieties, each with culturally based particularities and expectations.

It is hardly novel to suggest that musical reactions and assessments are dependent upon the listener's prior conditioning and exposure. Musical conventions, like a modulation or turn of phrase, arouse generalized emotions for listeners familiar with those devices. Music tied to a holiday or special event brings entire communities into shared sentiments connected with that day. Melodies are often linked to one's past, stirring feelings and memories of a particular time, place or relationship.

But these observations can be taken too far. Even without the questioning voice of postmodernism, it is clear that how we think and feel about music is largely the product of our composite identities. Yet postmodern claims are softened by the fact that musical signatures and strains are felt in similar ways across wide audiences (within a cultural setting). If we concede that musical appraisal is essentially subjective, then consensus response is a valuable rubric. Musical conventions, figurations, parameters, conclusions and anticipations were not forced upon us or dictated from on high. They developed over time through an organic and collective process of experimentation, consolidation and familiarization. As such, standard reactions and attitudes toward musical stimuli are firmer than postmodernists would contend.

No experience, musical or otherwise, is entirely pure or unadulterated. However, this does not mean that qualities attributed to music are simply imaginary. Music appreciation occupies a middle ground, in which sounds are inextricably combined with multi-dimensional experiences. The music's essence is both intrinsic and entangled with the listener's personal history. The two cannot be separated.

Notes

1. Jean-Paul Sartre, *Literature and Existentialism*, trans. Bernard Frechtman (New York: Citadel, 1994), 68.
2. Ibid.

3. Dwight L. Bolinger, *The Symbolism of Music* (Yellow Springs, OH: Antioch Press, 1941), 27.

4. Umberto Eco, *The Role of the Reader: Explorations in the Semiotics of Texts* (Bloomington, IN: Indiana University Press, 1979), vii.

5. Umberto Eco, *Six Walks in Fictional Woods* (Cambridge, MA: Harvard University Press, 1994), 3.

Suggestions for Further Reading

Aitkin, Hugh. *The Piece as a Whole: Studies in Holistic Musical Analysis*. Westport, CT: Greenwood, 1997.
Bolinger, Dwight L. *The Symbolism of Music*. Yellow Springs, OH: Antioch Press, 1941.
Cumming, Naomi. *The Sonic Self: Musical Subjectivity and Signification*. Bloomington: Indiana University Press, 2000.
Eco, Umberto. *The Role of the Reader: Explorations in the Semiotics of Texts*. Bloomington, IN: Indiana University Press, 1979.
_____. *Six Walks in Fictional Woods*. Cambridge, MA: Harvard University Press, 1994.
Hallam, Susan, Ian Cross, and Michael Thaut, eds. *Oxford Handbook of Music Psychology*. New York: Oxford University Press, 2008.
Hughes, Robert. *Nothing If Not Critical: Essays on Art and Artists*. New York: Random House, 2012.
Jones, Mari Reiss, Richard R. Fay, and Arthur Popper, eds. *Music Perception*. New York: Springer, 2010.
Lehrer, Keith. *Art, Self and Knowledge*. New York: Oxford University Press, 2011.
Nussbaum, Charles O. *The Musical Representation: Meaning, Ontology, and Emotion*. Cambridge, MA: MIT Press, 2007.

16

LISTENING

The previous chapter looked at the part that listeners play in creating musical meaning. The present chapter focuses on another important piece of the listening experience: evaluation. Musical judgments arise very quickly—almost at the speed of instinct. This is because everything a person hears passes through layers of criteria forged from prior musical exposure. It is also true that because musical experiences are predominantly emotional, whatever reaction one has will invariably be subjective and subject to change with time. Music that clashes with one's preferences can be highly offensive, while sounds that resonate can bring immense comfort and satisfaction.

Evaluating Music

Leo Tolstoy's *Anna Karenina* begins with a maxim: "Happy families are all alike; every unhappy family is unhappy in its own way."[1] By this, Tolstoy meant that harmony in the home requires a checklist of essential ingredients: parental authority, child discipline, respectful discourse, mutual support, political agreement, good humor and so on. The list is long and largely unspoken, but failure in any one respect can upset the family balance. Happiness is predicated on success in numerous general areas, but unhappiness can result from varied sources of discord. There is no single-issue explanation for why one family is dysfunctional and another isn't, but functional families are functional for basically the same reasons.

Of course, not all inner-family differences are irreconcilable or severe enough to produce absolute unhappiness. Gradients of joy can be achieved without perfection. Few are the marriage and family counselors (or people in marriages and families) who would side wholeheartedly with Tolstoy's saying and all that it implies. Still, there is wisdom in the underlying premise: positive feelings about anything in life depend on a number of converging factors.

These factors tend to reveal themselves slowly within interpersonal relationships—familial, platonic, passionate and otherwise. It takes time to analyze our compatibility with another human being; the complexity of each person necessitates a thorough evaluation. The process is usually quicker in relationships with other things, such as food and recreation. In those cases, we rely on our senses for instant verdicts. But the rapidness with which these decisions are made does not mean they are casual or unrefined.

For example, musical judgments are usually formed within ten seconds of listening. That is all the time we need to assess whether or not we like what we hear. Our conclusion comes with such speed and certainty that it might seem arbitrary or unreflective. However, many categories of appraisal are present in the moment of listening. It is just that they are triggered automatically and are most often unconscious.

Without realizing it, we make musical decisions based on styles and genres, hooks and phrases, colors and moods, vocals and instruments, performance technique, recording quality and other features. The music needs to satisfy each area in order to be liked. As with Tolstoy's observation about family health, music that fails in just one way may cause disapproval. A lyric or guitar lick can spoil our relationship with the music.

This is not to say that musical judgment is always reflexive or cannot change over time. Elmer Bernstein argued this point with a crude analogy: "A piece of music is an art work, and to try to judge it by 'instinct' in four seconds has about as much validity as trying to evaluate the worth of a woman by the size of her bust."[2] Yet, even when the period of appraisal extends beyond a few seconds, music that is embraced must meet an assortment of usually unarticulated and always-personal requirements.

Subjective Sounds

Music is widely considered the most emotional of the arts. While other art forms may awaken ideas and images that act upon the feelings, music's first and most lasting impact is emotional. This is true when music aims at particular sentiments, and when it provides no definite clues as to an intended response. We are vulnerable to sounds that enter our awareness. They can deliver us to emotional states bearing no resemblance to our prior feelings. The speed with this occurs can make the emotions difficult to decode or articulate. Whether we are moved slightly or profoundly, music tends to inspire an immediate change (or changes) in mood. And since all this takes place in the private interior realm, the experience evades critical analysis.

As a predominantly emotional enterprise, music is saddled with the same term given to the emotions themselves: subjectivity. In music as elsewhere, this label is used in both a positive and negative sense. On the one hand, feelings derived from and felt toward music are biased—a uniformly ugly term. On the other hand, musical reactions and opinions are part of what makes us autonomous beings—a high and holy concept.

Musical bias is an inevitable byproduct of the listening experience. Each person filters auditory input through a singular and entangled web of perception and cognition. The type and magnitude of the elicited response rest on a host of conscious and unconscious forces, like personal history, cultural heritage, group affiliation, generational membership, general temperament and momentary frame of mind. As a result, reactions to music are not timeless or objective in the way that thoughts can be, but are embedded in a person's peculiar and non-replicable point of view. Judgments about music are, then, necessarily distorted: in whole or in large part, they involve feelings expressed as facts. These biases come to the surface in heated exchanges between fans of different artists, and when lists of the "best" composers/compositions/performers/songs are assembled and reacted to.

However, factors that contribute to bias become admirable when viewed from a different perspective. This is because musical opinions, when not at the center of contentious debates, reside in the sacred realm of self-knowledge. Tastes comprise an area of "me-ness": they are distinctive to the individual and their subjectivity needs no apology. Their basis in emotions shields them against rational and quantitative challenges. They retain personal validity no matter what anyone else says.

Musical preferences cannot be divorced from emotional responses. The former is essentially an expression of the latter. Even when we judge a piece using theoretical analysis or culturally accepted standards, our personal feelings play a determining role. We may decide that a piece or performance is "good" (problematic as that is), but we still might not like it. (It is also true that theoretical measurements and cultural assumptions are, at core, attempts to quantify emotional responses.)

Musical experiences are thoroughly subjective, with all the positive and negative meanings the term implies. Like the feelings music evokes, musical preferences are unabashedly our own.

Moved from Within

Force in music is usually understood metaphorically. Unlike the physical motion of water or wind, which can move objects between two points, musical force symbolically transports the hearer from one mental state to another. The sound's causal effect is akin to psychological manipulation: the listener is pushed and pulled into a particular mood. The sensation is commonly described as being "swayed," "bowled over," "carried along" and "taken away." The potency of such metaphorical movement is attested in diverse musical situations, including therapy, religious devotion, classical performances, patriotic displays and lullabies. In these settings, the listener is moved without actually moving.

Musical force can, however, manifest in another way. We detect movement in music partly because we experience it as a living organism, with coursing blood and appendages gesturing in various directions. As described above, this animation is often seen in the mind's eye and affects our psychological state. But it can also occur within our bodies.

According to Gary Ansdell, a research associate at the Nordoff-Robbins Music Therapy Centre in London, motion in music is more than just a mental inference or psychological response.[3] Music can stimulate a person's spirit or will, which then animates the body. Although music originates outside of the person, its mechanism differs from other exterior agents. For instance, when someone's leg is bent by an apparatus or machine, the action takes place outside the person and is not necessarily reflective of his or her wishes. The leg is acted upon as if it were an inanimate object. But when music compels the leg to move, the activity is generated from within. As Ansdell explains it, music communicates directly with the will, resulting in movement that is externally triggered yet internally generated.

Music therapists utilize this force to good effect. Many physical impairments can be overcome, circumvented or remediated through musical stimulation. The force of the music is such that it activates physical movement that is, under ordinary conditions, enormously difficult. The body translates the living essence of musical sound into fluid motion. This effect has been documented among patients with varying degrees of emotional constrictions, motoric impediments and physical damage.

In therapeutic settings and elsewhere, music motivates physical movement in three basic stages. First, the listener interacts with the sound, perceiving in it some type of motion (fast, slow, steady, disjointed, etc.). Second, the body aligns itself with the music's tempo and direction. Third, the body enacts the path of motion. Through this process, music becomes a vectoring force that literally moves us.

Taste Matters

Value in music is of two kinds. The first is formal, or value in the technical sense of the term. Within a musical system, there are agreed upon and objectively verifiable measurements for calculating elements such as tonality, texture, dynamics, temporal properties and structure. For example, theoretical analysis of Western concert repertoire includes specific names for chord types, normative concepts of articulation, parameters for simple and complex compositions, qualifications for themes and variations, and numerous other mechanical and quasi-mechanical computations.

The second kind of value is not so absolute. It is value in the humanistic sense, or the judgment of aesthetic qualities based on sensuous response. This is qualitative worth, in which subjective ideas like beauty, purpose, pleasantness, truth and goodness are applied to music. Such value exists on a continuum. An audience's impression of a piece can range from strong affinity to staunch dislike, with shades of nuance in between. These varied reactions are common despite attempts to standardize conceptions of excellence. Mozart is supposed to be received as beauty nearing perfection, even if a person does not resonate with it, while elevator music is supposed to be repugnant, even if one aimlessly rides up and down the shaft just to hear it.

True, one can never fully escape the musical pre-judgments that pervade a culture. Through cultural membership, we are involuntarily exposed to a set of consensus-driven artistic rules and expectations. Yet, on an individual level, there can be varying degrees of agreement and disagreement. This is because aesthetics are not inherent in the piece *or* in the mind of the listener. They arise from a transaction between the two.

Aesthetic valuation occurs in three successive stages: perception, statement of position, and reason for judgment. In a typical scenario, a listener hears a song, pronounces that it is boring, and explains that it lacks motion and variation. Another person might hear the same song and find it soothing for the same reasons. As a general rule, any piece is capable of attracting fans, no matter how vehement or widespread the opposition. The opposite goes for pieces widely regarded as good or pleasing: they still have their detractors.

Thus, the question follows: Is there any right or wrong way to feel about music? Critics and aestheticians would argue that there is. They point to the role of norms in determining things like attractiveness, balance and symmetry. By these guidelines, a selection can be certified as great, good, mediocre, bad, etc. An exception is made for works outside of one's purview, namely music of a foreign culture or subculture. For instance, the average American cannot accurately assess a gamelan performance, nor can a Baroque enthusiast give definitive appraisals of gansta rap. But critics object when similar leeway is given for music produced in one's own cultural setting.

Conclusions drawn by critics and aestheticians are often well reasoned and sometimes thought provoking. But they can also be overly academic and remote from the actual musical encounter. As much as they strive to distance music from arbitrary evaluations, the act of listening is by nature arbitrary. While music has absolute value in terms of its measurable components, the sensuous value we ascribe to it is the result of intimate contact. Norms and inherited assumptions can and do inform our decision-making, but the final judgment remains our own. Music is a matter of taste, and taste matters.

Comfort Music

Contact with the new and returning to the familiar are common occurrences among listeners of music. During the course of an average day and through the duration of an average life, a person is exposed to countless doses of music. Music is all around: on television, online, on the radio, on cellphones, in the grocery store, in children's mouths, in our own heads. Previously unheard material is always within access, whether it comes to us through active consumption or passive reception. And, because music is such a longstanding and boundlessly varied form of expression, no pair of ears will ever hear it all.

There is some attraction in music's apparent infiniteness. The appetite for the exotic, which exists in most people to a greater or lesser degree, can always feed upon new musical flavors. Yet, while much is gained from nibbling on diverse sounds, listeners eventually return to playlists of a much smaller size and scope. These individualized compilations are as distinct as the people who treasure them, and include selections of personal significance. The pleasure and assurance derived from such music is immediate, reliable and profound. It is audible comfort food.

Furthering the culinary analogy, the pull of familiar music has been likened to a hungry American traveling abroad. Native eateries have a certain appeal, offering unusual recipes and a doorway into local folkways. But for many tourists, restaurants serving familiar dishes are even more alluring. When navigating strange surroundings, the taste of home can simulate a sense of stability. A McDonald's hamburger helps to "normalize" cities as disparate and anxiety-inducing as Paris and Hong Kong.

The same occurs each time a person hears well-liked music. Recognizable sound patterns mitigate the complexities and uncertainties of existence. Of course, personal preference is the determining factor regulating which sounds bring this relief. But the effect is rooted much deeper than taste.

Researchers observe that when foreign noises are introduced into a wild biome, animals exhibit restlessness and other signs of distress. Once natural sounds are restored to purity, the reactions fade away.[4] In a similar and similarly basic way, the music we cherish provides an antidote to unwelcome noises, both literal and metaphorical. Having a special attachment to certain sounds is less about stubbornness or a fear of change, and more about seeking refuge from the clutter and stress that confront us daily. Our curiosity appreciates the exotic, but our nerves rely on the familiar.

Notes

1. Leo Tolstoy, *Anna Karenina* [1877] (New York: Dover, 2004), 1.
2. Elmer Bernstein, *Film Music Notebook*, Winter 1974–75, quoted in Nat Shapiro, *An Encyclopedia of Quotations About Music* (New York: Da Capo, 1978), 124.
3. See Rachel Verney and Gary Andsell, *Conversations on Nordoff-Robbins Music Therapy* (Gilsum, NH: Barcelona, 2010).
4. Krause, *The Great Animal Orchestra*, 188.

Suggestions for Further Reading

Bruscia, Kenneth E. *Defining Music Therapy*. Gilsum, NH: Barcelona, 1998.
Bunt, Leslie. *Music Therapy: An Art Beyond Words*. New York: Taylor and Francis, 2004.
Dickie, George. *The Century of Taste: The Philosophical Odyssey of Taste in the Eighteenth Century*. New York: Oxford University Press, 1995.
Dolan, Raymond J., and Tali Sharot, eds. *Neuroscience of Preference and Choice: Cognitive and Neural Mechanisms*. San Diego, CA: Academic, 2012.
Meyer, Leonard B. *Style and Music: Theory, History, and Ideology*. Chicago: University of Chicago Press, 1989.
Pellitteri, John. *Emotional Processes in Music Therapy*. Gilsum, NH: Barcelona, 2009.
Pitts, Stephanie. *Chances and Choices: Exploring the Impact of Music Education*. New York: Oxford University Press, 2012.
Rudd, Even. *Music Therapy: A Perspective from the Humanities*. Gilsum, NH: Barcelona, 2010.
Volpe, Galvano Della. *Critique of Taste*. New York: Verso, 1991.
Weber, William. *The Great Transformation of Musical Taste: Concert Programming from Haydn to Brahms*. New York: Cambridge University Press, 2009.

17

Ownership

The musical experience is autobiographical. Not only does the musician expose his or her innermost self to the listener, but the listener also filters the music through his or her own being. Every musical creation can be viewed as a record of personal influences, ideas, aptitudes, predilections, cultural location, and more. These same factors account for why a listener gravitates toward or steers away from a particular musical selection or style. At the same time, critics and academics can have significant influence when it comes to identifying "great" music. But, regardless of what others tell us, the music that occupies the most cherished individual space is that music in which we hear ourselves.

Self-Sounds

"I think therefore I am." This phrase has been repeated in countless writings, courses, discourses and ruminations since they first appeared in René Descartes' *Discourse on Method*.[1] Much of Western philosophy sides with this Cartesian principle, which argues that the act of thinking is the only certain proof that a thinker exists. While specific thoughts can (and should) be doubted if there is reason to do so, the fact that someone is thinking those thoughts cannot be challenged. It is the only thing one can be certain of.

Whether or not one agrees completely with this reductionist approach or accepts the mind-body dualism it rests upon, it does give due consideration to the connection between thought and identity. Ideas about the external world are born from the internal processes of perception, pondering and projection, which are necessarily subjective and usually malleable. One's notions about the world create the world for that person. The same goes for how one perceives oneself in the world, both in terms of self-image and the role that one plays. Thus, we might extend the aphorism "I think therefore I am" to include "What I think is who I am" (acknowledging that the first statement is objective and the second is subjective).

It is possible, then, to understand all works of the mind as autobiographical. Essays, equations, illustrations, engravings, enquiries and inscriptions need not tell an oral history or communicate a narrative to divulge details of the author's experience. The particular thoughts one thinks and the way those thoughts are expressed are, in a basic sense, who that person is. The creation defines the creator.

To be sure, each person who encounters the final product will interpret (or recreate) it all over again. Even the maker him or herself will appreciate it differently with each exposure. But regardless if the work is artistic, utilitarian or somewhere in between, it reveals the person's mind, and is thus the most that can be known of who that person is.

Music provides an illustration. Traces of influence, flashes of inspiration, flights of ingenuity, records of experience, translations of feelings, indications of aptitudes, attestations of predilections are all stored in the sounds and silences, rhythms and phrasings, harmonies and dynamics, articulations and voicings of a piece. It is the activity of the mind made audible. It is the self made audible.

Music is also autobiographical in that it captures a moment in time. It is a snapshot of a creative and reflective instance in one's always-changing existence. The sounds capture the nuances of the moment. They stem from a mind in constant shift. Music written at any other time would be different. Each piece is like a page in a diary.

Granted, the language of music can be abstract. It may contain the essence of the composer, but that essence is not always clear or universally understood (or understood the same way each time it is heard). This, too, is representative of the mind-located identity. Like all thoughts, musical thoughts are elusive and temporary. Yet they do not have to be definite or straightforward to be evidence of the thinker's realness or constitutive of the thinker's identity. To think up music is to exist; the music that is thought up is who the composer is.

Music Good and Bad

The God of Baruch Spinoza is not a personal or independent creator of the universe, but the universe itself. The deity, whom Spinoza called "God or nature," is the ultimate cause of all things because all things follow causally and necessarily from the divine essence. There is a definite order in the universe, and everything operates according to that structure. In this deterministic system, where the whole of nature proceeds "eternally from a certain necessity and with the utmost perfection," "bad" and "good" are illusory categories relative to human experience, and free will (as commonly conceived) is but a figment of human consciousness.[2] We are not free to do what we want: every action is conditioned by circumstances preceding it, those circumstances are determined by causes preceding them, and on and on. Things can only turn out one way: the way they do. As such, the appearance of rightness or absurdity, justice or unfairness in nature stems from our ignorance of the coherence of the universe and our demand that everything be arranged in accordance with human reason.

Arguing the merits and demerits of this concept is a favorite sport among philosophers. In some ways, Spinoza's ideas seem as radical today as when they led to his expulsion from Amsterdam's Jewish community in 1656. What is intriguing from a musical standpoint is an analogy he used to challenge conventional wisdom on morality: "As for the terms good and bad, they indicate no positive quality in things regarded in themselves but are merely modes of thinking, or notions which we form from the comparison of things one with another. Thus one and the same thing can be at the same time good, bad and indifferent. For instance, music is good for him that is melancholy, bad for him that mourns; for him that is deaf, it is neither good nor bad."[3]

As controversial as this evaluation may be, the comment on music deserves our consideration. There have been many attempts to devise standards and categories of good and bad music. Famously, sociomusicologist Simon Frith proposed four signifiers of bad pop recordings: tracks that rely on false sentiment; tracks featuring outmoded sound gimmicks; tracks displaying uneasy genre confusion; and tracks incompetently performed or produced.[4] Yet, aside from perhaps the last part, these are essentially matters of taste. To use a well-worn aphorism, "one man's trash is another man's treasure." Similar issues of preference and bias—which, we might add, are deterministically conditioned by circumstances like exposure and environment—cloud attempts to separate the trash from the treasure of any musical genre. Objective measurements simply do not (and cannot) exist.

Spinoza goes a step further in identifying the murkiness and subjectivity of musical judgment. Namely, he recognizes utility as a determining factor. Certain music may be appropriate or inappropriate for certain people in certain states at certain times. (Hence, the examples of the depressed person, the mourner and the person unable to hear.) It follows, then, that the perceived goodness or badness of a piece derives from two qualities: personal taste and situational function.

Spinoza sums up this non-absolutist, contextual approach thus: "By good I mean that which we certainly know to be useful to us." If the music is "good," it is because we like it and because we find it suitable for a particular situation. "Bad" music fails on both accounts. It is also true that one's opinion of a piece may shift from good to bad or vice versa depending on changes in aesthetic leanings and the contexts in which the music is heard. As Spinoza might say, the conditions, causes and effects leading up to the listening experience determine whether the music is heard as good or bad (or indifferent).

Judge for Yourself

"I don't believe any of you have ever read *Paradise Lost*, and you don't want to. That's something that you just want to take on trust. It's a classic … something that everybody wants to have read and nobody wants to read."[5] Mark Twain included this remark in a speech given at the Nineteenth Century Club in New York on November 20, 1900. His intent was not to shame modern readers for being disinterested in Milton's retelling of Adam and Eve—an epic that expands excessively on the size and scope and simple text of the original. Instead, he meant to illustrate how fashion in literature changes with the times. *Paradise Lost* and other hard-to-digest relics are known more by name than by content, and remain on lists of classics because the experts make it so, not because the public demands it.

The further removed we are from the time and culture that produces a so-called classic, the less we rely on our own opinions and the more we go by scholarly consensus. If we were to read *Paradise Lost*, we might enjoy it or we might not; we might be enthralled or we might wonder what all the fuss is about. But its status is predetermined, and our view of it is irreversibly tainted. It is great whether we like it or not, and we tend to blame ourselves—not the book—if it fails to capture our interest. For that reason, it is often safer to trust a work's pre-established classic-ness than to delve into it oneself.

Literary canons do, of course, serve practical purposes. If they did not exist, works like *Paradise Lost* would meet the same fate as "lesser" contributions of their day: extinction. Isolating a few works as "great" also helps keep track of history, since many more words are published than can be remembered or preserved. Furthermore, pantheons of greatness—whatever criteria they use—are valuable cultural inventories, cataloging how tastes and trends alter over time. These pragmatic considerations aside, there is something odd about accepting works as classics (or anything else) without actually experiencing them.

Art is made to be experienced. Whether it takes the form of literature, painting, music, theater, food, architecture or something else, art is not just the self-expression of its creator or even the creation itself. It also includes all that occurs when a person sees, touches, smells, tastes or hears it. In this sense, art is not complete (or even really art) unless and until it is interacted with.

In the moment of interaction, the work goes through a multilayered process of impulsive evaluation, informed by the experiencer's background, education, affiliation, disposition, etc. This is how we decide if we like it, hate it, or feel something in between. And whatever we feel is open to debate with others and subject to revision within ourselves.

Getting back to Twain's point, an artwork is most alive when it is fashionable (meaning current). Reactions are freely felt, opinions are freely expressed, pluses and minuses are freely discussed. By the time the experts give their appraisals, it is almost too late for us to have a pure response. This is especially so when the art in question is decades or centuries old. But the process is even skewed when critics review recent albums, movies, gallery shows and the like. The work is handed to us with a label, which we either accept or weigh against our feelings. But at least we have our own experience to draw from.

Music of Mine

The complaint is heard in every age, "How can anyone listen to that awful music?" The bewilderment is usually generational: the older generation cannot relate to the music of the youth, and the younger generation cannot tolerate the music of their elders. When the youngsters become parents themselves, their objections will mirror those that were once directed at them, and they will face the same opposition they exerted in their earlier years. The drama is repeated whenever two or more generations coexist on the planet. That is to say, it happens all the time.

The disagreement can be framed as rebellion and counter-rebellion. Adolescents push away from their parents, attach themselves to their peers, and assert their youthfulness through music of their own choosing. Meanwhile, the parents become more aggressive in their listening habits, turning their music louder to ensure that their offspring hear it (especially in closed confines like an automobile). Of course, this scenario is not an absolute given. Some families manage to exist in reasonable musical harmony. But disagreement is the norm.

Why is this so? Part of it has to do with the general dynamics of the parent-child relationship. However, there is a deeper reason. Neuroscientist Daniel J. Levitin explains that musical preferences are essentially fixed by age fourteen, setting the stage for a lifetime of stubborn listening.[6]

Adolescence is a period of tremendous physical and emotional change, and pubertal growth hormones coursing through the body make every experience seem important. This perceived importance does not fade away as we get older, but stays with us in the sanctified form of nostalgia. Musical experiences have a particularly lasting effect, mainly because adolescents are drawn to music as a source of comfort, guidance and identity-formation. And though our tastes can fluctuate as our attitudes shift and we encounter different sounds, the music we liked at age fourteen is favored throughout our lives.

This leads to unavoidable conflict. Whatever music one grew up with is cherished above the music of previous and subsequent eras. As a result, the preferences of youths and adults are never in alignment, no matter who occupies the role of child or adult at a given moment.

A manifestation of this can be seen in houses of worship, where melody choice is an especially heated topic. In that sacred environment, the term "traditional" is often affixed to the music of one's upbringing. Prayer settings heard or sung around age fourteen are judged to be correct and definitive—not necessarily because of any musical qualities, but because they are part of the soundtrack of that impressionable period. What tends to be forgotten is that those beloved melodies—however well established—were themselves once offensive to an older generation, just as the prayer-songs of today's youth disturb the ears of many elders.

What seems to be lacking here is empathy. Musical taste is shaped around the same time in everybody's life. However, because that time is relative to the year a person was born, the sounds adopted differ from those embraced by older and younger people (and those of the same age in different parts of the world). Thus, while we might not like or understand the music others hold dear, we can at least relate to the fondness they have for it.

Notes

1. René Descartes, *Discourse on Method and Meditations on First Philosophy*, part IV (1637).
2. Baruch Spinoza, *The Ethics*, part I., p. 32 (1677).
3. Ibid., part IV., p. 189
4. Simon Frith, "What Is Bad Music?" [2004], in *Taking Popular Music Seriously: Selected Essays* (Burlington, VT: 2007), 313–334.

5. Mark Twain, *Mark Twain's Speeches* (New York: Harper, 1910), 194.
6. Daniel J. Levitin, *This Is Your Brain on Music: The Science of a Human Obsession* (New York: Plume, 2007), 231.

Suggestions for Further Reading

Bowie, Andrew. *Aesthetics and Subjectivity: From Kant to Nietzsche*. Manchester: Manchester University Press, 2003.
Connell, John, and Chris Gibson. *Sound Tracks: Popular Music, Identity, and Place*. New York: Psychology, 2003.
Crafts, Susan D. *My Music: Explorations of Music in Daily Life*. Middletown, CT: Wesleyan University Press, 1993.
Frith, Simon, ed. *Music and Identity* (*Popular Music*, vol. 4). New York: Routledge, 2004.
Haas, Karl. *Inside Music: How to Understand, Listen To, and Enjoy Good Music*. New York: Anchor, 1991.
Karnes, Kevin. *Ethnicity, Identity, and Music: The Musical Construction of Place*. New York: Oxford University Press, 2008.
Katz, Ruth, ed. *Contemplating Music: Source Readings in the Aesthetics of Music*. New York: Pendragon, 1987.
Stokes, Martin, ed. *Ethnicity, Identity, and Music: The Musical Construction of Place*. New York: Berg, 1994.
Washburne, Christopher, and Maiken Derno, eds. *Bad Music: The Music We Love to Hate*. New York: Psychology, 2004.
Wilson, Carl. *Let's Talk About Love: A Journey to the End of Taste*. New York: Continuum, 2010.

18

Prejudice and Tolerance

Music evokes intense responses, both positive and negative. Music that is loved is loved very strongly; music that is disliked is hated with a passion. Yet, even with these staunch opinions, we tend to embrace a wide variety of music into our personal listening repertoires. This chapter explores the constant tension between prejudice and tolerance in our musical habits. It exposes the unfortunately common tactic of denigrating the musical tastes of others in order to elevate one's own. It concedes that all listeners are ideological in that they know what values they desire in music and have opinions about what is best for the music culture. It then challenges us to avoid harsh stances, lest we become musical bigots, and argues that much can be learned from reflecting on our own musical choices.

Prejudicial Listening

Anglo-Irish author Oliver Goldsmith made a hobby of observing people in taverns, coffee houses and other public gathering spots. One such occasion is recorded in his celebrated essay "National Prejudices," which describes a boisterous "pseudo-patriot" pontificating on the character of European nations to a group of like-minded men. He calls the Dutch "avaricious wretches," the French "flattering sycophants," Germans "beastly gluttons," Spaniards "surly tyrants." The speaker has only pleasant things to say of the English, the people to which he belongs. In his not-so-humble estimation, they excel all the world in "bravery, generosity, clemency, and in every other virtue."[1]

Not wanting to be dragged into the hysterics, Goldsmith strikes a ruminative pose and pretends to think about something else. But the speaker, betraying the insecurity typical of the assertive dogmatist, insists that he collect everyone's approval, even Goldsmith's. After some prodding, Goldsmith reluctantly drops the observer's cloak and assumes the role of participant.

With calm voice and careful words, he explains that he cannot make broad statements about any population. He then artfully demonstrates how negative portrayals can be spun into compliments: the Dutch are "frugal and industrious," the French "temperate and polite," Germans "hardy," Spaniards "staid." As for the English, they can just as easily be called "rash, headstrong, and impetuous." The essay concludes with a question that gets to the heart of the matter: "Is it not very possible that I may love my own country, without hating the natives of other countries?"

Prejudice derived from self-love is something most of us are guilty of. True, citizens of the contemporary West are, for the most part, less ardently nationalistic than the inhabitants of eighteenth-century Europe. But the larger point still resonates. Despite our increasing individualism, rising global awareness and the triumphs of multiculturalism, we have not outgrown the false premise that in order to applaud ourselves, we must also put down others.

For most of us, this impulse has migrated away from chauvinistic nationalism and into other facets of life. Its presence is obvious in historically contentious areas like religion, politics, ethnicity and class. But it also thrives in less severe, but no less sensitive, areas such as food, automobiles, clothing, sports, television and music. We are quick to attack the character of a blouse or sedan that is not our own, and freely exaggerate the virtues of things we possess or to which we are attracted.

Building up and tearing down are prevalent in musical discussions. It is not enough to simply enjoy or feel a connection to this song or that performer. It must also be better than the rest. No musical creation or creator can stand alone or be appreciated by itself. Comparisons have to be made. A recording cannot simply draw us in or escape our interest. It must be awesome or awful.

This impulse is present among professional critics and regular folks alike. Peruse any music-related online message board and discover droves of passionate fans making points and counterpoints, striking and counterstriking, defending and counter-defending. Jimi Hendrix versus Eric Clapton, Joni Mitchell versus Nina Simone, Richard Tucker versus Jan Peerce, the London Symphony Orchestra versus the Berlin Philharmonic. Bring up two names and watch the heated exchange unfold. Neither side is willing to concede that its evaluation is clouded in personal ties and tastes, or accept that there is something for everyone in the vast world of music. If your opinions clash with mine, yours must be certifiably inferior. And let me count the ways.

Returning to Goldsmith's essay, loves and hatreds surrounding nationalism and musical preferences seem to have common roots. In both cases, feelings are hyper-charged because they are part and parcel of self-identity. Elevating one's national affiliation or musical tastes is an act of self-elevation, as is the companion instinct to degrade the nationality and musical affinities of others.

It doesn't take much imagination to see the insecurity underlying these twin inclinations. The rhetoric intensifies as confidence decreases. If a person is self-assured and comfortable with his or her place in the world, then there is less need to boast or put down. What Reinhold Niebuhr wrote about fanatic religiosity applies to national and musical prejudices as well: "[It] is never rooted in faith but in doubt; it is when we are not sure that we are doubly sure."[2]

Musical Ideologies

As a label, "ideology" usually assumes a pejorative tone. To have an ideology is to be distorted and stubborn in one's thinking, intolerant of opposing points of view, forceful in asserting beliefs, willfully ignorant of contrary evidence. These are the so-called "isms," which are apparently outgrowths and concretizations of our brain's tendency to seek out patterns, embrace simplified explanations, adopt unifying theories, and welcome worldviews that mask the complexities of reality. Such systems help us to cope with and (at least pretend) to understand the world around us.

In truth, most of us hold ideas that could be classified as ideological, and no amount of defensiveness or lack of self-awareness can change that fact. Even an aversion to ideologies is itself an ideology. As cultural theorist Terry Eagleton stated, "As with bad breath, ideology is always what the other person has."[3] Our relationship with the term might improve if we adopted the confession of economist Paul Krugman, who, in accepting charges of being an ideologue, reduced ideology to two simple parts: (a) having values; (b) having some opinion about how the world works.[4]

The realm of music is no stranger to ideology. As an astonishingly diverse and remarkably evocative medium, music begs for simplifying classifications and generates pointed responses. These conditions lead to the drawing of (often-untenable) lines between "genres"—groups of pieces that share enough in common to make them a unit—and the construction of binaries, around which musical ideologies coalesce: authentic vs. inauthentic; hip vs. old-fashioned; pure vs. impure; ugly vs. beautiful; pristine vs. debased.

Whether or not we smell it on our own breath, our musical preferences tend to coagulate into musical ideologies, or allegiances to certain musical values and opinions about how the world of music should or should not work. The caricature of the classical music snob comes to mind. In his defense, and in our own, it is near impossible to uphold a completely non-judgmental stance on things musical. While we might concede philosophically that music criticism (sophisticated and garden variety alike) is planted in the soil of subjectivity, music's *raison d'être* is to move us, making it difficult to stand stoically still.

Personally, while I am convinced that aesthetics is not a science and that music is a receptacle for non-rational value judgments, I frequently catch myself turning the radio up in delight or off in disgust. Most of the time, musical ideology takes this harmless, visceral form. Other times, it gushes from influential pens and oozes into academic circles, as with Theodor Adorno's Marxist critique of popular music.[5] On thankfully rare occasions, musical ideology can have a damaging or even devastating effect, especially when it is part of a nationalist agenda, as with Hitler's censorship of Jewish musicians and Stalin's crusade against "formalism" (an amorphous concept that included modernist trends, like dissonance and atonality, and famously targeted Shostakovich and Prokofiev).

The issue, then, is not about whether we are ideological by nature or ideologues when it comes to music. As Eagleton and Krugman remind us, to be human is to be *homo ideologicus*—creatures driven by ideas, judgments, viewpoints and firm beliefs. The issue instead is one of degrees. To restate, ideology has accumulated negative connotations because of its potential for distasteful manifestations and harmful consequences. Ideology has led (and will continue to lead) to some terrible things. Plus, most of us fancy ourselves as open-minded, which is presumed to be the opposite of ideological. (This, even as we proudly identify as Democrats, Presbyterians, Capitalists, Mystics, Foodies, Deadheads, and countless other ideologies we prefer not to think of as ideologies.) All of this can be sorted out with a crude prescription: ideologies are unavoidable—just don't be a jerk.

Lessons from the Ear

In many circles and in much of contemporary discourse, dogmatism is held up as a paramount virtue. Consistency of belief, firmness of position and unwavering opinions, whether of a religious, political or other kind, are viewed as treasured and noble traits. Conversely, those who exhibit intellectual flexibility and openness to revision are thought untrustworthy or insincere. This attitude persists despite our being the inheritors of millennia of ideas, our knowledge of the swiftly changing world, and our awareness of the historical tragedies ideologies have wrought. It seems that no matter how antiquated or simplistic the mindset—and regardless of the quality or amount of contrary evidence—steadfastness and cocksureness are judged intrinsically virtuous.

Allegiance to narrow principles and provincial notions does have its benefits, not the least of which are a (false) reduction of life's complexities, a sense of stability in an unstable world, a solid foundation for self-identity and a basis for group cohesion—unrealistic and un-nuanced though some of this may be. But the truly critical mind is never satisfied with this type of thinking, since it necessarily involves surrendering to inherited assumptions and accepting conclusions arrived at by a person or persons other than oneself. More importantly, the supposed nobility of ideological stubbornness conflicts with another, more compelling, virtue: learning from experience.

Situations, circumstances, observations, readings, reflections, interactions, trial and error, cause and effect and other undertakings offer the open mind ample opportunities for reevaluation. The challenge is to keep a portion of our slate blank enough to accept, adopt and adapt new information, and to be willing to dismiss cherished views when they are proven faulty or insufficient. To quote nineteenth-century ethicist Thomas Fowler, "intellectual honesty requires that, if need be, we should sacrifice our consistency and our favorite dogmas on the altar of truth."[6]

In spite of its current unpopularity, this approach is more practical than radical, and far more ancient than it might appear. Its roots are planted in Greece and Rome, where minds as celebrated as Posidonius, Cicero and Seneca conceded that no single system of thought was adequate for understanding reality. Instead, these philosophical eclectics drew upon multiple theories and methods to gain insights into a subject or decipher a scenario. They favored reason over elegance, constructing sometimes-messy worldviews from existing beliefs and their own ideas.

Their apparent inconstancy was as pragmatic as it is opposed to conventions of modern discourse. Yet even the current-day dogmatist tends to be eclectic in some ways. A case in point is musical listening. If we were to take an inventory of the music we enjoy (or have enjoyed in the past), we would likely be astonished by the variety and lack of unifying characteristics. Most of us draw musical selections from abundant sources and styles. Others have a disciplined relationship with music, limiting themselves to a certain period or genre of recordings. But even when the range is relatively small, there is still diversification enough to dispute dogmatism.

Added to this, the way we listen to a piece at any given time tends to vary. Our hearing is usually directed toward one or more specific dimensions, be it melody, orchestration, rhythmic pattern, tonal density, timbre, coloration, phrasing or something else. Whether this variation of perception is conscious or unconscious, the result is that we are always processing musical sounds differently. The heterogeneity of our listening habits rivals that of our musical choices.

Like the philosophical eclectic who un-rigidly searches for ideas best suited to address an inquiry, the listener seeks out music that best matches personal leanings and the situation at hand. And like the adherent of eclecticism, whose outlook and theoretical tools are receptive to reassessment and modification, our musical preferences are subject to change. If at any time we were presented with a thousand recordings representing far-flung styles, we would find some of them bearable, others unlistenable and select a few as favorites. The determining factor would be this: whether or not the music "works."

Of course, there are ideological purists in every area of life, including music. They fancy themselves honorable conservationists, but are just as often stubborn fossilizers artificially removed from the evolving experience that is life. Musical purists are unable and unwilling to budge, even if there are practical reasons for doing so. Clinging is construed as righteousness.

But such purists, while adamant and often vociferous, are the musical minority. Most of us have eclectic ears: we are open to and excited about adding to our constantly adjusting playlists. We approach music not as dogmatists, but as experimenters whose views derive from exposure and analysis. Honest engagement in all aspects of life requires a similar level of open-mindedness. If only we would listen to our ears.

Reflecting on Experience

Experience alone does not teach. Our lives are made up of a constant succession of experiences, some dull, some profound and most somewhere in between. If ridden through without reflection, these occurrences might leave a subconscious imprint, but they do not necessarily make us wiser or more informed. In the 1970s, educational theorists David Kolb and Ron Fry proposed a model outlining the stages by which experience becomes learning.[7] Referred to as Kolb's cycle of experiential learning (or the Kolb cycle), it is a repeatable spiral consisting of four elements: concrete experience, reflective observation, abstract conceptualization and active experimentation. The experience itself—whether it is a day at the office or a stroll through the park—is only the beginning. Personal growth occurs through examination, abstraction and future application.

For most people some of the time (and some people most of the time), this is a natural process. There is a sense in which we are all born philosophers, or *homo philosophicus*. On occasion, we find ourselves asking deep questions, contemplating our purpose and pondering the things we have observed. Aristotle addressed this inclination in the opening line of *Metaphysics*: "All men by nature desire to know."[8] Yet knowing from experience is not as simple as experiencing an experience. It requires a few additional steps, not to mention a motivating sense of curiosity.

Of course, some things in life are riper for exploration than others. For instance, we might readily progress through the Kolb cycle when the concrete experience is mowing a lawn, but are less inclined to do so when the activity is listening to music. This is partly because of the relative abstractness of the musical experience. Being moved by a piece or selecting a track for a playlist are processes more impulsive than cognitive, and thus hard to penetrate with intellectual methods. It is also the case that musical affinities are a matter of taste: a sensitive part of the human makeup, and one particularly resistant to critique.

When it comes to music, most of us adhere to the unreflective phrase, "I know what I like and I like what I know." This principle of subjective preference helps to protect our musical opinions. We need not justify (or even understand) our like or dislike for a particular selection. We simply know our position. This has its advantages, as musical penchants do not usually hold up well under analysis. Critical evaluation and experimentation have little regard for those individualistic factors that shape our musical beliefs: exposure, upbringing, peer influence, cultural biases, inherited assumptions, generational trends, etc. None of this leads to an objective conclusion. The further and more honestly we pursue the steps of observation, conceptualization and experimentation, the shakier our convictions become.

In the end, there may be no scientific or otherwise satisfactory rationale for musical taste. However, the philosopher in us should not view this as an impediment, but as an invitation. The questions that arise from musical self-inventory are themselves invaluable teachers. Bertrand Russell made this point in *The Problems of Philosophy*. His eloquent words are applicable to all areas of thought—whether musical or existential: "Philosophy is to be studied not for the sake of any definite answers to its questions, since no definite answers can, as a rule, be known to be true, but rather for the sake of the questions themselves; because these questions enlarge our intellectual imagination and diminish the dogmatic assurance which closes the mind against speculation...."⁹

Notes

1. Oliver Goldsmith, *The Miscellaneous Works of Oliver Goldsmith*, vol. 1, ed. James Prior (London: John Murray, 1837), 220–223.
2. Reinhold Niebuhr, quoted in Howard Bloom, *Global Brain: The Evolution of Mass Mind from the Big Bang to the 21st Century* (New York: Wiley, 2000), 194.
3. Terry Eagleton, "Why Ideas No Longer Matter: Modern Politicians Deal Only in Facts, Not Philosophical Reasoning," *The Guardian*, March 22, 2004, <http://www.theguardian.com/books/2004/mar/23/immigrationpolicy.politics>
4. Paul Krugman, "Everyone Has an Ideology," *The New York Times*, April 13, 2011, <http://krugman.blogs.nytimes.com/2011/04/13/everyone-has-an-ideology/>
5. See Wesley Blomster, "Sociology of Music: Adorno and Beyond," *Telos* 28 (1976): 81–112.
6. Thomas Fowler, "The Ethics of Intellectual Work and Life," *International Journal of Ethics* 9 (1899): 305.
7. David Kolb and Ronald Fry, "Toward an Applied Theory of Experiential Learning," in *Theories of Group Processes*, ed. Cary L. Cooper (New York: John Wiley, 1975), 33–57.
8. Aristotle, *Metaphysics*, 980a 21.
9. Bertrand Russell, *The Problems of Philosophy* [1912] (Rockville, MD: Arc Manor, 2008), 104.

Suggestions for Further Reading

Beebee, Thomas O. *Ideology of Genre: A Comparative Study of Generic Instability*. University Park: Pennsylvania State University Press, 2004.
Brown, Steven, and Ulrik Volgsten, eds. *Music and Manipulation: On the Social Uses and Social Control of Music*. New York: Berghahn Books, 2005.
Carroll, Mark. *Music and Ideology*. Burlington, VT: Ashgate, 2012.
De La Fuente, Eduardo, and Peter Murphy, eds. *Philosophical and Cultural Theories of Music*. Boston: Brill, 2010.
Howard, Keith, ed. *Music as Intangible Cultural Heritage: Policy, Ideology, and Practice in the Preservation of East Asian Traditions*. Burlington, VT: Ashgate, 2012.
Kerman, Joseph. *Contemplating Music: Challenges to Musicology*. Cambridge, MA: Harvard University Press, 2009.
Krims, Adam, ed. *Music/ideology: Resisting the Aesthetic*. New York: Psychology, 1998.
Leppert, Richard, and Susan McClary, eds. *Music and Society: The Politics of Composition, Performance and Reception*. New York: Cambridge University Press, 1989.
Paddison, Max. *Adorno's Aesthetics of Music*. New York: Cambridge University Press, 1997.
White, Harry, and Michael Murphy, eds. *Musical Constructions of Nationalism: Essays on the History and Ideology of European Musical Culture, 1800–1945*. Cork: Cork University Press, 2001.

19

Religion

For most of human history, music has not been a central attraction, but an accompaniment to other human activities. Some suggest that music's original and still most valuable purpose is as an aid to religious worship. This chapter explores reasons for the pervasive relationship of music and religion. Themes include music's power to motivate religious revivals and vitalize liturgical rituals, confirm religious convictions and stimulate emotional cohesion, contribute extra-textual meaning, bind worshipers together, and draw out the non-cognitive aspects of belief. The chapter also notes that being religious is not necessarily a prerequisite for enjoying music created for religious purposes.

Reviving Tones

American Baptist preacher and musician Adoniram Judson Gordon wrote, "eras of spiritual refreshing in the Church of Christ have generally been eras of revival in popular and congregational singing."[1] This comment is specific to American Christianity and its various "Great Awakenings," but it can be applied cross-culturally and cross-religiously to revivals like Neo-Hassidism—a Jewish movement that draws much of its vigor from the songs of Shlomo Carlebach and others. As a rule, religious revivals are not innovative in the sense of presenting new doctrines or ideas. Their originality lies instead in how they package and present existing material in new and emotionally convincing ways. As the "re" of the term connotes, the objective is not creation but restoration, renewal, reassertion, reconnection, reinvigoration, revitalization and return. The success or failure of a revival depends on how effective it is in converting inherited views and established thoughts into vibrant sources of energy. This is why group singing is so heavily relied upon.

Of all the arts, music is understood as the most closely associated with religious life. The freeness and intensity with which music interacts with non-rational strata of our consciousness is perceived as a deeply spiritual matter. The sensation is amplified in group settings, where communal song brings individuals to shared sentiments, common physiological reactions and strengthened ties to one another. When the context is religious, music-stimulated group energy is naturally translated into divine or spiritual energy. The content of the songs and the conditions in which they are sung add a powerful interpretive layer.

Musical responses play a crucial part in cultivating large-scale religious revivals and sustaining them over time. Again, the messages that are sung are typically conventional (though they can be phrased in fresh and relevant ways). What is novel and attractive is how the messages are experienced. As Gordon observed, revival songs tend to be popular and congregational: they embrace current musical tastes and encourage collective participation. Both of these elements—trendiness and communal engagement—contribute mightily to rekindling interest and enthusiasm in the religion.

In this sense, lyrical content—whether hymnal, liturgical, scriptural or other—is less important than how it is performed and received. This reflects a general musical truth: even when tones are used to transmit texts, they are perceived to explore and express levels and kinds of feelings that elude or transcend the words themselves. This has significance for religious revivals, which, as mentioned, are concerned with reigniting feelings rather than inventing ideologies. And it is for this reason that "eras of spiritual refreshing," as Gordon called them, are almost always propelled by song.

Emotion, Spirit and Sound

Benjamin Ray includes this optimistic observation in his textbook, *African Religions*: "Through ritual man transcends himself and communicates directly with the divine. The coming of divinity to man and of man to divinity happens repeatedly with equal validity on almost every ritual occasion."[2] The thought of a ritual—or another periodic activity—having the same impact or perceived potency each time it is performed is foreign to most people. Human beings are complicated creatures, and the potential elements of complication—interpersonal conflicts, financial worries, professional turmoil, indigestion, etc.—tend to hamper full engagement. Even the most devout will admit that spiritual highs are much less common than spiritual middles or lows. Perhaps things are different in generic Africa, though that is unlikely.

Added to this is the nature of ritual itself. In order to earn its designation, a ritual must be standardized, controlled and occasional. Several benefits stem from this predictability, not the least of which are feelings of stability and authenticity. But the religious ideals of attentiveness and elevation are often lost in repetition. The struggle to find personal meaning in religious ritual is as prevalent as ritual itself. This is especially so in liturgical traditions, where participants are expected to absorb themselves in texts they have read or heard hundreds of times before.

Music is typically turned to as a tool for fixing fractures in devotional concentration. There is an implicit awareness that text alone is not always compelling or stimulating enough to envelope the distracted worshiper, and musical strains are employed to do the trick—or at least aid the process. Of course, musical solutions are not infallible: liturgies are sung in faith communities the world over yet the challenge of focus still persists. Nevertheless, music's unshakable place in religious services owes greatly to its ability to ameliorate—though not alleviate—barriers to concentration.

The success of music in this regard derives from the close proximity of spirituality and emotions. On some level, these sensations are indistinguishable. A flush of emotions felt in a religious setting—a holy site or house of prayer—and/or linked to texts considered holy—scripture or liturgy—is likely to be designated spiritual. Likewise, a peak or epiphanic moment outside of a formal setting may be understood as spiritual depending on the outlook and vocabulary of the actor(s). Thus, a more precise classification might be that a spiritual experience is an idiosyncratically determined species of emotional experience.

Whether such emotions are a sign of something beyond, a pathway to self-realization, or a combination of the two is, from an experiential standpoint, inconsequential. The important takeaway is that the emotional part of the human persona must be activated in order for worshipers to feel the "coming of divinity to man and of man to divinity," as Ray puts it.

Herein lies the fundamental value of sacred music. Music serves to dramatize prayer, giving the language a personality and making it come to life. Music also generates psychophysical responses, steering the mind and body to feel a certain way. This influence can be traced to culturally conditioned reactions to musical techniques, such as tension and release, as well as personal and communal associations, such as nostalgic memories. In the end, the effect of the music becomes its character: calming, disconcerting, charming, invigorating, depressing, etc.

Again, music's emotionalizing function is not a sure-fire way of drawing people into prayer or of retaining their attention. Old tunes, like old texts, can become dry after too many repetitions, and a given piece must be at least moderately attractive (not repulsive) to the individual. But under ideal conditions, music prompts emotional responses, which kindle spiritual connotations, thereby triggering thoughts of a heavenly source.

Music and Coherence

Religious faith is commonly conceived of as cognitive. Those who are drawn to beliefs and practices are, by implication, convinced of their hypotheses, evidence and/or explanatory reasoning. Adherents accept the claims—or many of the claims—as consistent with reality, and assert the overall truth of the religious system. While this intellectual component is certainly crucial, a religion's emotional resonance is nearly (if not equally) as important. Believers pressed to justify their allegiances frequently bypass logical arguments altogether, citing instead confirmatory experiences. These might include a personal encounter with otherness, a feeling of profound consolation, or some other sensation that evades scientific validation but is felt to be real. To quote nineteenth-century preacher and theologian Jonathan Edwards, "True religion in great part consists in the affections."[3]

There is a growing body of psychological and neurological studies showing the extent to which we attach emotional attitudes to concepts. When appraising the value of an idea, we rely not only on reasoned thought but also on the sentiments we ascribe to that idea. Thus, the discerned accuracy or inaccuracy of a religious concept hinges in part on its ability to address specific human needs, such as social bonding, avoidance of anxiety, moral certainty and life after death. This is not mere wish fulfillment, but a rational choice informed by irrational and usually subconscious desires. As philosopher Paul Thagard puts it in his theory of emotional coherence, "people adopt and maintain religious beliefs for a combination of evidential and emotional reasons that provide satisfaction of cognitive and emotional constraints."[4]

Worship music is one area in which the intellectual and sentimental regularly converge. For reasons still not fully understood, combinations of pitches, timbres, rhythms, durations and dynamics effortlessly penetrate the seat of sentiments. When words are added to music, they tend to take on the character dictated by the tones. In most cases, the songwriter seeks to match a text with corresponding sounds, thereby reinforcing the thematic content. However, the force of music is such that upbeat lyrics sung to a sad melody will be perceived as sorrowful, while melancholy words set to a gleeful tune are felt, on some level, to be uplifting.

Whether the music matches the basic meaning of the language or shades it in a particular direction, the emotions stirred act as a type of confirmation.

In devotional settings, this effect serves as affirmation of themes and ideas present in a prayer. With the aid of melody, a prayer of peace becomes a sensation of peace, a prayer of hope becomes a sensation of hope, a prayer of compassion becomes a sensation of compassion, and so on. Worship music can satisfy more general concerns as well, like the need for communal bonding and connection to heritage.

In these instances and more, exposure to music creates or enhances the emotional coherence of a religious system. It is an area of experience wherein cognition and affections seamlessly merge, and truth is as much a matter of feeling as it is of thought

Music as Contagion

The cohesive power of song is well exploited by groups of all sorts. In settings religious and secular, familiar melodies are used to consolidate feelings and energies and fuse communal consciousness. This transition from individuals to community owes in part to lyrical content. The words that are sung tend to emphasize the ethos of the collective or some aspect of its convictions or heritage. This is demonstrated whenever a national anthem is performed publically or a generation-defining song is sung at a frat house. But an argument can be made that music, more than message, is what truly brings the group into an experience of itself.

To illustrate this point, it will suffice to describe a typical congregational gathering. As the service time approaches, people—young, old, and in between—file into the sanctuary at irregular intervals and scatter into pews or chairs. Some arrive in families or in small groups; others come alone or with a companion. Most take to chatting; a few sit in quiet contemplation. They have entered a shared space, yet they are, for the moment, a loose assortment of people filling a room. A clergyperson offers perfunctory remarks to quiet the crowd. Some congregants straighten up in their seats. Others reach into their pockets to turn off their cellular phones. The atmosphere slowly begins to change. But it is not until the first syllable is sung that the group really takes shape. Congregants join their voices and perk their ears as the song continues. Their attention turns effortlessly to one another. The tones bring them out of their own thoughts and into a mutual moment. They are no longer "I" but "we."

Some version of this scenario is repeated in other singing communities. Yet, as with all commonplace phenomena, it is easier to acknowledge than to account for. Among the potential explanations is emotional contagion, a concept pulled from the psychological literature.

Broadly defined, emotional contagion is the automatic tendency to mimic and synchronize vocalizations, gestures, postures, facial expressions and movements of another person or persons, thereby generating emotional convergence. In the words of Gerald Schoenewolf, it is "a process in which a person or group influences the emotions or behavior of another person or group through the conscious or unconscious induction of emotion states and behavioral attitudes."[5]

Unconscious mood transfer is innate to the human species. It can be relatively mild, as with the child who feels happy when she sees someone else smiling. It can also have serious consequences, as when fear and loathing infect a crowd to the point of mob violence. Whether the scale is small or large and whether the outcome is positive or negative, emotional contagion illustrates our susceptibility to the feelings of others.

This process is indicative of communal singing. To a certain extent, lyrics and physical space can stimulate infectious emotions. Language and architecture are known to impact mood and influence demeanor. However, because singing involves a series of movements that can be imitated, the music (apart from text and location) is the primary source of contagion. Most participants intuitively unite in pitch, rhythm, volume, tone quality, swaying, toe tapping, mannerisms and a host of unconsciously coordinated actions.

These infectious elements, combined with music's inborn emotional qualities, promote solidarity of a visceral and lasting kind. Put succinctly, people merge together when they sing together.

Music Itself

Conventional thought holds that liturgical song is of two basic kinds. The first is logogenic (word-born), where rhythm, shape, movement, phrasing and cadences are directed by the ebb and flow of a text. This is essentially musical grammar—sometimes called speech-melody or stylized speaking—and is the dominant trait of scriptural cantillation and modal prayer chant. The second type is melogenic (melos-born), where words are fitted to the music. This includes prayer-songs in which musical considerations, like meter and melody, outweigh textual concerns. There is room in each of these categories for simple and complex music, literal and interpretive approaches, prosaic and creative treatments.

While the full range of liturgical music can be divided between these groupings, there is a third, somewhat different class that deserves our attention: pathogenic. Strictly defined, pathogenic (emotion-born) songs are distinguished by vocables: meaningless or nonlexical syllables sung to deliver melodies. This is a common feature of Native American songs and the wordless tunes of Hassidic Jewish origin. The music is devoid of verbal syntax and substance, and emotional outlet is the foremost purpose.

Although pathogenic songs are technically extra-liturgical—they do not involve prayer-texts—many who attend liturgical worship experience the music in a pathogenic way. This is especially so in settings where texts are in a foreign language and/or contain ideas foreign to a participant's worldview. An example would be a Jewish congregant who is an atheist and does not understand (or care to understand) Hebrew, but still finds satisfaction in synagogue song. He may be an object of pity for the pious clergyperson or the high-minded composer; but he is common—perhaps the majority in some places—and his experience is as authentic as anyone else's.

Whether the design of a prayer-song is logogenic or melogenic, the music has an essence and vitality of its own. Of course, the skilled composer or presenter will use musical devices to bring out qualities they find in the text, and they generally expect worshipers to pick up on the word-music interplay. However, once notions and emotions are translated into sound, they tend to take on an independent life. Although the text is the reason for the music, it is not always the reason a person is attracted to the music. (In fact, one's affection for a song may be diminished when he or she discovers its meaning.)

If we expand the discussion of liturgical song to include the experiential aspect, then pathogenic becomes a legitimate and profitable classification. This approach is consistent with the updated understanding of ritual music, which sees text as one of several components of musical worship.

In contemporary scholarship, ritual music addresses the entirety of the rite: words, actions, artifacts, music and physical space. This holistic view looks beyond language and transcends debates about the appropriateness or inappropriateness of a particular musical setting. It is the rite—not just the message—that shapes and reinforces identities and brings meaning to the lives of participants. The words may or may not be understood and may or may not be relevant for everyone in attendance. But there is acknowledged value in all elements of the rite, including the music itself.

Collective Voice

Religion always involves community. It is learned in social contexts, grounded in shared ideas, built upon social relations and sustained by collective actions. As Émile Durkheim reminded us, a religion is a system of beliefs and practices that unites individuals in a single moral community called a church (or another faith-specific synonym).[6] While there is space for personal practice—and while such practice is vital for retaining members and strengthening the whole—religion is not an individualized spiritual path. There is no religion without a church.

In both Judaism and Christianity, the congregation is the most significant and influential level of social organization. It draws adherents together in a common location and provides them with opportunities for shared devotional, educational, gastronomical and recreational experiences. Because a congregation's central aim is to foster and maintain communal cohesion, group singing has long been its most trusted aid.

The effectiveness of congregational song is rooted in the nature of the congregation itself. It thus behooves us to look more closely at what a congregation is and what it seeks to achieve. For this, we turn to John Locke, the English physician and Enlightenment philosopher. Locke's most cogent description of a congregation is found in *A Letter Concerning Toleration*. Published amidst fears that Catholicism was taking over England, the short treatise cautions against government-imposed religion. In Locke's view, religious tolerance is key to maintaining civil order, whereas civil unrest is the natural response to magistrates who attempt to outlaw religious sects and denominations. Since genuine religious converts are gained through persuasion and not coercion, governments have no right to intrude upon matters of the soul. In Locke's eloquent words, "the power of civil government relates only to men's civil interests, is confined to the care of the things of this world, and hath nothing to do with the world to come."[7]

Against this backdrop, Locke defined a congregation as a "voluntary society of men, joining themselves together of their own accord, in order to the public worship of God, in such a matter as they judge acceptable to them, and effectual to the salvation of their souls."[8] This observation pertains specifically to Protestant contexts, where affiliation choices can be many. Under ideal conditions, individuals are free to join in or drop out according to their comfort or discomfort with doctrines, rituals, policies, membership and so on. Thus, to a certain and important extent, those who gather together *want* to gather together.

The voluntariness of congregational affiliation—which obviously varies from place to place—is precisely why communal song is so valuable. Congregants need compelling reasons to congregate. It is one thing to share values, views and heritage, and another thing to engage in them. What group singing accomplishes is a kind of transformation. Voices united turn common beliefs (lyrical content) and identity-affirming sounds (melody) into a lived collective experience.

It is often said that song is the glue that keeps a congregation together. Ideologically and emotionally reinforcing music replenishes and rededicates group commitment. Without group singing—and other means of creating palpable unity—the church risks losing its appeal and dissolving away.

The Body Thinks

The scene is not uncommon. A group gathers to study the ancient language of a scriptural passage or liturgical text. As they delve into the themes and imagery, judgments are made and ideological lines are drawn. One person accepts it as unquestioned truth. Another finds it hopelessly linked to a distant time. Someone else searches for hidden meaning. Another relates it to current events. The points they argue and sides they take reflect the group's composition: a traditionalist, a rationalist, a mystic and a political activist. As always, their lively exchange ends in respectful disagreement. They put down their books, finish their coffee, shake each other's hands, walk into the sanctuary, and disperse among the congregation. In a few minutes, they will be singing the words they were just debating. And they will be happily absorbed in the melody.

To the casual observer, this scene illustrates the dichotomy between study and song. The first is an intellectual activity, inviting scrutiny, deconstruction, reconstruction and reasoned dispute. The second is an emotional experience, disarming the analytical urge and inviting the flow of passions. Because the first involves critical thought and the second uncritical feeling, studying is generally viewed as more virtuous. To be moved by music containing words we struggle with is a case of lower capacities overtaking higher faculties.

There is, however, another, less hierarchical way of looking at it. Anthropologist Michelle Rosaldo challenged us to appreciate emotions as "embodied thoughts."[9] They are not, she contended, involuntary or irrational exertions of the animal self, but the result of a deliberate and engaged body. Like cognition, emotion is a genuine and considered expression of who we are. It is the body's way of reasoning.

As word-centric beings, we tend to dismiss the non-verbal realm of feelings as primal or crude. We take a dualistic stance, dividing thought and emotion into firm categories. We appraise the mind as literally and figuratively above the body. The intellect is the basis of our superiority as a species; feelings arise from our base biology. According to Rosaldo, this viewpoint is a reflection of culture rather than reality. While the mind processes information in words, the body processes information in sensations. One is not necessarily better or more efficient than the other. Both constitute our humanity.

This perspective helps us decipher the liturgical scenario above. Despite the differing views expressed around the study table, the heterogeneous group joins in the joyful singing of passages they had argued over moments before. Objections they raised with the text and one another remain unresolved. But as the words melt into music, so do their intellects melt into feelings. Their thinking brains are quieted; their thinking bodies stimulated. The debate is put on hold until next time.

Feeling Belief

Anthropologists place the world's religions into several categories, including animism, ancestor cult, nature religions, polytheism and monotheism. Each of these broad groupings contains a diversity of convictions, practices and mythologies reflective of the fertility of human imagination. Religion, it seems, is as variegated as humanity itself. Still, it is possible to locate shared purposes within these sundry (and in many ways incompatible) systems. For instance, they all strive to help people deal with uncertainties, provide meaning for their lives, give answers to difficult questions and promote social cohesion. While no particular belief or practice is common to or deemed valid by every group, these aims are universal.

A rationalist might argue that the extreme variety of religious beliefs is evidence of their falsity. If each claims to be the absolute truth, then none of them can be absolutely true. It might also be asserted that scientific research and other modern advances have made and will continue to make religious answers obsolete. Even sacred subjects like the soul, morality and apparent glimpses of the afterlife have been shown to have brain-based origins. At the same time, it is clear that the core issues religions address are inherent to the human condition. If centuries of philosophical inquiry and empirical data have taught us anything it is that life is uncertain, unpredictable and devoid of absolute meaning. That religions construct order in this chaos is justification for their persistence, even in the age of science.

It would be a mistake to dismiss religious beliefs as merely wishful. Though faith derives from and appeals to the intellect, it is not without experiential confirmation. Believers genuinely feel that they are in contact with supernatural forces. Proof of divine concern is not always observable in the course of everyday life, but there are certain feelings that provide assurance. Knowledge of horrors and tragedies might pose a challenge to belief, but sensations mitigate doubt.

It is no coincidence that cultures far and wide associate singing with the supernatural and infuse religious activities with song. Religion needs singing. It is a primary mode by which convictions become feelings. Songs yield tangible results. Of course, this can be attributed to music-triggered emotional and neurological responses. But in the context of worship and the mind of the believer, it is confirmation of faith.

Music's role in supporting belief can be traced to prehistoric times. Archaeological ruins indicate that rituals were often performed in rooms and caverns with the liveliest acoustics. Paleolithic paintings are generally clustered on the most resonant cave walls, suggesting that they were used in conjunction with ritualistic chant. Neolithic stone configurations, like Avebury and Stonehenge, were similarly composed of echoing rocks. As society advanced, the association of vibrant sounds with the holy found its way into sacred architecture, where reverberating sanctuaries symbolically convey a back-and-forth between humanity and the supernatural.

It is not necessary to accept this devotional interpretation to understand music's confirmatory power. Whether we are religious or not, we remain a species attracted to the emotionalizing effects of song and vibrant acoustics. Their impact is enough to convince us that what is being sung is right and valid. While the beliefs themselves might not resonate with people outside of a particular worldview, we can at least appreciate the persuasive hold of the music.

Beauty Before Content

"I take satisfaction in belonging to a species of creatures with the ability not only to conceive and perform, but also respond appreciatively to such a work."[10] This declaration comes from Nelson Edmondson's thoughtful essay, "An Agnostic Response to Christian Art." Edmondson, an emeritus professor of art and art history at Michigan State University, is the agnostic in the title. The "work" he is referring to is any classic of Christian art, graphic or musical. His attraction to such pieces, despite his lack of faith and regardless of his artistic ability, is a hallmark of our species. We need not be wrapped up in an artwork's message or subject matter to be moved by it, or to appreciate the skill involved in its creation. Intellectual investment can deepen our involvement, but absence of commitment does not eliminate our emotional susceptibility. To a great extent, the meaning of the work is secondary to its aesthetic force.

If any example proves this point, it is the confession of evolutionary biologist and self-professed "militant atheist," Richard Dawkins. Dawkins recalls an appearance he had on *Desert Island Discs*, a British radio show. When asked to choose the eight records he would take with him on a desert island, he included "*Mache dich mein Herze rein*" from J. S. Bach's *St. Matthew Passion*. "The interviewer was unable to understand how I could choose religious music without being religious," Dawkins recalls. "You might as well say, how can you enjoy *Wuthering Heights* when you know perfectly well that Cathy and Heathcliff never really existed?"[11]

The beauty of Bach's oratorio does not spring from the text, but from his own musical imagination. In Bach's time and place, the church was the only institution that could have supported an opus of such grandeur. The words, culled from the Gospel of Matthew and librettist Picander (Christian Friedrich Henrici), provided Bach a platform upon which to apply his genius. But financial source and linguistic ingredients should not be confused with inspiration. There are numerous cases of composers jumping between sacred and secular subjects, and rarely do they make discernable distinctions. Bach can be grouped among them. Their style, passion, and approach remain virtually the same. Moreover, there are some composers, like Ralph Vaughan Williams, who suspend their own agnosticism to sincerely and convincingly set religious words to music.

More important, our response to these creations is not determined by their ideational content. The music or visual art tends to hit us before we realize what it conveys, and even after we recognize the image or implication, we can stay enthralled. The same occurs when we gravitate to a pop song. The lyrics might be repugnant, imbecilic, or otherwise offensive (if they are intelligible at all), but the music still moves us.

Notes

1. Adoniram Judson Gordon, *Congregational Worship* (Boston: Young and Bartlett, 1874), 60.
2. Benjamin Ray, *African Religions: Symbol, Ritual, and Community*, 2nd ed. (Upper Saddle River, NJ: Prentice Hall, 1999), 17.
3. Jonathan Edwards, *A Treatise Concerning Religious Affections* [1746] (New York: Cosimo, 2007), 27.
4. Paul Thagard, "The Emotional Coherence of Religion," *Journal of Cognition and Culture* 5:1–2 (2005): 64.
5. Gerald Schoenewolf, "Emotional Contagion: Behavioral Induction in Individuals and Groups," *Modern Psychoanalysis* 15 (1990): 50.

6. Émile Durkheim, *The Elementary Forms of Religious Life* [1912], trans. Karen E. Fields (New York: Free Press, 1995), 44.
7. John Locke, *A Letter Concerning Toleration* [1689] (Huddersfield, UK: J. Brook, 1796), 14.
8. Ibid.
9. Michelle Z. Rosaldo, "Toward an Anthropology of Self and Feeling," in *Culture Theory: Essays on Mind, Self and Emotion*, ed. Richard Shewder and Robert LeVine (New York: Cambridge University Press, 1984), 137–157.
10. Nelson Edmondson, "An Agnostic Response to Christian Art," *Journal of Aesthetic Education* 15:4 (1981): 31.
11. Richard Dawkins, *The God Delusion* (New York: Houghton Mifflin Harcourt, 2006), 253.

Suggestions for Further Readings

Beck, Guy L. *Sacred Sound: Experiencing Music in World Religions*. Waterloo: Wilfred Laurier University Press, 2006.
Begbie, Jeremy S., and Steven R. Guthrie, eds. *Resonant Witness: Conversations Between Music and Theology*. Grand Rapids, MI: Eerdmans, 2011.
Blackwell, Albert L. *The Sacred in Music*. Louisville, KY: Westminster John Knox Press, 1999.
Bohlman, Philip V., Edith L. Blumhofer, and Maria M. Chow, eds. *Music in American Religious Experience*. New York: Oxford University Press, 2006.
Friedmann, Jonathan L., comp. *Music, Theology and Worship: Selected Writings, 1841–1896*. Jefferson, NC: McFarland, 2011.
_____. *The Value of Sacred Music: An Anthology of Essential Writings, 1801–1918*. Jefferson, NC: McFarland, 2009.
Leaver, Robin A., and Joyce Ann Zimmerman, eds. *Liturgy and Music: Lifetime Learning*. Collegeville, MN: Liturgical Press, 1998.
Marini, Stephen. *Sacred Song in America: Religion, Music, and Public Culture*. Urbana and Chicago: University of Illinois Press, 2003.
Sullivan, Lawrence E., ed. *Enchanting Powers: Music in the World's Religions*. Cambridge, MA: Harvard University Press, 1997.
Viladesau, Richard. *Theology and the Arts: Encountering God through Music, Art and Rhetoric*. New York: Paulist, 2000.

20

Spirituality

Music has been called the most spiritual of the arts. The basis for this claim is twofold: music is auditory and thus lacks a physical substance, and music primarily impacts the ineffable realm of emotions. This chapter elaborates on the spiritual component of musical phenomena. It begins with Kurt Vonnegut's argument that all music is spiritual. From there, it describes music's ability to change moods, inspire epiphanies, bypass the confusion of words, induce peak experiences, expand consciousness, inspire supernatural imagery, and transcend the intellect.

Music of Champions

In the preface to *Breakfast of Champions*, Kurt Vonnegut describes the book as a fiftieth-birthday present to himself. It is a gift more therapeutic than celebratory. He likens the novel to "a sidewalk strewn with junk, trash which I throw over my shoulders as I travel in time back to November eleventh, nineteen hundred and twenty-two."[1] The junk consists of childish drawings (of assholes, flags, underpants, and so on), characters recycled from previous stories, and absurd science-fiction plots he never intended to develop into books. At the end of the confessional prelude, Vonnegut assures the reader that while this garbage must be emptied, he does not want to throw away any "sacred things." The sacraments he cites are Armistice Day, *Romeo and Juliet*, and all music.

The categories these things represent are fairly conventional. Most religious systems include holidays, stories and music deemed sacred. But Vonnegut's choices are more personal. He was a humanist without creedal ties. Armistice Day, which happened to be his birthday, was an important part of his childhood (he had no similar regard for the Veteran's Day that would replace it). He considered Shakespeare the wisest of human beings (though, he admitted, that wasn't saying much). He was less selective when it came to music. In fact, he was not selective at all.

20. Spirituality

Is there any wisdom in Vonnegut's view that all music is sacred? Strictly speaking, sacred music is an established taxonomic classification. It is music performed or composed for religious use and/or created under religious influence. It goes by many names: worship music, religious music, liturgical music, devotional music, ecclesiastical music, etc. But Vonnegut was not referring to any specialized musical purpose or context. To him, music—generically and without judgment—is a sacred thing.

To understand this viewpoint, we should look at the word "sanctity," which derives from the Latin term *sanctum*, or "set apart." Specifically, it denotes something that is set apart from the profane or ordinary.

Music fits this description in at least seven ways: (1) It is perceived as distinct from other noises; (2) Words set to music rise above everyday speech; (3) Our propensity for music-making distinguishes us from other animals; (4) Musical sounds penetrate otherwise untapped areas of consciousness; (5) Music has "extra-physical" power over our emotions; (6) Music is suggestive of a force greater than ourselves; (7) Any music can be set apart as special by an individual.

As inherently judgmental creatures, we might not agree with Vonnegut's uncritical appraisal. We might also be cautious not to take his statement too seriously, given his track record of sarcasm and his usual penchant for sharp criticism. However, it is reasonable to accept his words at face value. All music likely *was* sacred to him, even as most other things were not (and many things were merely trash).

Breakfast of Champions was not the only place Vonnegut expressed this opinion. Elsewhere, he contrasted the brokenness he saw in the world with the purity he heard in music. This is most clearly written in his collection of essays, *A Man Without a Country*: "No matter how corrupt, greedy, and heartless our government, our corporations, our media, and our religious and charitable institutions may become, the music will still be wonderful."[2]

Music Shapes the World

As he grew older, Tomas Edison became increasingly fascinated with the alleged mystical powers of sound and music. Inspired by the spiritualism and paranormal craze of the decades surrounding the turn of last century, Edison announced in 1920 that he was developing a machine that could communicate with the dead. He reasoned that if a spirit world actually existed, an extremely sensitive device was needed to converse with it. A little closer to reality, Edison conducted a series of Mood Change Parties, in which participants listened to recordings and filled out charts documenting their responses. The goal was to link mood changes—worried to carefree, nervous to composed, etc.—with corresponding musical stimuli.

One of these "parties" took place in a Yale University psychology class. As a newspaper described it, it aimed "toward alleviating neurotic conditions, with a view of discovering psychological antidotes for depressed conditions of mind whether due to fatigue or disappointment."[3] Similar experiments were conducted at other Ivy League schools, giving an air of legitimacy to the proceedings despite company documents showing little serious interest in the project's scientific merits or lack thereof. Not surprisingly, both the séance device and the Mood Change Parties were, more than anything, elaborate marketing ploys.

Whatever the motives, the machine designed for the deceased and the parties intended for the living grew from Edison's awareness that sound could manipulate the psychological atmosphere. Pseudoscientific claims aside, it is clear that certain tone patterns used in certain environments can cause us to feel *as if* something otherworldly is occurring (hence the effect of science fiction film scores). Likewise, a group of people with common cultural backgrounds (such as Yale students in the 1920s) usually have shared reactions to changes in tone sequences—the differences being only in degree.

In both cases, too, sound-triggered transformations are perceived not just in the internal realm of emotions, but also in the surrounding environment. The room itself is felt to shift from heavy to light, tense to relaxed, sterile to active, etc. But these are really psychological shifts. From a philosophical standpoint, this adds support to the notion that the mind shapes the world around us. Before we can begin to apply rational thought, subconscious processes organize data coming to us through our senses, and largely determine what it is we are experiencing. Musical sounds strike us on such an all-consuming and mind-altering level that the emotions stirred interiorly tend to influence how we perceive the exterior world.

In Edison's experiments, this was demonstrated both in the presumed way that aural changes could create an ambience conducive to communicating with the dead, and the more realistic idea that the mood of a party—not just those in attendance—could change in accordance with listening selections. In this modest sense, music can be said to shape the world around us.

Spirit in Sound

"Wagner is my religion."[4] Thus said an enthusiast when asked by a friend why he had not been attending church. The response was certainly not a comment on Wagner the man, whose character and views are even less worthy of devotion than the average person. Nor was it meant to imply that Wagner's music was sufficient to replace the multi-layered and multi-faceted complexity of religious affiliation. Not coincidentally, the quip hearkened back to words penned by Wagner himself, namely: "I found true art to be at one with true religion," and "[I]f we obliterate or extinguish music, we extinguish the last light God has left burning within us."[5]

What, if anything, should be gleaned from the remarks of Wagner and the extoller of his musical virtues? Is it not careless to compare works of music to religious beliefs and practices? How can listening to music possibly fulfill the duties and obligations placed on the religiously observant? Is human-made music really comparable to the light of God? Are these statements hyperbolic or intentionally provocative?

These and similar questions appear on their face to be reasonable challenges. Surely, it is impossible for music to replace the awesomeness of a deity or the dogma, ritual and pageantry a deity commands. But this line of questioning does not accurately address the "music as religion" position. It is better to ask if and how, on an experiential level, music satisfies central aims and expectations of religious adherence.

A musical experience might involve a series of quasi-religious epiphanies. Attaining them depends on a number of conditions, not the least of which are the listener's orientation and attributes of the music itself. Just as religious practices yield varying and circumstantially shaped results, epiphanic musical moments can sometimes be unobtainable, at times fleeting and other times long-lasting. Any discussion of the overlap of music and religion must therefore begin with recognition that we are dealing with ideals.

Potential musical revelations include the following: Penetrating tones might stimulate deep introspection; Emotional and kinesthetic reactions might suggest the indwelling presence of a spiritual force; The arrangement of sonic materials might evoke a sense of cosmic order; The abundance of sound might suggest a transcendent power; The creativity the music exudes might inspire renewed faith in humanity; The listener might be motivated to translate the music into positive action. In these and other ways, musical and religious engagement can have similar (or even identical) benefits.

R. Heber Newton, a turn-of-the-twentieth-century Episcopalian writer and priest, supplied a summation of this effect in his treatise, *The Mysticism of Music*. In characteristically eloquent language, he compared the feelings roused at a concert with those derived from religious activities: "Here is the broad thought known to all who love music intelligently, that it expresses, outside of the church, the highest principles of religion and morality, as they influence the sentiments and actions of men. Music vindicates thus the cardinal principle of religion, its central article of faith—that human life, as such, is divine, that the secular is after all sacred."[6]

What Heber observed and what has been described above is probably closer to spirituality than religion proper. Religion is a technical term encompassing an intricate network of social, historical, cultural, doctrinal, aesthetic and ritual elements. Music alone cannot replace such a system. But, again, this misses the point. Religion and secular music converge in the arena of outcomes. They might differ in substance and intention, but can be directed toward like ends.

Spirituality of the Human

Many secular people are averse to the term "spirituality." To them, it connotes something hopelessly religious, patently unscientific and irrationally romantic. These objections are not unfounded. The popularization of spirituality in the twentieth century owed to theologians like Rudolf Otto, religious enthusiasts like William James, and New Age groups like the Theosophical Society. We have inherited the term from pious sources, associate it with mystics and proselytizers, and encounter it in devotional discourse. As a result, the very idea of "secular spirituality" might seem a careless cooption of a faith-filled concept or, worse, a laughable oxymoron.

But a growing number of secularists are adopting "spirituality" as a useful designation. They discard the supernaturalism of an immortal soul, divine entity or astral plane, but recognize opportunities for transcendence in human qualities such as compassion, love, harmony and contentment. These ideals exist prior to and independent of religious doctrine. Without relying on otherworldly interpretations or deistic explanations, secular spirituality seeks inner tranquility, pursues higher virtues and cultivates awareness of something greater than our physical selves.

While this process takes place in the realm of cognition, the overall effect is, by definition, beyond the ordinary experiences of mind and matter. It is thus better to describe it by way of example than to rely upon the limited resources of language.

There is a church in Albuquerque, New Mexico, that boasts of offering Sunday services "minus religion." It is called the Church of Beethoven, a congregation dedicated to presenting "professional live music performances of the highest quality, together with other artistic expressions from fields including poetry ... in a manner that transcends the commonplace."[7] The church gathers each week for a one-hour program, typically consisting of a short musical selection, a poetry reading, a two-minute "celebration of silence," and a substantial work of chamber music. According to its founder, Felix Wurman, the gathering places music "as the principal element, rather than as an afterthought."[8]

It is no coincidence that music plays a key role in many of the world's religions. Melodic expression, it is widely believed, helps prepare us for transcendence. Yet music designed for sacred purposes is generally used in support of words ("worship music" usually refers to song-settings of poetry and prayer). Such music is programmatic, guided by textual narratives and meant to convey specific extra-musical themes. In contrast, most of the music performed at the Church of Beethoven is absolute, or music for its own sake. For example, a past service consisted of Bach's Sonata in E-minor, Höller's SCAN for Solo Flute, and Mozart's Quartet for Flute, Violin, Viola and Cello. The intent behind this music is not religious per se. However, as the church insists, these performances can foster the ecstasy and communal bonding one would expect from a religious service—just without the dogma.

Music has the potential to bring us to a higher place. This can occur within or outside expressly ecclesiastical contexts, and may be achieved with music made for many purposes. The Church of Beethoven embraces this realization. It offers an alternative to conventional worship services, which are cluttered with rules of doctrine and practice. Its gatherings are, in a way, "pure" activities, unhindered by agenda or ideology. The same applies when we find spiritual uplift in a child's joy, the sight of nature and other this-worldly pleasures. Spirituality belongs to us all.

Musical Peaks

Music is a common element of trance. Musical sounds combine with other sensual cues—like incense and bright ornate colors—to bring individuals into feelings of euphoria and a perceived connection with a sacred realm. In the Santería religion of West Africa and the Caribbean, songs with repetitive and extended rhythmic patterns are played to call upon deities, known as *orishas*. A typical ceremony begins with *oro seco*, dry drumming without singing, followed by a salute to Elegúa, the messenger between gods and humans. Next comes the *oro cantado*, or sung prayer, during which individual *orishas* respond to set rhythms and musical themes, and enter the bodies of consecrated priests—a sensation called "mounting the horse." The musicians and dancers, propelled by polyrhythmic textures and repetitious melodies, continue performing for many hours. The emotions and physical exertion escalate as the ceremony carries on. The end goal is spirit possession, in which *orishas* are believed to work within the possessed and deliver messages, advice and healing.

This is just one culturally and religiously specific example of how rhythm, melody, dance and belief merge to inspire feelings of transcendence. The type and level of rapture will vary according to factors like physical space, group makeup, belief system and style and duration of the musical episode. How and for what reason the trance is induced is situational: it takes different forms and is interpreted differently depending on whether the context is Hassidic, Dervish, Santerian or something else. Moreover, similar feelings can be aroused at secular venues like a rave or rock concert, and can potentially be achieved in unplanned and informal dance sessions done in private.

The diversity of perceived causes and meanings indicates two things. First, human beings seem to be drawn to this kind of experience. We have an instinctual urge for ecstatic moments and use music and dance to reach them. Second, it is in the level of interpretation—prior to and afterward —that we assign meaning to what takes place. The kinds of responses that occur are essentially identical from person to person and group to group, but the environments and explanations span a wide spectrum of possibilities. Many of them involve some form of theological language, as with the notion of *orishas* possessing their invokers. But is this a necessary component?

Dance trances, in all their multifarious incarnations, exemplify what Abraham Maslow called peak experiences. Maslow, a humanist psychologist, rejected the premise that supernatural forces ignite feelings regarded as spiritual. Instead, he saw these "peaks" as perfectly natural moments of self-actualization: especially exciting events involving sudden feelings of wholeness, elation, epiphany and awe. These wondrous instances can be triggered by an assortment of inducements, including love, works of art, the beauty of nature and music.

In *The Farther Reaches of Human Nature*, Maslow cites listeners of classical music who describe themselves being delivered to "great joy," "ecstasy," "visions of another world" and "another level of living."[9] A few sentences later, he notes the consciousness-altering effect of music when it "melts over, fuses over, into dancing or rhythm." According to Maslow, the potential outcome of such peak experiences is manifold. They can release creative energy, affirm the value of existence, renew a sense of purpose and promote oneness with the universe. And the mark they leave can be permanent, reorienting the individual for the better.

Again, none of this depends on an external power; it all takes place within the "farther reaches" of the body and mind. In this sense, there is no inherent contrast between spiritual/religious experiences and peak/highly emotional experiences. They are one and the same. The only difference is whether religious or secular language is used to contextualize and interpret what has occurred. Regardless of how we choose to frame such experiences, they demonstrate the human propensity—and need—for extraordinary moments.

Consciousness, Cognition and Music

An issue of *The International Journal for the Psychology of Religion* published over a decade ago includes two conflicting articles on the nature of spiritual awareness. The first, by Robert A. Emmons, argues for what he terms "spiritual intelligence."[10] The second, by John D. Mayer, challenges Emmons's formulation, replacing it with "spiritual consciousness." More than a semantic squabble, their contrasting approaches address whether or not spirituality should be viewed as a form of cognitive activity or as an enigmatic element of consciousness.

Emmons offers a five-part definition of spiritual intelligence: (1) the capacity for transcendence; (2) the ability to enter into heightened states; (3) the ability to find sacredness in relationships and everyday actions; (4) the ability to use spiritual resources to solve problems; (5) the capacity for virtuous behavior. The problem with this list, in Mayer's view, is its reliance on "ability" and "capacity"—language ordinarily reserved for discussions of mental aptitude and high-level reasoning. In classical discourse, abstract thought is the first hallmark and foremost attribute of intelligence. It involves executing various kinds of mental transformations, such as identifying patterns, generalizing information, registering similarities, contrasting dissimilarities and performing other regulated cognitive functions. From Mayer's perspective, forcing spirituality into this limiting arena of cognition is more indicative of a desire to raise the prestige of spirituality than an accurate representation of what it entails.

As a corrective, Mayer modifies Emmons's intelligence model to convey what psychologists call "structuring" or "developing" consciousness. He removes spirituality from the realm of reasoning and places it in the mysterious territory of consciousness, where it resides as a phenomenon distinct from rational systems of thought and an activity grounded in mechanisms of an intuitive, rather than cerebral, kind. He rephrases Emmons's characteristics thus: (1) *attending* to the unity of the world and transcending one's existence; (2) *consciously* entering into heightened states; (3) *attending* to the sacred in relationships and everyday actions; (4) *structuring* consciousness so that life problems are seen in light of ultimate concerns; (5) *desiring* to act in a virtuous way (italics from the original). These are processes (as opposed to mental exercises) and give preference to sensations—attending, altering, entering, desiring, etc.—over logic and reasoning.

To be sure, cognition can and usually does play a supporting role in spirituality. Religious stories, mythologies, doctrines, customs and interpretations provide language with which to frame the experience. These conceptions may be rehearsed beforehand, recalled during the act, or reflected upon afterward. But such discernment is ultimately separate from the experience itself. Indeed, the main reason spiritual pursuits elicit feelings of transcendence is because they are, at root, non-rational or supra-rational. They exist apart from ordinary mental states. Thus, argues Mayer, spiritual consciousness should not be confused with intelligence, where abstract thought reigns supreme, and should instead be embraced as a distinct way of knowing, where sensations are processed as meaning-giving and life-changing currents.

Such extra-mental awareness is commonly instigated and sustained through music. The naturalness with which music lends itself to this undertaking has made it a staple of spiritual practices worldwide. To paraphrase English theater critic Jeremy Collier, exposure to musical sounds activates passions that destroy reason. Stated more positively, if we allow ourselves to succumb to and be absorbed in musical stimuli, we can reach a level and category of consciousness discrete from the usual modes of cognition.

This does not mean that all music or all musical contexts are equally conducive to spirituality or will promote that end with equal effect. Nor is it always possible to keep the brain's interpretive functions and critical faculties sufficiently in abeyance to be fully exposed to musical inducements. But the extent to which music is used in public devotion, private meditation and other spiritual praxes proves its potency as a vehicle for transcendence. More importantly, it demonstrates an inherent distinction between mental processing and spiritual consciousness, without depreciating the latter. Spirituality may not be intelligence, but it is indispensable just the same.

Inventing the Supernatural

The conjuring of supernatural explanations for natural phenomena is a hallmark of religious thought. Ancient civilizations freely invented extra-physical explanations for the sun's apparent rise and fall, the occurrence of earthquakes and droughts, the origins of plants and animals, and the collapse of kingdoms. In the spirit-filled world of the ancients, fortunes, failures, ailments, recoveries, victories, tragedies and all manner of circumstances were attributed to divine intervention. The characteristics of the deities and the ways in which they were worshiped varied from place to place, as each group drew upon its own surroundings and experiences. Similar cultural variations persist in religious systems of our day. And despite the great extent to which physical and social sciences have explained things once thought mysterious, the devout continue to frame material existence in supernatural language and imagery.

The concoction of religious ideas to comprehend nature is apparent throughout the history and diversity of religion. Less often considered is how religious notions were devised to account for events of our minds, or inner nature. Dreams, for instance, were (and sometimes still are) believed to be a mechanism of prophecy, revelation or divine inspiration, rather than an involuntary succession of images, sensations and scenarios that occur during certain stages of sleep. Likewise, psychiatric and mood disorders were (and sometimes still are) attributed to demons or divine punishment, rather than genetic, circumstantial or chemical causes.

The ubiquitous association of music and religion can be grouped with the supernatural explications for human nature. Music's often-overwhelming and usually unavoidable hold on our emotions has long been a source of theological discourse. The interaction of this abstract art with our inner being is felt as evidence of a spiritual force. There is no shortage of literature describing how music is a portal to human-divine communion, a conduit for the divine presence, a pathway to the heavenly plane.

The intersection of music and theology is so widely asserted that some commentators refer to worship music as "sung theology" or "theology sung." Contrary to what might be assumed, this is not because worship songs typically involve prayerful words set to music—and thus expose practitioners to theological themes—but rather because our encounter with music transcends the ordinary and hints at something beyond ourselves.

As with other areas of consciousness, religious reasons for music's impact can only resonate with the theologically or spiritually oriented. The philosophical materialists among us require a material explanation. However, as much success as researchers have had deciphering sources of dreams, mental disorders and other arenas of the mind, music remains largely inexplicable. Despite many reasonable theories and promising discoveries, we cannot yet state precisely why we respond to music the way we do.

Of course, the absence of scientific consensus does not make supernatural claims any more valid. Explaining a mystery with a fantasy is a fruitless endeavor. Instead, music demonstrates that we need not fully understand what is happening outside or inside of us to appreciate our experience of it.

Experiencing Music

Music is often referred to as an ineffable art form. The immediacy and intensity with which it manipulates our mind and mood exceeds the ability of words to describe. Yet despite—or perhaps because of—music's mysterious influence, the religiously devout regularly rush to identify its effect as a divine energy or spiritual force. On the opposite end of the worldview spectrum, scientists have reduced the thrill and charm of music to a surge of dopamine and a decrease in the body's post-stress responses. While some explanations have greater veracity than others, they all run counter to claims of ineffability. Indeed, for something allegedly beyond description, there is an enormous amount of attempted elucidations.

An additional irony arises when religious adherents criticize scientists for stripping musical experience of its mystery. In their view, attributing rushes of emotion to chemical reactions obscures and cheapens what is really happening: human-divine contact. But heaping religious terminology on feelings induced by music equally diminishes its enigmatic nature. Labeling it the spirit of God, a holy encounter, or another mystic formulation does not expand our conception. It reduces it.

From an experiential standpoint, it matters little whether our interaction with music is spiritual, material or something in between. Any interpretation—realistic or not—is ultimately separate from the experience itself. This is so regardless if our response is conditioned—as with a religious person hearing religious music in a religious setting—or reflective—as with the researcher who analyzes a musical episode after it has taken place. For an experientialist, who considers experience a valid source of knowledge, it is not the explication that is important, but the occurrence itself. Our musical reactions have intrinsic truth and inherent value prior to and apart from our efforts to explain them.

As intuitive as this might appear, our species is ever consumed with curiosity and a stubborn need for answers. These impulses are intensified when our emotions are strong and circumstances seem out of our control. Such is our relationship with music. However, if we wish to honor and uphold music's inexpressible essence, we must be willing to subdue our urge to describe it. Again, most of us enter the musical experience in a state of wonder and susceptibility. But preserving these pre-cognitive sensations is a challenge, particularly after the sounds have passed and we are left to decipher what has occurred.

This does not mean that every proposed reason for why and how we respond to music should be dismissed out of hand. But there is beauty and virtue in allowing music to be an activity apart. The emotional abandon it promotes and mystery it inspires is particularly beneficial for the rationalist, who is normally engaged in critical evaluation of "life, the universe and everything" (to use Douglas Adams' phrase). We all need a healthy release from our hyperactive brains now and again. Even if music's impact could be fully explained, it is probably best to just surrender to its power and enjoy the ride.

Notes

1. Kurt Vonnegut, *Breakfast of Champions: A Novel* (New York: Random House, 1973), 5.
2. Kurt Vonnegut, *A Man Without a Country* (New York: Seven Stories, 2005), 66.
3. "Note Changes in Mood Caused by Hearing Music," *New Haven Sunday Register*, May 22, 1921.
4. R. Heber Newton, *The Mysticism of Music* [1915], in *The Value of Sacred Music: An Anthology of Essential Writings, 1801–1918*, comp. Jonathan L. Friedmann (Jefferson, NC: McFarland, 2009), 73.
5. Ibid.
6. Ibid., 74.
7. Jonathan L. Friedmann, *Synagogue Song: An Introduction to Concepts, Theories and Customs* (Jefferson, NC: McFarland, 2012), 89.
8. Felix Wurman, quoted in Ibid.
9. Abraham H. Maslow, *The Farther Reaches of Human Nature* (Chapel Hill, NC: Maurice Bassett, 1973), 176.
10. John D. Mayer, "Spiritual Intelligence or Spiritual Consciousness?" *International Journal for the Psychology of Religion* 10:1 (2000): 47–56; Robert A. Emmons, "Spirituality and Intelligence: Problems and Prospects," *International Journal for the Psychology of Religion* 10:1 (2000): 57–64.

Suggestions for Further Reading

Aldridge, David, and Joerg Fachner, eds. *Music and Altered States: Consciousness, Transcendence, Therapy and Addictions.* Philadelphia: Jessica Kingsley, 2005.
Cobussen, Marcel. *Thresholds: Rethinking Spirituality Through Music.* Burlington, VT: Ashgate, 2008.
Crowe, Barbara J. *Music and Soulmaking: Toward a New Theory of Music Therapy.* Lanham, MD: Scarecrow, 2004.

Hale, Susan Elizabeth. *Sacred Space, Sacred Sound: The Acoustic Mysteries of Holy Places.* Wheaton, IL: Quest, 2007.

Jordan, James Mark. *The Musician's Soul: A Journey Examining Spirituality for Performers, Teachers, Composers, Conductors, and Music Educators.* Chicago: GIA, 1999.

St. Vincent, Justin, ed. *The Spiritual Significance of Music.* Auckland: Xtreme Music, 2009.

Schnebly-Black, Julia, and Stephen Moore. *The Rhythm Inside: Connecting Body, Mind, and Spirit Through Music.* Van Nuys, CA: Alfred Music, 2003.

Solomon, Robert C. *Spirituality for the Skeptic: The Thoughtful Love of Life.* New York: Oxford University Press, 2002.

Sylvan, Robin. *Traces of the Spirit: The Religious Dimensions of Popular Music.* New York: New York University Press, 2002.

Van der Leeuw, Gerardus. *Sacred and Profane Beauty: The Holy in Art.* New York: Oxford University Press, 2006.

Bibliography

Addis, Laird. *Of Mind and Music*. Ithaca, NY: Cornell University Press, 2004.

Aitkin, Hugh. *The Piece as a Whole: Studies in Holistic Musical Analysis*. Westport, CT: Greenwood, 1997.

Aldridge, David, and Joerg Fachner, eds. *Music and Altered States: Consciousness, Transcendence, Therapy and Addictions*. Philadelphia: Jessica Kingsley, 2005.

Alleyne, Richard. "Babies Are Born to Dance to the Beat." *The Telegraph*, March 15, 2010. <http://www.telegraph.co.uk/science/science-news/7450560/Babies-are-born-to-dance-to-the-beat.html>.

Alperson, Philip, ed. *What Is Music? An Introduction to the Philosophy of Music*. University Park: Pennsylvania State University Press, 2010.

Alves, William. *Music of the Peoples of the World*. Belmont, CA: Cengage, 2012.

Andrews, Robert, ed. *The Concise Columbia Dictionary of Quotations*. New York: Columbia University Press, 1992.

Appell, Glenn, and David Hemphill. *American Popular Music: A Multicultural History*. Belmont, CA: Cengage, 2010.

Archer, Peter. *The Quotable Intellectual*. Avon, MA: Adams, 2010.

Arnstein, Flora J., Albert I. Elkus, and Stewart W. Young, *Oscar Weil: Letters and Papers*. San Francisco: Book Club of California, 1923.

Augustine. *St. Augustine on the Psalms*. New York: Newman, 1961.

Ball, Philip. *The Music Instinct: How Music Works and Why We Can't Do Without It*. New York: Oxford University Press, 2010.

Bannan, Nicholas, ed. *Music, Language, and Human Evolution*. New York: Oxford University Press, 2012.

Beck, Guy L. *Sacred Sound: Experiencing Music in World Religions*. Waterloo: Wilfred Laurier University Press, 2006.

Beebee, Thomas O. *Ideology of Genre: A Comparative Study of Generic Instability*. University Park: Pennsylvania State University Press, 2004.

Beeching, Angela Myles. *Beyond Talent: Creating a Successful Career in Music*. New York: Oxford University Press, 2005.

Begbie, Jeremy S., and Steven R. Guthrie, eds. *Resonant Witness: Conversations between Music and Theology*. Grand Rapids, MI: Eerdmans, 2011.

Bergeron, Katherine, and Philip V. Bohlman, ed. *Disciplining Music: Musicology and Its Canons*. Chicago: University of Chicago Press, 1992.

Berkeley, George. *A Treatise Concerning the Principles of Human Knowledge* [1710]. Whitefish, MT: Kessinger, 2004.

Berkowitz, Aaron. *The Improvising Mind: Cognition and Creativity in the Musical Moment*. New York: Oxford University Press, 2010.

Berman, Morris. *Coming to Our Senses: Body and Spirit in the Hidden History of the West*. New York: Bantam, 1989.

Berry, Wallace. *Structural Functions in Music*. New York: Dover, 1987.

Bierce, Ambroze. *The Collected Works of*

Ambrose Bierce, vol. VII: *The Devil's Dictionary*. New York: Neale, 1911.
Blacking, John. *How Musical is Man?* Seattle: University of Washington Press, 1973.
Blackwell, Albert L. *The Sacred in Music*. Louisville, KY: Westminster John Knox Press, 1999.
Blanning, T. C. W. *The Triumph of Music: The Rise of Composers, Musicians and Their Art*. Cambridge, MA: Harvard University Press, 2008.
Blomster, Wesley. "Sociology of Music: Adorno and Beyond." *Telos* 28 (1976): 81–112.
Bloom, Howard. *Global Brain: The Evolution of Mass Mind from the Big Bang to the 21st Century*. New York: Wiley, 2000.
Boardman, Eunice, ed. *Dimensions of Musical Thinking*. New York: Rowman and Littlefield, 1989.
Bohlman, Philip V. *The Study of Folk Music in the Modern World*. Bloomington: Indiana University Press, 1988.
———, Edith L. Blumhofer, and Maria M. Chow, eds. *Music in American Religious Experience*. New York: Oxford University Press, 2006.
Bolinger, Dwight L. *The Symbolism of Music*. Yellow Springs, OH: Antioch Press, 1941.
Bowie, Andrew. *Aesthetics and Subjectivity: From Kant to Nietzsche*. Manchester: Manchester University Press, 2003.
Brabazon, Tara. *Popular Music: Topics, Trends, and Trajectories*. London: Sage, 2012.
Bradbury, Ray. *Zen in the Art of Writing*. New York: Bantam, 1992.
Brady, Erica. *A Spiral Way: How the Phonograph Changed Ethnography*. Jackson: University Press of Mississippi, 1999.
Bronowski, Jacob. *The Identity of Man*. Garden City, NY: American Museum Science, 1965.
Brown, Steven, and Ulrik Volgsten, eds. *Music and Manipulation: On the Social Uses and Social Control of Music*. New York: Berghahn Books, 2005.
Brownell, John. "Analytical Modes of Jazz Improvisation." *Jazzforchung/Jazz Research* 26 (1994): 9–29.
Bruscia, Kenneth E. *Defining Music Therapy*. Gilsum, NH: Barcelona, 1998.
Bunt, Leslie. *Music Therapy: An Art Beyond Words*. New York: Taylor and Francis, 2004.
Byrne, David. *How Music Works*. San Francisco: McSweeney's, 2012.
Cahn, William L. *Creative Music Making*. New York: Psychology, 2005.
Carlyle, Thomas. *Works*, vol. 27. New York: Charles Scribner's Sons, 1904.
Carroll, Mark. *Music and Ideology*. Burlington, VT: Ashgate, 2012.
Chanan, Michael. *Repeated Takes: A Short History of Recording and Its Effects on Music*. New York: Verso, 1995.
Changizi, Mark. *Harnessed: How Language and Music Mimicked Nature and Transformed Ape to Man*. Dallas, TX: BenBella, 2011.
Charlton, David, ed. *E. T. A. Hoffmann's Musical Writings: Kreisleriana, the Poet and the Composer, Music Criticism*. New York: Cambridge University Press, 1989.
Chase, Ava R. "Music Discriminations by Carp (Cyprinus Carpio)." *Animal Learning & Behavior* 29:4 (2001): 336–353.
Chorus America. *The Chorus Impact Study: How Children, Adults, and Communities Benefit from Choruses*. Washington, D.C.: Chorus America, 2010.
Chua, Daniel K. L. *Absolute Music and the Construction of Meaning*. New York: University of Cambridge Press, 1999.
Churchland, Patricia S. *Braintrust: What Neuroscience Tells Us About Morality*. Princeton, NJ: Princeton University Press, 2011.
Clarke, Donald. *The Rise and Fall of Popular Music*. New York: St. Martin's Griffen, 1995.
Clarke, Eric, Nicola Dibben, and Stephanie Pitts. *Music and Mind in Everyday Life*. New York: Oxford University Press, 2010.
Clarke, Eric, and Simon Emmerson, eds. *Music, Mind and Structure (Contempo-*

rary Music Review 3:1). New York: Taylor and Francis, 1989.

Cobussen, Marcel. *Thresholds: Rethinking Spirituality Through Music*. Burlington, VT: Ashgate, 2008.

Cochrane, Tom, Bernardino Fantini, and Klaus R. Scherer, eds. *The Emotional Power of Music: Multidisciplinary Perspectives on Musical Arousal, Expression, and Social Control*. New York: Oxford University Press, 2013.

Cohen, Ronald D. *Folk Music: The Basics*. New York: Routledge, 2006.

Connell, John, and Chris Gibson. *Sound Tracks: Popular Music, Identity, and Place*. New York: Psychology, 2003.

Cook, Nicholas. *Beyond the Score: Music as Performance*. New York: Oxford University Press, 2014.

———. *A Guide to Musical Analysis*. New York: Oxford University Press, 1987.

———. *A Very Short Introduction to Music*. New York: Oxford University Press, 1998.

———, and Mark Everis, eds. *Rethinking Music*. New York: Oxford University Press, 1999.

Copland, Aaron. *Music and Imagination*. Cambridge, MA: Harvard University Press, 1980.

Crafts, Susan D. *My Music: Explorations of Music in Daily Life*. Middleton, CT: Wesleyan University Press, 1993.

Črnčec, Rudi, Sarah J. Wilson, and Margot Prior. "The Cognitive and Academic Benefits of Music to Children: Facts and Fiction." *Educational Psychology: An International Journal of Experimental Educational Psychology* 26:4 (2006): 579–594.

Crocker, Richard L. *A History of Musical Style*. New York: Dover, 1986.

Crofton, Ian, and Donald Fraser, comp. *A Dictionary of Musical Quotations*. New York: Macmillan, 1985.

Crowe, Barbara J. *Music and Soulmaking: Toward a New Theory of Music Therapy*. Lanham, MD: Scarecrow, 2004.

Cumming, Naomi. *The Sonic Self: Musical Subjectivity and Signification*. Bloomington: Indiana University Press, 2000.

Dahlhaus, Carl. *Esthetics of Music*. New York: Cambridge University Press, 1982.

———. *The Idea of Absolute Music*. Chicago: University of Chicago Press, 1991.

Danto, Arthur C. *What Art Is*. New Haven, CT: Yale University Press, 2013.

Darwin, Charles. *The Descent of Man*. New York: D. Appleton, 1871.

———. *The Expression of the Emotions in Man and Animals*. New York: D. Appelton, 1872.

Davidson, Jane W. "What Type of Information Is Conveyed in the Body Movements of Solo Musician Performers?" *Journal of Human Movement Studies* 6 (1994): 279–301.

Davie, Cedric Thorpe. *Musical Structure and Design*. New York: Dover, 1966.

Davies, Stephen. *Musical Works and Performances: A Philosophical Exploration*. New York: Oxford University Press, 2001.

———. *Themes in the Philosophy of Music*. New York: Oxford University Press, 2003.

Dawkins, Richard. *The God Delusion*. New York: Houghton Mifflin Harcourt, 2006.

De La Fuente, Eduardo, and Peter Murphy, eds. *Philosophical and Cultural Theories of Music*. Boston: Brill, 2010.

Deland, Lorin F., ed. *The Musical Record: A Journal of Music, Art, Literature* (May 1895).

Deliège, Irène, and Geraint A. Wiggins, ed. *Musical Creativity: Multidisciplinary Research in Theory and Practice*. New York: Psychology, 2006.

Demorest, Steven M., and Steven J. Morrison. "Does Music Make You Smarter?" *Music Educators Journal* 87:2 (2000): 33–39, 58.

DeNora, Tia. *Music in Everyday Life*. New York: Cambridge University Press, 2000.

Descartes, René. *Discourse on Method and Meditations on First Philosophy*, part IV (1637).

Deutsch, Diana. *The Psychology of Music*. Waltham, MA: Academic, 2013.

de Waal, Frans. *The Bonobo and the Athe-*

ist: *In Search of Humanism Among the Primates*. New York: W. W. Norton, 2013.

Diamond, Jared. *Guns, Germs, and Steel: The Fates of Human Societies*. New York: W. W. Norton, 1999.

Dickie, George. *The Century of Taste: The Philosophical Odyssey of Taste in the Eighteenth Century*. New York: Oxford University Press, 1995.

Dickreiter, Michael. *Score Reading: A Key to the Music Experience*. New York: Hal Leonard, 2000.

Dissanayake, Ellen. *Homo Aestheticus: Where Art Comes From and Why*. Seattle: University of Washington Press, 1992.

Dolan, Raymond J., and Tali Sharot, ed. *Neuroscience of Preference and Choice: Cognitive and Neural Mechanisms*. San Diego, CA: Academic, 2012.

Donovan, Siobhán, and Robin Elliott, ed. *Music and Literature in German Romanticism*. Rochester, NY: Camden House, 2004.

Dunbar, Robin. *The Science of Love*. Hoboken, NJ: Wiley, 2012.

Durkheim, Émile. *The Elementary Forms of Religious Life* [1912]. Translated by Karen E. Fields. New York: Free Press, 1995.

Dutton, Denis. *The Art Instinct: Beauty, Pleasure, and Human Evolution*. New York: Bloomsbury, 2009.

Eagleton, Terry. "Why Ideas No Longer Matter: Modern Politicians Deal Only in Facts, Not Philosophical Reasoning." *The Guardian*, March 22, 2004. <http://www.theguardian.com/books/2004/mar/23/immigrationpolicy.politics>

Eco, Umberto. *The Role of the Reader: Explorations in the Semiotics of Texts*. Bloomington, IN: Indiana University Press, 1979.

———. *Six Walks in Fictional Woods*. Cambridge, MA: Harvard University Press, 1994.

Edmondson, Nelson. "An Agnostic Response to Christian Art." *Journal of Aesthetic Education* 15:4 (1981): 31–44.

Edwards, Jonathan. *A Treatise Concerning Religious Affections* [1746]. New York: Cosimo, 2007.

Eggebrecht, Hans Heinrich. *Understanding Music: The Nature and Limits of Musical Cognition*. Burlington, VT: Ashgate, 2010.

Einstein, Alfred. *A Short History of Music*. New York: Alfred A. Knopf, 1954.

Eliade, Mircea. *The Myth of the Eternal Return*. Princeton, NJ: Princeton University Press, 1991.

Emmons, Robert A. "Spirituality and Intelligence: Problems and Prospects." *International Journal for the Psychology of Religion* 10:1 (2000): 57–64.

Empson, Barry. "Schoenberg's Hat: Objects in Musical Space." In *Frameworks, Artworks, Place: The Space of Perception in the Modern World*, edited by Timothy J. Mehigan. Amsterdam: Rodopi, 2008. 83–96.

Erickson, Robert. *Sound Structure in Music*. Berkeley: University of California Press, 1975.

Ericsson, K. Anders, ed. *The Road to Excellence: The Acquisition of Expert Performance in the Arts and Sciences, Sports, and Games*. New York: Psychology, 2014.

Fekete, S., C. Winding, and T. Rülicke. "Effect of Human as Well as Rodentized Mozart and Bach Music on the Open-Field Activity of BALB/c Mice." Paper presented at the CEELA-II Triannual Conference, Budapest, 2012.

Ferguson, Donald N. *The Why of Music: Dialogues in an Unexplored Region of Appreciation*. Minneapolis: University of Minnesota Press, 1969.

Fowler, Thomas. "The Ethics of Intellectual Work and Life." *International Journal of Ethics* 9 (1899): 296–349.

Freedberg, David, and Vittorio Gallese, "Motion, Emotion and Empathy in Esthetic Experience." *Trends in Cognitive Sciences* 5:197 (2007): 197–203.

Friedman, Daniel. "Art and Nature: Beauty and Spirituality." In *Secular Spirituality: Passionate Journey to a Rational Judaism*, edited by M. Bonnie Cousens.

Farmington Hills, MI: Milan, 2003. 101–108.

Friedmann, Jonathan L., comp. *Music, Theology and Worship: Selected Writings, 1841–1896*. Jefferson, NC: McFarland, 2011.

_____, ed. *Quotations on Jewish Sacred Music*. Lanham, MD: Hamilton, 2011.

_____. *Synagogue Song: An Introduction to Concepts, Theories and Customs*. Jefferson, NC: McFarland, 2012.

_____, comp. *The Value of Sacred Music: An Anthology of Essential Writings, 1801–1918*. Jefferson, NC: McFarland, 2009.

Frith, Simon, ed. *Music and Identity* (Popular Music, vol. 4). New York: Routledge, 2004.

_____. *Performing Rites: On the Value of Popular Music*. Cambridge, MA: Harvard University Press, 1998.

_____. *Taking Popular Music Seriously: Selected Essays*. Burlington, VT: 2007.

Fuller, Thomas. *History of the Worthies of England*, vol. 1. London: Thomas Tegg, 1840.

Gabrielsson, Alf. *Strong Experiences with Music: Music Is Much More Than Just Music*. New York: Oxford University Press, 2011.

Gaffurius, Franchinus. *Practica musicae*, Book 1 (Millan: 1496).

Galewitz, Herb, ed. *Music: A Book of Quotations*. New York: Dover, 2001.

Gelbart, Matthew. *The Invention of Folk Music and Art Music: Emerging Categories from Ossian to Wagner*. New York: Cambridge University Press, 2007.

Gladwell, Malcolm. *Outliers: The Story of Success*. New York: Hachette, 2008.

Godøy, Rolf Inge, and Marc Leman, eds. *Musical Gestures: Sound, Movement, and Meaning*. New York: Routledge, 2010.

Goldsmith, Mike. *Discord: The History of Noise*. New York: Oxford University Press, 2012.

Goldsmith, Oliver. *The Miscellaneous Works of Oliver Goldsmith*, vol. 1. Edited by James Prior. London: John Murray, 1837.

Gordon, Adoniram Judson. *Congregational Worship*. Boston: Young and Bartlett, 1874.

Gordon, Edwin. *The Aural/Visual Experience of Music Literacy: Reading and Writing Music Notation*. Chicago, GIA: 2004.

Govaner, Alan B. *Everyday Music: Exploring Sounds and Cultures*. College Station: Texas A&M University Press, 2012.

Gracyk, Theodore. *Listening to Popular Music, Or, How I Learned to Stop Worrying and Love Led Zeppelin*. Ann Arbor: University of Michigan Press, 2007.

_____. *On Music*. New York: Routledge, 2013.

_____, and Andrew Kania, eds. *The Routledge Companion to Philosophy of Music*. New York: Routledge, 2011.

Granat, Helen. *Wisdom Through the Ages: A Collection of Favorite Quotations*. Victoria, BC, Canada: Miklen, 1998.

Grant, Ulysses S. *Personal Memoirs of Ulysses S. Grant* [1885–1886]. New York: Cosimo, 2007.

Gronow, Pekka, and Ilpo Saunio. *International History of the Recording Industry*. New York: Bloomsbury, 1999.

Haas, Karl. *Inside Music: How to Understand, Listen To, and Enjoy Good Music*. New York: Anchor, 1991.

Haeckel, Ernst. *The History of Creation, or, The Development of the Earth and Its Inhabitants by the Action of Natural Causes*. New York: D. Appleton, 1892.

Hale, Susan Elizabeth. *Sacred Space, Sacred Sound: The Acoustic Mysteries of Holy Places*. Wheaton, IL: Quest, 2007.

Hallam, Susan, Ian Cross, and Michael Thaut. *Oxford Handbook of Music Psychology*. New York: Oxford University Press, 2008.

Hanchett, Henry Granger. *The Art of the Musician: A Guide to the Intelligent Appreciation of Music*. New York: Macmillan, 1905.

Hansen, Dee, and Elaine Bernstorf. "Linking Music Learning to Reading Instruction." *Music Educators Journal* 88:5 (2002): 17–21, 52.

Hegel, Georg Wilhelm Friedrich. *Aesthetics: Lectures on Fine Art*. Translated by

T. M. Knox. Oxford: Oxford University Press, 1975.

Heline, Corinne. *Music: The Keynote of Human Evolution.* Santa Barbara, CA: J. F. Rowny Press, 1965.

Hendy, David. *Noise: A Human History of Sound and Listening.* New York: HarperCollins, 2013.

Herbert, Trevor. *Music in Words: A Guide to Researching and Writing about Music.* New York: Oxford University Press, 2009.

Herzog, George. "Music's Dialects: A Non-Universal Language." *Independent Journal of Columbia University* 6:10 (1939): 1–2.

Higgins, Kathleen Marie. *The Music Between Us: Is Music a Universal Language?* Chicago: University of Chicago Press, 2012.

Hoffmann, E. T. A. *Werke.* Edited by Georg Ellinger. Berlin: Deutsches, 1900.

Holoman, Kern D. *Writing About Music: A Style Sheet.* Berkeley: University of California Press, 2008.

Horn, Stacey. "Singing Changes Your Brain." *Time,* August 16, 2013. <http://ideas.time.com/2013/08/16/singing-changes-your-brain/>

"How Many Melodies Are There in the Universe?" Everything2. <http://everything2.com/title/How+many+melodies+are+there+in+the+universe%253F>.

Howard, Keith, ed. *Music as Intangible Cultural Heritage: Policy, Ideology, and Practice in the Preservation of East Asian Traditions.* Burlington, VT: Ashgate, 2012.

Howard, Vernon Alfred. *Charm and Speed: Virtuosity in the Performing Arts.* New York: Peter Lang, 2008.

Hoy, Ronald R. "Acute as a Bug's Ear: An Informal Discussion of Hearing in Insects." In *Comparative Hearing: Insects,* edited by Ronald R. Hoy, Arthur N. Popper and Richard R. Fray. New York: Springer, 1998. 11–17.

Hughes, Robert. *Nothing If Not Critical: Essays on Art and Artists.* New York: Random House, 2012.

Hugo, Victor. *William Shakespeare.* London: Hauteville, 1864.

Hull, Geoffrey P., Thomas William Hutchison, and Richard Strasser. *The Music Business and Recording Industry: Delivering Music in the 21st Century.* New York: Taylor and Francis, 2011.

Huron, David. *Sweet Anticipation: Music and the Psychology of Expectation.* Cambridge, MA: MIT Press, 2006.

Huxley, Aldous. *Music at Night and Other Essays.* Leipzig: Albatross, 1931.

_____. *The Perennial Philosophy.* New York: Harper, 1940.

Ingarden, Roman. *The Work of Music and the Problem of Its Identity.* Berkeley: University of California Press, 1986.

Inglis, Ian. *Performance and Popular Music: History, Place and Time.* Burlington, VT: Ashgate, 2013.

Izdebski, Krzysztof. *Emotions in the Human Voice: Foundations.* San Diego, CA: Plural, 2007.

James, William. *The Varieties of Religious Experience.* London: Longmans, Green, 1905.

Janes, E. "The Emotions in Music" [1874]. In *The Value of Sacred Music: An Anthology of Essential Writings, 1801–1918,* compiled by Jonathan L. Friedmann. Jefferson, NC: McFarland, 2009. 91–98.

Jankélévitch, Vladimir. *Music and the Ineffable.* Translated by Carolyn Abbate. Princeton, NJ: Princeton University Press, 2003.

Jenner, Gustav. "Johannes Brahms as Man, Teacher, and Artist." In *Brahms and His World,* edited by Walter Frisch and Kevin C. Karnes. Princeton, NJ: Princeton University Press, 2009. 381–424.

Jones, Mari Reiss, Richard R. Fay, and Arthur Popper, eds. *Music Perception.* New York: Springer, 2010.

Jordan, James Mark. *The Musician's Soul: A Journey Examining Spirituality for Performers, Teachers, Composers, Conductors, and Music Educators.* Chicago: GIA, 1999.

Jordania, Joseph. *Why Do People Sing? Music in Human Evolution.* Tbilisi: Logos, 2011.

Juslin, Patrik N., and Petri Laukka. "Communication of Emotions in Vocal Expression and Musical Performance: Different Channels, Same Code?" *Psychological Bulletin* 129 (2003): 770–814.

Kappas, Arvid, Ursula Hess, and Klaus R. Scherer. "Voice and Emotion." In *Fundamental od Nonverbal Behavior*, edited by Robert Stephen Feldman and Bernard Rimé. New York: Cambridge University Press, 1991. 200–238.

Karnes, Kevin. *Ethnicity, Identity, and Music: The Musical Construction of Place*. New York: Oxford University Press, 2008.

Karpf, Anne. *The Human Voice: The Story of a Remarkable Talent*. New York: Bloomsbury, 2011.

Katsh, Shelley, and Carol Merle-Fishman. *The Music Within You*. Gilsum, NH: Barcelona, 1998.

Katz, Ruth, ed. *Contemplating Music: Source Readings in the Aesthetics of Music*. New York: Pendragon, 1987.

Kerman, Joseph. *Contemplating Music: Challenges to Musicology*. Cambridge, MA: Harvard University Press, 2009.

Kierkegaard, Søren. *Either-Or*. Translated by Water Lowrie. Princeton, NJ: Princeton University Press, 1974.

Kivy, Peter. *Authenticities: Philosophical Reflections on Musical Performance*. Ithaca, NY: Cornell University Press, 1995.

———. *Introduction to a Philosophy of Music*. New York: Clarendon, 2002.

Klickstein, Gerald. *The Musician's Way: A Guide to Practice, Performance, and Wellness*. New York: Oxford University Press, 2009.

Kolb, David, and Ronald Fry. "Toward an Applied Theory of Experiential Learning." In *Theories of Group Processes*, edited by Cary L. Cooper. New York: John Wiley, 1975. 33–57.

Krause, Bernie. *The Great Animal Orchestra: Finding the Origins of Music in the World's Wild Places*. New York: Little, Brown, and Co., 2012.

———. *Wild Soundscapes: Discovering the Voice of the Natural World*. Berkeley: Wilderness, 2002.

Krims, Adam, ed. *Music/ideology: Resisting the Aesthetic*. New York: Psychology, 1998.

Krugman, Paul. "Everyone Has an Ideology." *The New York Times*, April 13, 2011. <http://krugman.blogs.nytimes.com/2011/04/13/everyone-has-an-ideology/>

Langer, Susanne K. *Philosophy in a New Key: A Study in the Symbolism of Reason, Rite, and Art*. New York: Mentor, 1964.

Langlois, Judith H., and Lori A. Roggman. "Attractive Faces are Only Average." *Psychological Science* 1:2 (1990): 115–121.

Leaver, Robin A., and Joyce Ann Zimmerman, eds. *Liturgy and Music: Lifetime Learning*. Collegeville, MN: Liturgical Press, 1998.

Lee, Harper. *To Kill a Mockingbird*. New York: HarperCollins, 1988.

Legdin, Stephanie P. *Discovering Folk Music*. Santa Barbara, CA: ABC-CLIO, 2010.

Lehmann, Andreas C., John A. Sloboda, and Robert H. Woody. *Psychology for Musicians: Understanding and Acquiring the Skills*. New York: Oxford University Press, 2007.

Lehrer, Keith. *Art, Self and Knowledge*. New York: Oxford University Press, 2011.

Leppert, Richard, and Susan McClary, eds. *Music and Society: The Politics of Composition, Performance and Reception*. New York: Cambridge University Press, 1989.

Lévi-Strauss, Claude. *The Raw and the Cooked*. Translated by John and Doreen Weightman. New York: Harper and Row, 1969.

Levitin, Daniel J. *This is Your Brain on Music: The Science of a Human Obsession*. New York: Plume, 2007.

———. *The World in Six Songs: How the Musical Brain Created Human Nature*. New York: Penguin, 2008.

Lewis, Bernard. *History: Remembered, Recovered, Invented*. New York: Simon & Schuster, 1987.

Lippman, Edward A. *Musical Aesthetics:*

The Nineteenth Century. New York: Pendragon, 1986.

Locke, John. *A Letter Concerning Toleration* [1689]. Huddersfield, UK: J. Brook, 1796.

Loersch, Chris, and Nathan L. Arbuckle. "Unraveling the Mystery of Music: Music as an Evolved Group Process." *Journal of Personality and Social Psychology* 105 (2013): 777–798.

London, Fran. "An Insider's View: How We Traveled from Obscurity to the Klezmer Establishment in Twenty Years." In *American Klezmer: Its Roots and Offshoots*, edited by Mark Slobin. Berkeley: University of California Press, 2002. 206–210.

Lussy, Mathis. *Musical Expression, Accents, Nuances, and Tempo, in Vocal and Instrumental Music*. Stockbridge, MA: Hard Press, 2012.

Machin, David. *Analysing Popular Music: Image, Sound and Text*. London: Sage, 2010.

Marini, Stephen. *Sacred Song in America: Religion, Music, and Public Culture*. Urbana and Chicago: University of Illinois Press, 2003.

Marler, Peter R., and Hans Slabbekoorn. *Nature's Music: The Science of Birdsong*. San Diego, CA: Academic, 2004.

Martinelli, Dario. *Of Birds, Whales, and Other Musicians: An Introduction to Zoomusicology*. Scranton, PA: University of Scranton Press, 2009.

Maslow, Abraham H. *The Farther Reaches of Human Nature*. Chapel Hill, NC: Maurice Bassett, 1973.

Masson, Jeffrey Moussaieff, and Susan McCarthy. *When Elephants Weep: The Emotional Lives of Animals*. New York: Random House, 1995.

Mattick, Paul. "The Institutions of Art." Paper presented at the Forty-Seventh Annual Meeting of the American Society for Aesthetics, New York City, October 25, 1989.

Mayer, John D. "Spiritual Intelligence or Spiritual Consciousness?" *International Journal for the Psychology of Religion* 10:1 (2000): 47–56.

Mazzola, Guerino, Joomi Park, and Florian Thalmann. *Musical Creativity: Strategies and Tools in Composition and Improvisation*. New York: Springer, 2011.

McAllister, Lesley Sisterhen. *The Balanced Musician: Integrating Mind and Body for Peak Performance*. New York: Rowman and Littlefield, 2012.

Meyer, Leonard B. *Emotion and Meaning in Music*. Chicago: University of Chicago Press, 1956.

_____. *Style and Music: Theory, History, and Ideology*. Chicago: University of Chicago Press, 1989.

Miller, Geoffrey. "Sexual Selection for Cultural Displays." In *The Evolution of Culture: An Interdisciplinary View*, edited by Robin Dunbar, et al. Edinburgh: Edinburgh University Press, 1999. 71–91.

Mithen, Steven. *The Singing Neanderthals: The Origins of Music, Language, Mind and Body*. London: Weidenfeld and Nicolson, 2005.

Morley, Iain. *The Prehistory of Music: Human Evolution, Archaeology, and the Origins of Musicality*. New York: Oxford University Press, 2013.

Morrison, Grant. *Animal Man: Deus Ex Machina*. New York: DC Comics, 2003.

Mudge, Alden. "Ron Rash: Shaped by the Land, Torn Apart by Intolerance." *BookPage*, April 2012. <http://bookpage.com/interviews/8796-ron-rash#.UznOXihq594>

Murch, Walter. "Hyser Memorial Lecture." Paper presented at the Audio Engineering Society 117th Convention, San Francisco, October 30, 2004.

Nagyvary, Joseph. "A Comparative Study of Power Spectra and Vowels in Guarneri Violins and Operatic Singing." *Savart Journal* 1:3 (2013): 1–30.

Nattiez, Jean-Jacques. *Music and Discourse: Toward a Semiology of Music*. Princeton, NJ: Princeton University Press, 1990.

Neer, Richard. *FM: The Rise and Fall of Rock Radio*. New York: Random House, 2001.

Nettl, Bruno. *The Study of Ethnomusicology: Thirty-One Issues and Concepts*. Champaign: University of Illinois Press, 2005.

Newton, R. Heber. *The Mysticism of Music* [1915], in *The Value of Sacred Music: An Anthology of Essential Writings, 1801–1918*, compiled by Jonathan L. Friedmann (Jefferson, NC: McFarland, 2009), 73–90.

"Note Changes in Mood Caused By Hearing Music." *New Haven Sunday Register*, May 22, 1921.

Nussbaum, Charles O. *The Musical Representation: Meaning, Ontology, and Emotion*. Cambridge, MA: MIT Press, 2007.

Oberman, Heiko Augustinus. *Luther: Man Between God and the Devil*. New Haven, CT: Yale University Press, 2006.

Odena, Oscar, ed. *Musical Creativity: Insights from Music Education Research*. Burlington, VT: Ashgate, 2013.

O'Hara, Kenton, and Barry Brown. *Consuming Music Together: Social and Collaborative Aspects of Music Consumption Technologies*. New York: Springer, 2006.

Oppezzo, Marily, and Daniel L. Schwartz. "Give Your Ideas Some Legs: The Positive Effect of Walking on Creative Thinking." *Journal of Experimental Psychology* (2014): 1–11.

Paddison, Max. *Adorno's Aesthetics of Music*. New York: Cambridge University Press, 1997.

Patel, Aniruddh D. *Music, Language, and the Brain*. New York: Oxford University Press, 2010.

Pellitteri, John. *Emotional Processes in Music Therapy*. Gilsum, NH: Barcelona, 2009.

Philip, Robert. *Performing Music in the Age of Recording*. New Haven, CT: Yale University Press, 2004.

Pinker, Steven. *How the Mind Works*. New York: W. W. Norton, 1997.

———. *The Language Instinct*. New York: W. Morrow, 1994.

Pitts, Stephanie. *Chances and Choices: Exploring the Impact of Music Education*. New York: Oxford University Press, 2012.

Poultney, David. *Studying Music History: Learning, Reasoning, and Writing about Music History and Literature*. Upper Saddle River, NJ: Prentice Hall, 1996.

Power, Scott. *Musician's Little Book of Wisdom*. Merrillville, IN: ICS, 1996.

Prager, Brad. *Aesthetic Vision and German Romanticism: Writing Images*. New York: Camden House, 2007.

Rauscher, Frances H., et al. "Music Training Causes Long-Term Enhancement of Preschool Children's Spatial-Temporal Reasoning." *Neurological Research* 19 (1997): 2–8.

Ray, Benjamin. *African Religions: Symbol, Ritual, and Community*, 2nd ed. Upper Saddle River, NJ: Prentice Hall, 1999.

Rebuschat, Patrick, ed. *Language and Music as Cognitive Systems*. New York: Oxford University Press, 2012.

"Researchers Reconstructed Love Song of Prehistoric Bushcricket." Sci-News.com, February 7, 2012. <http://www.sci-news.com/paleontology/article00173.html>

Rice, Timothy. *Ethnomusicology: A Very Short Introduction*. New York: Oxford University Press, 2014.

Richards, Laura J. *Music as an Asset to Spirituality* [1928]. Whitefish, MT: Kessinger, 2011.

Ridley, Aaron. *The Philosophy of Music: Theme and Variations*. Edinburgh: Edinburgh University Press, 2004.

Rink, John. *Musical Performance: A Guide to Understanding*. New York: Cambridge University Press, 2002.

Robinson, Jennifer, ed. *Music and Meaning*. Ithaca, NY: Cornell University Press, 1997.

Rorem, Ned. *Music from Inside Out*. New York: George Braziller, 1967.

Rosaldo, Michelle Z. "Toward an Anthropology of Self and Feeling." In *Culture Theory: Essays on Mind, Self and Emotion*, edited by Richard Shewder and Robert LeVine. New York: Cambridge University Press, 1984. 137–157.

Ross, Alex. "Why So Serious? How the Classical Concert Took Shape." *The New Yorker*, September 8, 2008. <http://www.newyorker.com/arts/critics/musical/2008/09/08/080908crmu_music_ross?currentPage=all>

Rothenberg, David. *Bug Music: How Insects Gave Us Rhythm and Noise*. New York: Macmillan, 2013.

———. *Why Birds Sing: A Journey into the Mystery of Bird Song*. New York: Basic, 2006.

———, and Marta Ulvaeus, eds. *The Book of Music and Nature: An Anthology of Sounds, Words, Thoughts*. Middleton, CT: Wesleyan University Press, 2013.

Rothko, Mark. *The Artist's Reality: Philosophies of Art*. New Haven, CT: Yale University Press, 2006.

Rowell, Lewis. *Thinking About Music: An Introduction to the Philosophy of Music*. Amherst: University of Massachusetts Press, 1983.

Rudd, Even. *Music Therapy: A Perspective from the Humanities*. Gilsum, NH: Barcelona, 2010.

Russell, Bertrand. *The Conquest of Happiness* [1930]. New York: Routledge, 2006.

———. *The Problems of Philosophy* [1912]. Rockville, MD: Arc Manor, 2008.

Sacks, Oliver. *Musicophilia: Tales of Music and the Brain*. New York: Vintage, 2008.

St. Vincent, Justin, ed. *The Spiritual Significance of Music*. Auckland: Xtreme Music, 2009.

Saminsky, Lazare. *Music of the Ghetto and the Bible*. New York: Bloch, 1934.

Sartre, Jean-Paul. *Essays on Existentialism*. New York: Citadel, 1965.

———. *L'Imaginaire*. Paris: Gallimard, 1940.

———. *Literature and Existentialism*. Translated by Bernard Frechtman. New York: Citadel, 1994.

Schenker, Heinrich. "Eugen d'Albert." *Die Zukunft* 9 (1894): 33.

Scherer, Klaus R. "Expression of Emotion in Voice and Music." *Journal of Voice* 9:3 (1995): 235–238.

Schnebly-Black, Julia, and Stephen Moore. *The Rhythm Inside: Connecting Body, Mind, and Spirit Through Music*. Van Nuys, CA: Alfred Music, 2003.

Schoenberg, Arnold. *Style and Idea: Selected Writings*. Edited by Leonard Stein, and translated by Leo Black. Berkeley: University of California Press, 2010.

Schoenewolf, Gerald. "Emotional Contagion: Behavioral Induction in Individuals and Groups." *Modern Psychoanalysis* 15 (1990): 49–61.

Schulkin, Jay. *Reflections on the Musical Mind: An Evolutionary Perspective*. Princeton, NJ: Princeton University Press, 2013.

Scruton, Robert. *Beauty: A Very Short Introduction*. New York: Oxford University Press, 2011.

———. *Understanding Music: Philosophy and Interpretation*. New York: Bloomsbury, 2009.

Seeger, Anthony. *Why Suyá Sing: A Musical Anthropology of an Amazonian People*. Urbana: University of Illinois Press, 2004.

Shapiro, Nat. *An Encyclopedia of Quotations About Music*. New York: Da Capo, 1978.

Shepherd, John, et al. *Whose Music? A Sociology of Musical Languages*. New Brunswick, NJ: Transaction, 2008.

Shepherd, Tim, and Anne Leonard, ed. *The Routledge Companion to Music and Visual Culture*. New York: Routledge, 2013.

Slobin, Mark. *Folk Music: A Very Short Introduction*. New York: Oxford University Press, 2011.

Slonimsky, Nicolas, ed. *Lexicon of Musical Invective: Critical Assaults on Composers Since Beethoven's Time*. Seattle: University of Washington Press, 1965.

Solomon, Robert C. *Spirituality for the Skeptic: The Thoughtful Love of Life*. New York: Oxford University Press, 2002.

Spencer, Herbert. *Essays: Scientific, Political, and Speculative*, vol. 2. London: Williams and Norgato, 1891.

Spinoza, Baruch. *The Ethics*, part I. (1677).

Stokes, Martin, ed. *Ethnicity, Identity, and*

Music: *The Musical Construction of Place*. New York: Berg, 1994.

Sullivan, Lawrence E., ed. *Enchanting Powers: Music in the World's Religions*. Cambridge, MA: Harvard University Press, 1997.

Sylvan, Robin. *Traces of the Spirit: The Religious Dimensions of Popular Music*. New York: New York University Press, 2002.

Talbot, Michael, ed. *Musical Work: Reality or Invention?* Liverpool, UK: University of Liverpool Press, 2000.

"Teen Becomes a Musical Genius." *Mail Online*, November 21, 2013. <http://www.dailymail.co.uk/news/article-2511439/Denver-teen-Lachlan-Connors-musical-genius-suffering-concussion.html>

Thagard, Paul. "The Emotional Coherence of Religion." *Journal of Cognition and Culture* 5:1–2 (2005): 58–74.

Thomson, Virgil. *Music with Words: A Composer's View*. New Haven, CT: Yale University Press, 1989.

Titon, Jeff, et al. *Worlds of Music: An Introduction to the Music of the World's Peoples*. Belmont, CA: Thomson.

Tolstoy, Leo. *Anna Karenina* [1877]. New York: Dover, 2004.

Turing, Alan M. "Computing Machinery and Intelligence." *Mind* 59:236 (1950): 433–460.

Twain, Mark. *Mark Twain's Notebook*. Edited by Albert Bigelow Paine. New York: Harper, 1935.

_____. *Mark Twain's Own Autobiography: The Chapters from the North American Review*. Madison: University of Wisconsin Press, 1924.

_____. *Mark Twain's Speeches*. New York: Harper, 1910.

Tzu, Sun. *The Art of War*. Translated by Lionel Giles. Radford, VA: Wilder, 2008.

Van der Braembussche, A. A. *Thinking Art: An Introduction to Philosophy of Art*. New York: Springer, 2009.

Vandercook, H. A. *Expression in Music*. New York: Hal Leonard, 1989.

Van der Leeuw, Gerardus. *Sacred and Profane Beauty: The Holy in Art*. New York: Oxford University Press, 2006.

Verney, Rachel, and Gary Andsell. *Conversations on Nordoff-Robbins Music Therapy*. Gilsum, NH: Barcelona, 2010.

Viladesau, Richard. *Theology and the Arts: Encountering God through Music, Art and Rhetoric*. New York: Paulist, 2000.

Vines, Bradley W. et al. "Music to My Eyes: Cross-Modal Interactions in the Perception of Emotions in Musical Performance." *Cognition* 118 (2011): 157–170.

Volpe, Galvano Della. *Critique of Taste*. New York: Verso, 1991.

Vonnegut, Kurt. *Breakfast of Champions: A Novel*. New York: Random House, 1973.

_____. *Cat's Cradle: A Novel*. New York: Random House, 2009.

_____. *A Man Without a Country*. New York: Seven Stories, 2005.

Wade, Bonnie C. *Thinking Musically: Experiencing Music, Expressing Culture*. New York: Oxford University Press, 2013.

Wallin, Nils Lennart, Björn Merker, and Steven Brown, ed. *The Origins of Music*. Cambridge, MA: MIT Press, 2001.

Washburne, Christopher, and Maiken Derno, eds. *Bad Music: The Music We Love to Hate*. New York: Psychology, 2004.

Watanabe, Shigeru, and Katsufumi Sato. "Discriminative Stimulus Properties of Music in Java Sparrows." *Behavioural Processes* 47:1 (1999): 53–57.

Weisbard, Eric. *Listen Again: A Momentary History of Pop Music*. Durham, NC: Duke University Press, 2007.

White, Harry, and Michael Murphy, eds. *Musical Constructions of Nationalism: Essays on the History and Ideology of European Musical Culture, 1800–1945*. Cork: Cork University Press, 2001.

"Why Music?" *The Economist*, December 18, 2008. <http://www.economist.com/node/12795510>

Williams, Andrew. *Portable Music and Its Functions*. New York: Peter Lang, 2007.

Williamson, John, ed. *Words and Music*. Liverpool: Liverpool University Press, 2005.
Wilson, Carl. *Let's Talk About Love: A Journey to the End of Taste*. New York: Continuum, 2010.
Wood, Christopher. *An Elgar Companion*. Derbyshire, UK: Moorland, 1982.
Zbikowski, Lawrence M. *Conceptualizing Music: Cognitive Structure, Theory, and Analysis*. New York: Oxford University Press, 2002.
Zuckerkandl, Victor. *Man the Musician*. Princeton: Princeton University Press, 1976.
_____. *Sound and Symbol: Music and the External World*. New Haven, CT: Princeton University Press, 1969.

Index

absolute music 96–97, 173
Academy for Jewish Religion, California 3
Acheulean hand axes 83
Adams, Douglas 179
Adorno, Theodor 150
African Religions 156
"American Pie" 104
amusia 19, 38
Andersen, Hans Christian 72
Animal Man 65
Anna Karenina 133
Ansdell, Gary 136
anthrophony 81
Appalachia 42
appearance emotionalism 53
Arbuckle, Nathan L. 30
Aristotle 77, 153
Armistice Day 168
Armstrong, Louis 89
The Art Instinct 94
The Art of the Musician 43
The Art of War 117–118
Augustine of Hippo 73
Austen, Jane 114

Bach, J.S. 5, 35, 84, 166, 173
Ball, Philip 49
Bartók, Béla 119
battle trance 29
Beethoven, Ludwig van 11, 35, 60, 71, 91, 95, 114, 130, 172–173
Berkeley, George 80
Berlin Philharmonic 148
Berlioz, Hector 119
Berman, Morris 12
Bernstein, Elmer 134
bias 147–152
Bierce, Ambrose 17–18
Billboard 36
biophony 79, 81
birdsong 28, 78, 79, 80, 81–83, 84
Bizet, Georges 119
Bloch, Ernest 10

"Bohemian Rhapsody" 104
Bolinger, Dwight L. 126–127
The Bonobo and the Atheist 46
Boston Herald 50
Bradbury, Ray 110
Brahms, Johannes 18, 71, 115
Breakfast of Champions 168–169
Britten, Benjamin 114
Bronowski, Jacob 12–13
Brownell, John 61
Byrne, David 57, 122–123

Cage, John 20
Cale, John 20
Carlebach, Shlomo 155
Carlyle, Thomas 90, 92
Cassiodorus 54
Changizi, Mark 78
choral music 29–30
Chorus America 29
Church of Beethoven 172–173
Churchland, Patricia S. 79
Cicero 151
Civil War 2, 38–39
Clapton, Eric 148
Cohen, Leonard 36
Coleman, Ornette 21
Collier, Jeremy 176
computers 35–36
congregational singing 161–163
The Conquest of Happiness 103
Cook, Nicholas 97
Copland, Aaron 14, 36–37
Cornell University 84
Craig, Wallace 83
criticism 133–138, 141–143

Darwin, Charles 4, 26–27, 30–31, 53–54, 109
Davidson, Jane W. 44–45
Davies, Stephen 52, 53
Dawkins, Richard 166
Delius, Frederick 119

Descartes, René 140
The Descent of Man 26–27, 30
Desert Island Discs 166
The Devil's Dictionary 17
de Waal, Frans 46
Diamond, Jared 113
Dickens, Charles 114
A Dictionary of Musical Quotations 11
Discourse on Method 140
Dissanayake, Ellen 87
Dolphy, Eric 21
Dunbar, Robin 31
Durkheim, Émile 162
Dutton, Denis 83, 94
Dylan, Bob 36, 126

Eagleton, Terry 149–150
Eco, Umberto 128–129
The Economist 31
Edison, Thomas 57–58, 169–170
Edmondson, Nelson 165
Edwards, Jonathan 158
Egyptians 57
Einstein, Alfred 24–25
Elgar, Edward 11
Eliade, Mircea 65
Emmons, Robert A. 175–176
Emotion and Meaning in Music 106
emotional coherence 158–159
emotional contagion 159–160
emotions 42, 71–73, 156–158, 163–165
empathy 45–46
Encyclopædia Britannica 16
endorphins 30
Enigma Variations 11
Eno, Brian 20
Ericsson, K. Anders 110
eternal return 65–66
ethnomusicology 18–19, 86, 88, 98
ethology 81–82
Everything2 118
evolution 25–32, 49, 78–79, 82–83, 89, 94, 100, 111, 120, 166
existentialism 63–64
The Expression of the Emotions in Man and Animals 53

The Farther Reaches of Human Nature 174
Finch, Atticus 9–10
Folk Music: A Very Short Introduction 90
Fowler, Thomas 151
free jazz 17
Freedberg, David 46
Freud, Sigmund 114
Friedman, Daniel 121–122
Friedmann, Elvia 3

Frith, Simon 142
Fry, Ron 152–153
Fuller, Thomas 40
functional music 99–100, 141–143
Funktionslust 82–83

Gaffurius, Franchinus 76–77
Gallese, Vittorio 46
Genesis 103
geophony 81
gifted listener 14
Goethe, Johann Wolfgang von 14, 71
Goldsmith, Oliver 147–149
Gordon, Adoniram Judson 155–156
Gospel of Matthew 166
Grant, Ulysses S. 38–39
The Great Animal Orchestra 78, 80–81
Great Awakenings 155
Greeks 57, 71, 151
Guarneri violin 54–55
Guns, Germs, and Steel 113
Guns N' Roses 104
Guthrie, Woody 20

Haeckel, Ernst 26
Hanchett, Henry Granger 43
Harnessed 78
Hassidism 161, 174
Hegel, Georg Wilhelm Friedrich 21
Heine, Heinrich 71
Hendrix, Jimi 148
Heraclitus of Ephesus 106
Herzog, George 19
Hitler, Adolf 150
Hoffer, Eric 114
Hoffmann, E.T.A. 71
Höller, York 173
Homo Aestheticus 87
Hooker, John Lee 84
Horn, Stacy 29
How the Mind Works 31
Hoy, Ronald R. 84
Hugo, Victor 72
Huron, David 50
Huxley, Aldous 69–70

The Identity of Man 12
ideology 149–150
L'Imaginaire 59
improvisation 35, 61, 82, 98, 104, 111, 112, 113
The International Journal for the Psychology of Religion 175
The International Silver String Submarine Band 45
Isidore of Seville 54

Index

James, William 64, 172
Janes, E. 42
Jankélévitch, Vladimir 9–10
jazz 17, 20, 31, 35, 49, 61, 62, 63, 82, 91, 97, 104, 111, 118
Jenner, Gustav 115
Joplin, Janis 36
Jordania, Joseph 28
Journal of Experimental Psychology 115
Journal of Personality and Social Psychology 29
Jubilus 73

Kant, Immanuel 114
Kierkegaard, Søren 64
Kodály, Zoltán 88–89
Kolb, David 152–153
Kolb Cycle 152–153
Konecni, Vladimir 53
Krause, Bernie 78, 80–81
Krugman, Paul 149–150

Langer, Susanne K. 60
Langlois, Judith H. 51
The Language Instinct 94
Lao Tzu 70
Law, William 70
Lee, Harper 9–10
Leonardo da Vinci 76
A Letter Concerning Toleration 162
Lévi-Strauss, Claude 78
Levitin, Daniel J. 145
Lewis, Bernard 66
Little Rascals 45
Living Links Center 46
Locke, John 162
Loersch, Chris 30
logogenic music 160
Lohengrin 18
London, Frank 91–92
London Symphony Orchestra 148
love songs 26–28
lyrics 73–74

"Mache dich mein Herze rein" 166
A Man Without a Country 169
Maslow, Abraham 174–175
Masson, Jeffrey Moussaieff 82
Mattick, Paul, Jr. 94
Mayer, John D. 175
McDonald's 138
McLean, Don 104
melogenic music 160
Metaphysics 153
Meyer, Leonard B. 106–107
Michigan State University 165

Miller, Geoffrey 31
Milton, John 114, 143
minimalism 107
mirror neurons 46–47
Mitchell, Joni 148
Mithen, Steven 26
Mood Change Parties 169–170
Morrison, Grant 65
Morton, John 3
Moses und Aron 50
Mozart, Wolfgang Amadeus 18, 91, 121–122, 137, 173
Mozart Effect 6
Murch, Walter 57–58
Music: A Book of Quotations 11
Music and the Ineffable 9–10
Music as an Asset to Spirituality 119
Music at Night 69
music theory 12–13, 43
musical gravity 76–77
Musical Times 50
The Mysticism of Music 171–172

Nagyvary, Joseph 54–55
Native American songs 161
Nattiez, Jean-Jacques 83–84
Neanderthals 26
Neo-Hassidism 155
New England Conservatory 91
New York Times 89
New Yorker 95
Newton, R. Heber 171–172
Niebuhr, Reinhold 149
Nietzsche, Friedrich 114
Nineteenth Century Club 143
Ninth Symphony (Beethoven) 60, 95
Nordoff-Robbins Music Therapy Centre 136
notism 61–62
"November Rain" 104

ontological time 21–22
Oppezzo, Marily 115
Orishas 173–174
oro cantado 173
Oscar Weil: Letters and Papers 2
Otto, Rudolf 172
Oxford University 31
oxytocin 30

Paradise Lost 143
Parker, Charlie 20–21, 61, 92
Parry, Hubert 11
Passover 65
pathogenic music 160–161
Peerce, Jan 148

The Perennial Philosophy 69–70
Perlman, Itzhak 55
Peruvian flute 92
Philosophy in a New Key 60
Picander (Christian Friedrich Henrici) 166
Pinker, Steven 31–32, 93–94
Piss Christ 18
Plato 54
Polynesian music 3
Porter, Cole 113
Posidonius 151
Practica musicae 77
The Problems of Philosophy 153–154
Proceedings of the National Academy of Sciences 27
Prokofiev, Sergei 150
psychological time 21–22
Puccini, Giacomo 13
Pulley, Emily 55
Putterman, Daniel Campos 3

qawwali 107
Queen 104
Quotations on Jewish Sacred Music 11

Rash, Ron 41–42
Ravel, Maurice 34–35
Ray, Benjamin 156–157
recording 57–58, 65–66
repetition 48–49
Ricci, Ruggiero 18
Richards, Laura J. 119
Robert, Daniel 27
Roggman, Lori A. 51
The Role of the Reader 128
Rollins, Sonny 61
Romeo and Juliet 168
Rorem, Ned 72
Rosaldo, Michelle 163–164
Ross, Alex 95
Rossini, Gioachino 18
Rothenberg, David 82–83
Rowell, Lewis 16
Russell, Bertrand 103, 153

Sacred Service (Avodath Kodesh) 10
St. Matthew Passion 166
Saminsky, Lazare 10
Santería 173–174
Sartre, Jean-Paul 59, 63, 125–126
Schenker, Heinrich 112
Schlegel, Karl Wilhelm Friedrich 71
Schlösser, Louis 11
Schoenberg, Arnold 49–50, 84, 102
Schoenewolf, Gerald 160
Schopenhauer, Arthur 21

Schubert, Franz 71
Schuller, Gunter 61
Schumann, Robert 71, 114
Schwartz, Daniel L. 115
Seeger, Anthony 109
Seneca 151
serialism 17, 50
Serrano, Andres 18
Shakespeare, William 168
Sharlin, William 3, 62, 120–121
A Short History of Music 24
Shostakovich, Dimitri 150
silence 69–70
Simone, Nina 118, 148
The Singing Neanderthals 26
Slobin, Mark 90
Society for Humanistic Judaism 121
Sonic Youth 20
Spinoza, Baruch 141–143
spiritual intelligence 175–176
Stalin, Joseph 150
Stanford University 115
"The Star-Spangled Banner" 100
Stevens, Wallace 40
Stewart, Rod 36
Stewart, Stan 3
Stone, Jon R. 2
Stradivarius violin 55
Stravinsky, Igor 18, 104
Sufism 107, 174
Sun Tzu 117
A Survivor from Warsaw 50
Suyá 108–109
The Symbolism of Music 126

Talbot, Michael 98
Tchaikovsky, Pyotr Ilyich 114
Thagard, Paul 158
Theosophical Society 172
Thinking on Music 1
three-minute rule 102, 103–104, 111
Tieck, Ludwig 71
To Kill a Mockingbird 9–10
Tolstoy, Leo 133–134
Tucker, Richard 148
Turing, Alan 35
Twain, Mark 19, 20–21, 143–144

University of Liverpool 98
University of Reading 26
University of Western Australia 44
University of York 28

The Varieties of Religious Experience 64
Vaughan Williams, Ralph 119, 166
Verdi, Giuseppe 119

Veteran's Day 168
Villa-Lobos, Heitor 18
Vines, Bradley W. 45
visual cues 44–45
Vivaldi, Antonio 128
Vonnegut, Kurt 74, 168–169

Wagner, Richard 13–14, 18, 96, 170–171
Waits, Tom 36
Weil, Oscar 2
Wendte, Charles William 72
West Point 37
When Elephants Weep 82
Why Birds Sing 82
Why Do People Sing? 29
Why Suyá Sing 109

Wurman, Felix 173
Wuthering Heights 166

Xingu River 108

Yale University 170
"Yankee Doodle" 37, 42
Yerkes Primate Center 46
Yoruba 126

Zappa, Frank 20
Zentner, Marcel 28
zero-energy hypothesis 60
zoomusicology 84
Zuckerkandl, Victor 37

www.ingramcontent.com/pod-product-compliance
Ingram Content Group UK Ltd.
Pitfield, Milton Keynes, MK11 3LW, UK
UKHW042010140426
5217IPUK00015B/1082